THE ILLUSTRATED HISTORY OF WORLD WAR I

THE ILLUSTRATED HISTORY OF WORLD WAR I

ANDY WIEST

CHARTWELL BOOKS, INC.

Published by
CHARTWELL BOOKS, INC.
A Division of BOOK SALES, INC.
114 Northfield Avenue
Edison, New Jersey 08837

Dedicated to my wife Jill, whose unfailing support made this possible

ISBN: 0-7858-1424-8

Editorial and design by
Amber Books Ltd
Bradley's Close
74–77 White Lion Street
London N1 9PF

Project Editor: Charles Catton
Editor: Vanessa Unwin
Design: Zoe Mellors
Picture Research: Lisa Wren/ Charles Catton

Printed in Singapore

CONTENTS

Eduard Palm

CHAPTER 1

The Road to War

MANY EUROPEANS GREETED THE OUTBREAK OF THE GREAT WAR WITH ENTHUSIASM, INCLUDING THIS GERMAN CROWD SENDING ITS MEN OFF TO WAR. THE FIRST MODERN, INDUSTRIAL WAR WAS EXPECTED TO BE A QUICK VICTORY – THE WORLD DID NOT REALISE THE HORRORS THAT LAY AHEAD.

Not only had France been defeated, she had been humiliated. The desire for revenge and the redemption of Alsace-Lorraine would later come to dominate French foreign policy. Germany had created a bitter enemy.

BISMARCK AND FRANCE

RIGHT: OTTO VON BISMARCK, THE ARCHITECT OF GERMAN UNIFICATION, STROVE TO AVOID FUTURE CONFLICT.

In some ways World War I can be seen as a continuation of the Franco-Prussian War. Otto von Bismarck, Chancellor of Germany, had used war to unify his country in the 1860s. The final war against France ended in German victory, another French Revolution and the Treaty of Frankfurt. Bismarck had always been careful not to press his victories too far, seeking only to unify his own nation, but with the Treaty of Frankfurt he made critical errors in judgement. Germany seized the disputed border states of Alsace and Lorraine from the French. In addition, the treaty called for a German occupation of France until war reparations had been paid in full. Finally, the Germans proclaimed the founding of the German Empire in a lavish ceremony in the Hall of Mirrors in the Palace of Versailles, the very symbol of French power. Not only had France been defeated, she had been humiliated. The desire for revenge and the redemption of Alsace-Lorraine would later come to dominate French foreign policy. Germany had created a bitter enemy.

The ever-practical Bismarck set out to limit the scope of his mistake. His goal was to isolate the French diplomatically, curtailing their hopes of a war of revenge, and he did this through a cunning series of diplomatic manoeuvres. He had little to worry about with Britain, which chose its usual isolationist pattern when it came to European politics, and Italy remained a firm friend. Russia and Austria proved more tricky to deal with, for they were often at each others' throats over disputes in the Balkans. Austria hoped to expand into the region, while Russia saw herself as the region's Slavic protector, and openly coveted land access to the Dardanelles. Thus, Bismarck was unable to cement alliances with

OVERVIEW

The aftermath of the Franco-Prussian War of 1870 caused continental Europe to enter into an entangling system of competing military alliances. The alliance groupings, led by Germany and France respectively, were roughly equal in size. Britain had always remained aloof from military alliances, but a near-loss in the Boer War convinced the United Kingdom to rethink its isolationism. Much enmity existed between France and Britain, leaving Germany the logical choice as an alliance partner. However, bumbling diplomacy by Kaiser Wilhelm II forced Britain into an Entente (friendly agreement) with France, thus altering the tenuous European balance of power.

Suddenly tragedy struck, placing the alliance systems at odds. The dramatic assassination of Archduke Franz Ferdinand, the heir to the Austrian throne, served to set in motion a spiral of events that inexorably led to the beginning of the most important war of the twentieth century.

both countries, so he chose the next best thing. Germany signed a military alliance with Austria, and then quickly signed the secret Reinsurance Treaty with Russia. By 1888 all was well in Bismarck's diplomatic world. France was isolated and Germany led the only alliance system on the continent. However, all of Bismarck's careful work was at great risk, for in 1888 Germany crowned a new Kaiser: Wilhelm II.

THE KAISER AND FOREIGN POLICY

The new Kaiser, unlike his grandfather, would stamp his personality upon the foreign policy of his nation. Wilhelm II was a complex, sometimes comic, man. He was quite vain, possessing more lavish military uniforms than there were days in the year to wear them. The flamboyant Kaiser longed to transform his nation into the pre-eminent power in the world, at that time a position occupied by Great Britain.

As the grandson of Queen Victoria, Wilhelm loved Britain, but he was also intensely jealous of the island nation. The power wielded by Bismarck, and the Chancellor's pacific foreign policy, perturbed the Kaiser. As a result, he dismissed Bismarck in 1890, having allowed the Chancellor to remain in office even that long only out of a sense of decorum. The foremost diplomatic genius of German history, and the architect of the Empire was gone, leaving the German ship of state under the control of an inexperienced hothead with grand designs.

One of the Kaiser's first diplomatic manoeuvres was an unmitigated disaster: he allowed the Reinsurance Treaty with Russia to lapse. This left the Russians with no certain friends

KAISER WILHELM II OF GERMANY.

THE KAISER

Kaiser Wilhelm II ascended to the throne of Germany in 1888. His parents were Frederick III and the eldest daughter of Queen Victoria. Self-confident and vain, the Kaiser chafed at Bismarck's power, and dismissed the architect of German unification in 1890. Having seized control over most of German foreign policy, the Kaiser began to lead Europe down the road to war. Historians still debate Wilhelm's motivations. Did he crave European dominance, or did he merely set into motion a catastrophic series of events that he was unable to control? The Kaiser and his personality are central to the story of the coming of the Great War.

Wilhelm hoped that Germany could supplant Great Britain as the world's pre-eminent power and thus achieve Germany's 'place in the sun'. To this end, he supported naval and military build-ups which would spark a major arms race and alienate Germany from her potential ally, Great Britain.

The Kaiser practiced a bellicose style of foreign policy, often issuing veiled threats of war over rather trivial issues. In the end, his policies backfired, driving both Russia and Britain into agreements with France. Once the war began, he tried to play the role of wartime leader, but soon found himself under the control of his own military machine. As Germany succumbed to defeat and revolution, Wilhelm abdicated the throne on 9 November 1918 and fled to exile in the Netherlands. If the Kaiser had truly wanted war in an effort to achieve European hegemony, he had failed to understand the nature and risks of modern war.

RIGHT: THE GUNS OF ONE OF THE NEW GERMAN BATTLESHIPS IN ACTION.

BELOW: ADMIRAL ALFRED VON TIRPITZ, THE CHIEF NAVAL ADVISOR TO KAISER WILHELM II AND FOUNDER OF THE GERMAN HIGH SEAS FLEET. HIS PROGRAMME OF SHIP BUILDING HELPED TO SPARK A BITTER NAVAL ARMS RACE WITH GREAT BRITAIN.

and in a very precarious situation in Europe. The answer to the Russian dilemma was all too obvious: turn towards France. Both nations were now outcasts looking on as Germany seemed to dominate matters on the continent. More for reasons of mutual defence than outright friendship, Russia and France signed the Dual Alliance in 1904. In four short years, Wilhelm II destroyed Bismarck's carefully laid plans. France now had an ally, and Germany found herself in an unenviable position, located between two, possibly hostile, powers. The Kaiser recouped some of his losses by adding Italy to his own alliance with Austria, creating the Triple Alliance. However, the balance of power had begun to shift away from Germany and towards France, a nation still bent on revenge against Germany for the Treaty of Frankfurt.

Adding to Germany's diplomatic problems, the Kaiser began to dabble in naval issues. Adhering to the ideas of A.T. Mahan, he came to believe that Germany had to possess a large navy to be a truly great world power. As a result, in 1898 Germany passed a naval law that would lead to the construction of the High Seas Fleet. Such a development could not go unnoticed by Great Britain, a nation that relied on dominance over the world's oceans for sheer survival. However, in 1898 the fledgling German navy was not large enough yet to constitute a threat. In the eyes of most Britons, the threat still emanated from the age-old enemy: France. The Kaiser, though, had struck upon the one issue that could drive Britain into the arms of France. To Wilhelm, his navy was, in the main, a diplomatic tool. To Britain, the navy was the difference between life and death.

BRITAIN AND THE ENTENTE

The United Kingdom, since her foray into continental war in the Napoleonic era, had been content, in the main, to remain somewhat isolated from Europe, preferring to concentrate her energies on the formation of a world empire. However, matters in the empire itself forced Britain to reconsider her isolation. The arch-imperialist Cecil Rhodes of South Africa sought to expand the British Empire northward to include the diamond-rich Boer Republics. He hoped that the tiny Boer population would put up but scant resistance, and began to apply pressure on them to test their resolve. The Boers, however, held firm, and both sides began to arm for war. In a surprising move, the Boers launched a pre-emptive strike in 1899 by invading South Africa.

The war should have been a mismatch of epic proportions, for it pitted around 200,000 Boer farmers against the world's leading empire. However, initially the Boers won victory after victory and laid siege to several important South African cities. Only after a massive infusion of men and materiel did the forces of the British Empire gain the upper hand.

HMS *DREADNOUGHT*

Developed by Admiral Fisher and launched in 1906, HMS *Dreadnought* represented a revolution in naval design and armament. The ship was powered by a new turbine engine that allowed *Dreadnought* to ride lower in the water, thus making her a smaller target. In addition, the state-of-the-art powerplant made the *Dreadnought* the fastest capital ship afloat, capable of reaching speeds of up to 39 nautical kph (21 knots). Finally, the *Dreadnought* was the first 'all big gun' battleship. Previous battleships had carried an assortment of weaponry designed for many tasks. The new ship's armament consisted of 10 30cm (12in) guns that were designed to be fired together; each could hurl a shell weighing more than 453kg (1000lb) a distance of 16km (10 miles). Thus the new ship could outrun, outmanoeuvre and outfight any capital ship afloat. It was reckoned that the *Dreadnought* alone, combining speed and firepower, could fight most navies of the world to a standstill and as a result, it had rendered all existing capital ships obsolete. Nations around the globe scrambled to develop and construct their own fleets of 'all big gun' ships, giving rise to an entire class of capital ship named after the *Dreadnought*. The Germans quickly began construction of German Dreadnoughts, sparking a bitter naval arms race with Britain that would be instrumental in pushing the British ever-closer to an alliance with France. The ship that had changed the naval world was herself slightly outdated at the outbreak of World War I. Although she served with the British Grand Fleet throughout the conflict and rammed and sunk one U-boat in 1915, she otherwise saw no significant action.

HMS *DREADNOUGHT*, A SINGLE SHIP THAT SPARKED A NAVAL REVOLUTION.

Right: Though most naval theorists believed that the war at sea would be one of climactic battle between capital ships, it was the submarine, almost ignored in 1914, that would rise to challenge British dominance of the seas. Here the German U-boat *U-15* navigates the Kiel Canal in the early days of the war.

Even then, the Boers struggled doggedly on, utilising guerrilla tactics. In the end, British forces had to employ a system of concentration camps to force the Boers to their knees, and the war dragged on into 1902. The poor showing in the Boer War forced British leaders to reconsider many policies. What would the outcome have been if Britain had faced a continental foe? As a result, the British began a programme of army reform, but more importantly, began the search for allies.

At first Britain made diplomatic overtures to Germany - often an ally in wars past - concerning a partnership. The Kaiser, however, was instrumental in rebuffing the British advances. To this day historians argue over Wilhelm's rationale, for an Anglo-German alliance would have been well-nigh unstoppable. It seems, though, that the Kaiser desperately craved control over any alliance with Britain. He desired the British alliance, but wanted to make certain that the British would realise that their role would be secondary. To achieve this end, Germany chose to demonstrate its international and military power, including naval power, in an effort to make Britain seek an eventual alliance on terms more favourable to Germany. Such a risk seemed worth taking, for few in Germany believed that Britain could ever come to an agreement with the ancient enemy France. Thus the Kaiser thought he had plenty of time to bring his version of an Anglo-German alliance to fruition. He was wrong.

Several events, domestic and international, served to lessen the hostility between Britain and France and to draw the old adversaries together. In 1903 the British monarch, Edward VII, made a public visit to France. Many thought the journey unwise, believing

Germany chose to demonstrate its international and military power, in an effort to make Britain seek an eventual alliance on terms more favourable to Germany. Such a risk seemed worth taking, for few believed that Britain could ever come to an agreement with France.

CURRAGH MUTINY

The Liberal Party in Britain had long been in favour of Irish Home Rule – rule centred in Catholic Dublin – but any efforts toward that end had always floundered in the conservative House of Lords.

A constitutional crisis in 1909, partly due to new taxes to pay for the expensive Dreadnought build-up, stripped the House of Lords of its veto power. Finally, a Home Rule bill passed the Commons in 1912, due for implementation in 1914. However, Home Rule was anathema to the Protestant community of northern Ireland and they began to gather arms to resist it. Furthermore, their supporters in Britain, the Unionists, pleaded with the Government to exempt them from Home Rule. This went against the dreams of most Catholic Irish nationalists and, as a result, they too began to procure arms to defend the Home Rule policy.

A MEETING OF MEMBERS OF SINN FEIN.

Britain was faced with a dire situation: the threat of civil war loomed in Ireland as the date for Home Rule approached. In early 1914, as events in Europe began a slow march toward war, the British Government ordered cavalry troops from their base in Curragh in southern Ireland to move northwards in order to surpress any civil unrest which might break out there. But the leading officers in the cavalry unit peacefully resigned en masse rather than be a party to forcing loyal subjects out of the United Kingdom. It quickly became apparent to all that many other officers in the British Army shared the same Unionist beliefs.

Events in Ireland came to a head in June and July 1914, effectively blinding the British Government to the coming of war in Europe. Ultimately, the advent of hostilities with the common enemy, Germany, put off the reckoning in Ireland until 1916.

The Russo-Japanese war lasted a little over one year and resulted in a Russian defeat. The strain it placed on the archaic Russian system also caused a societal breakdown and the outbreak of a revolution aimed at moderate reform.

RIGHT: BRITISH TROOPS IN ACTION IN THE BOER WAR.

BELOW: GENERAL JAN CHRISTIAN SMUTS (CENTRE) PICTURED DURING THE BOER WAR IN WHICH HE FOUGHT AGAINST BRITAIN. DURING THE GREAT WAR, THOUGH, SMUTS AND OTHER BOER MODERATES FOUGHT FOR BRITAIN.

that a significant proportion of the French population still viewed Britain as an enemy. It was feared that an adverse reaction by the French public to the presence of the British monarch could do irreparable damage to Franco-British relations. However, Edward VII received a grand welcome, and was a gracious and sensitive visitor. It was only a first step, but the visit did much to allay the fears of many on both sides of the English Channel.

In the Far East the impending collapse of China caused great tension between Japan and Russia, the two powers most interested in competing over the spoils. Japan, an island nation that modelled itself somewhat after Britain, was a rising naval power in the Pacific. In an effort to solidify their Pacific dominance, the Japanese sought out an alliance with Britain, the one European power with significant naval resources located in the Far East. The two nations signed an alliance in 1902, freeing the Japanese to focus their strength on Russia in the continuing struggle over hegemony in China. Japan used its new-found security in the Pacific to launch a surprise attack on the Russian Pacific fleet at Port Arthur in 1904, thus beginning the Russo-Japanese War.

The Russo-Japanese war lasted a little over one year and resulted in a Russian defeat. The strain it placed on the archaic Russian system also caused a societal breakdown and the outbreak of a revolution aimed at moderate reform. The war signified the rise of Japan as an important power, but also caused speculation concerning the dwindling strength of Russia. The French were very concerned with their alliance partner's sorry showing, and came to realise that Russian aid might not be sufficient in any future conflict. As a result, the burgeoning friendship with Britain became that much more important to French policy.

Naval matters were paramount in forging a close bond between Britain and France. By 1903 the growing size of the German High Seas Fleet was causing concern to British military and political leaders. They were certain that German naval production could never produce a navy equal to that of the United Kingdom. However, while the British Navy was scattered all over the globe to secure far-flung British interests, the German Navy was located exclusively in the North Sea. The Kaiser's naval advisor, Admiral Alfred von Tirpitz, saw this as an opportunity. He reasoned that Germany only had to produce a navy less than half the size of the British Navy. Since Britain would never recall her entire fleet, the smaller German Navy, concentrated as it was, would pose a significant threat to Britain. The naval balance of power in the North Sea could then be used as a trump card to force the British into an alliance with Germany under German control. The Kaiser accepted Tirpitz's plan, hoping to forge his desired partnership with a subservient Britain. However, the Germans had erred. Once again, Britain viewed naval threats as matters of life or death. As a result, Britain sought to do the unthinkable: settle her colonial disputes around the globe, thereby freeing the navy for concentration in the North Sea against the budding German threat.

ABOVE: A BOER COMMANDO (IRREGULAR UNIT) POSES FOR A PHOTOGRAPH DURING THE BRIEF BOER OCCUPATION OF NATAL. THE GUERRILLA TACTICS OF THE BOERS FORCED THE BRITISH TO USE CONCENTRATION CAMPS TO SECURE VICTORY.

In 1904 Britain came to terms with France at last and signed the Entente Cordiale. This friendly agreement settled all outstanding colonial disputes between the rival nations, especially in Africa, which had been a stumbling block. In 1907 Britain also signed an Entente ending colonial disputes with Russia, mainly in Asia. Although Britain had not signed alliances with France and Russia, the advent of the Triple Entente represents a fundamental revolution in diplomatic affairs. Since the 100 Years War, France and Britain had been enemies. Now the aggressive diplomacy of the Kaiser had driven the erstwhile adversaries together. Having blundered so badly, the Kaiser now attempted to shatter the Entente that he had helped to create.

TENSION RISES

The Anglo-French Entente had solved lingering disputes over Morocco, the British ceding control over their areas to the French. As France moved to take possession of the new protectorate, the Kaiser decided to use the issue to place pressure on the Entente and force its collapse. In a grandstand play, the Kaiser himself turned up at the Moroccan port of Tangiers in March 1905, proclaiming himself to be in full support of Moroccan independence. He then went on to demand an international conference to discuss the Moroccan issue, offering veiled threats of war as the only alternative to international mediation. Thus began the First Moroccan Crisis.

THE SITUATION IN 1914

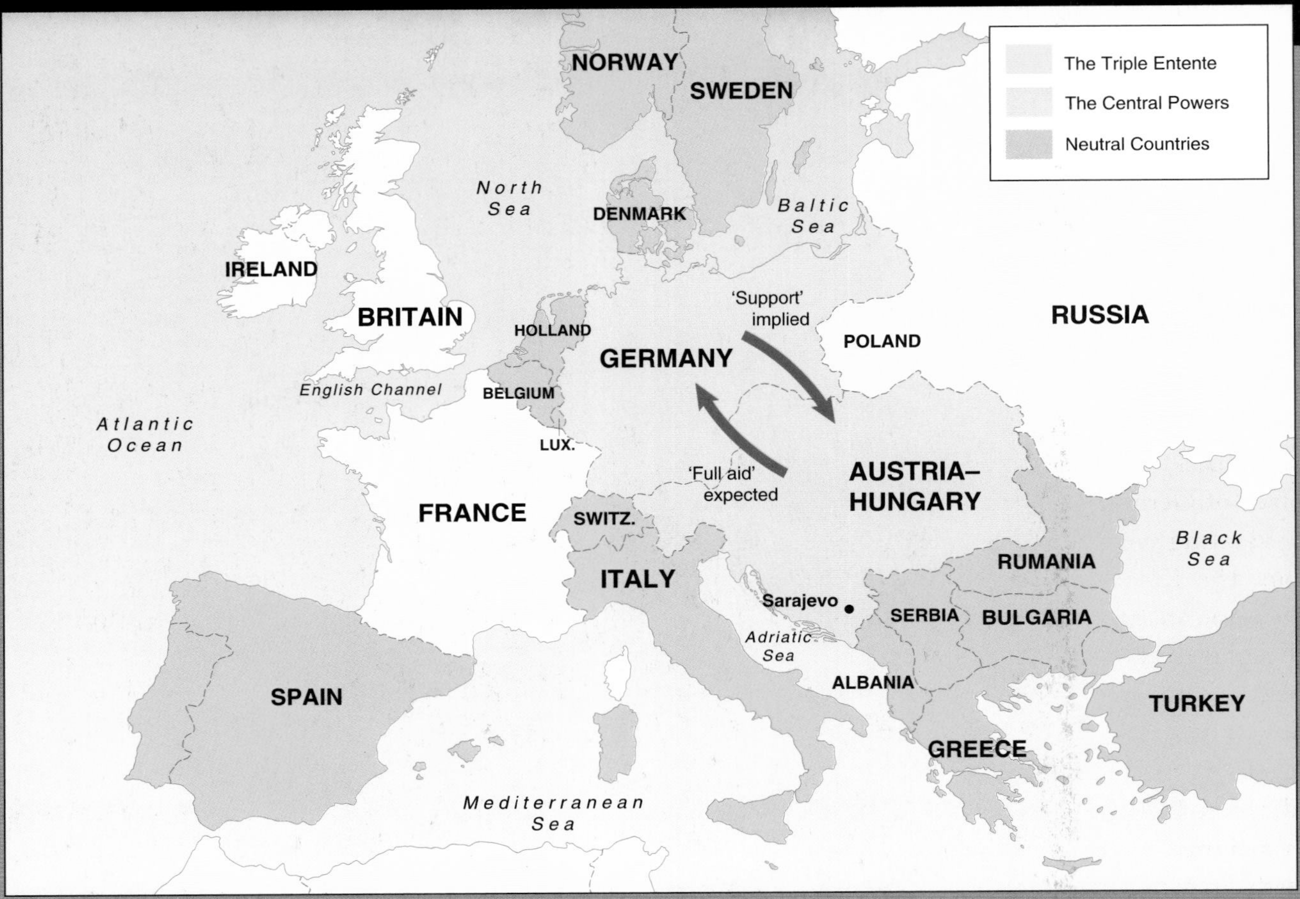

The Triple Entente
The Central Powers
Neutral Countries

NORWAY
SWEDEN
North Sea
DENMARK
Baltic Sea
IRELAND
BRITAIN
HOLLAND
GERMANY
'Support' implied
POLAND
RUSSIA
English Channel
BELGIUM
LUX.
Atlantic Ocean
'Full aid' expected
AUSTRIA–HUNGARY
FRANCE
SWITZ.
Black Sea
RUMANIA
ITALY
Sarajevo
SERBIA
BULGARIA
Adriatic Sea
ALBANIA
SPAIN
TURKEY
GREECE
Mediterranean Sea

RIGHT: In the wake of the problems exposed by the Boer War, Britain revamped her military training system to create a more professional force. The training of these troops would serve them well at Mons.

In 1906 the leading nations of Europe gathered at Algeciras to discuss the future of Morocco and, by default, the European balance of power. The conference was disastrous for Germany, proving that her efforts to use force to destroy the Entente had failed miserably. The British fully supported France and did not back down in the face of German 'sabre rattling'. In addition, the Kaiser was perplexed to find that the majority of European powers backed France on the Moroccan issue. Indeed, even Italy, Germany's alliance partner, sided with France, leaving only Austria loyal to the German cause.

Above: Archduke Franz Ferdinand and his wife make their way to their car on the fateful day of their assassination.

Left: Gavrilo Princip and his fellow conspirators stand trial for the assassination of the Archduke. It was the shots fired by Princip that helped lead to the outbreak of World War I.

The results of the conference were even worse than the Kaiser could have imagined. By now, it had become quite clear to many in Britain that Germany was the main threat to the security of continental Europe. The British and French military staffs began secret discussions on how best to employ British might in a coming war. It was decided that Britain would send the majority of its standing army to France in the event of a German invasion. The British Expeditionary Force (BEF), as it came to be known, was quite tiny - numbering something like 100,000 men - but could play a critical role in a war between the rather evenly matched foes France and Germany.

After failing to rend the Entente asunder through diplomatic means, the Kaiser turned to other methods of applying force to separate Britain and France. In 1906 Britain had

Above: Mourners line the streets to watch the funeral procession of Archduke Franz Ferdinand. Aghast at his assassination, many Austrians demanded revenge for his death.

revolutionised naval warfare at a stroke by launching the mighty HMS *Dreadnought*, deemed so powerful by contemporary experts that it made all other warships redundant. The warship solidified Britain's naval mastery, but also made it very precarious. In 1905, before it appeared, the British held such a lead in warship numbers that the German Navy posed little serious threat. After it appeared, the *Dreadnought* represented such a quantum leap in ship design that great numbers of British ships were now almost useless. The British Navy's lead over the German Navy had effectively been reduced to just one ship; only ships of the *Dreadnought*'s class now mattered.

The Kaiser saw his opening and seized upon it with abandon; Germany was now to develop its own Dreadnoughts, and sought to build them at a frenetic pace and challenge Britain for dominance of the seas. But Britain could not allow this to happen, for the navy was the very life of the country. So the British resolved to construct two Dreadnoughts for each one constructed by Germany. A very bitter and expensive naval arms race had begun. Germany, which a short period before had been Britain's hereditary ally against France, was becoming her national enemy.

In 1911 Morocco once again became the focus of a European crisis. After a riot against foreigners, the Kaiser ordered the German gunboat *Panther* to the Moroccan port of Agadir, ostensibly in an effort to protect German interests in the area, but really to show French weakness to Britain. He had calculated that this would force the British to come to the belated conclusion that strong Germany was a better alliance partner than weak France. But the diplomatic effort to wreck the Entente failed yet again, and had additional, unforeseen consequences for Germany. In the wake of the Second Moroccan Crisis, Britain came to an unprecedented naval agreement with France; they removed their fleet from the Mediterranean Sea, leaving it to the protection of the French. In return, the British promised to defend the English Channel against any German aggression in case of war. The Entente was now a true military alliance in all but name.

It seemed that imminent conflict had been averted. However, the alliance systems were firmly in place, awaiting only a spark to ignite a conflagration of war. The spark would come from the Balkans.

THE BALKAN CRISIS AND THE COMING OF WAR

In the wake of diplomatic failure in 1911 the Kaiser began to temper his aggressive actions and relations between the dominant powers in Europe became pacific: to many it seemed that imminent conflict had been averted. However, the alliance systems were firmly in place, awaiting only a spark to ignite a conflagration of war. The spark would come from the Balkans. These tiny nations, most importantly Serbia, had only recently won their freedom from the tottering Ottoman Empire. In the wake of the Turkish retreat, the different ethnic and religious groupings of the Balkans struggled for dominance in a series of wars.

Adding to this confusion were Austrian desires for expansion into the Balkans and their recent extension of rule over the Balkan Slavs to include those settled in Bosnia. Furthermore, Russia had designs on control of the Straits and a perceived Slavic ethnic kinship with the Balkan people. Indeed, the Russians and the Serbs completed a military alliance of their own aimed at Austria. Thus Austria and Russia were at cross-purposes, enmeshed in a diplomatic struggle amid a very unstable Balkan political situation.

On 28 June 1914 an assassin's bullet rang out, shattering the delicate European diplomatic calm. Archduke Franz Ferdinand, heir to the Austrian throne, was in Sarajevo, ostensibly on a goodwill tour. However, there could be little doubt that he was there, in part, to demonstrate Austrian regional dominance over Serbia. Many Slavs lived under the perceived heel of the Austrian Empire, and the Archduke's presence was a provocation to the Serbs, especially to the nationalist leadership of Serbia, who longed to bring all Slavic peoples in the Balkans under their control and out of Austria's sphere of influence. Gavrilo Princip, a member of the Serbian ultra-nationalist group, the Black Hand (which might have enjoyed covert

BELOW: THIS *PUNCH* CARTOON DEPICTS THE AUSTRIAN EAGLE ATTACKING THE SERBIAN COCKEREL – HOWEVER, THE RUSSIAN BEAR LURKS IN THE BACKGROUND, READY TO COME TO SERBIA'S AID.

Serbian governmental support), journeyed to Sarajevo with several other assassins to take their revenge on the Austrian leadership. Initial efforts to assassinate the Archduke had come to nothing, but Princip found himself in a coffee shop lamenting his failure when the Archduke's open car stopped outside. Princip took his pistol, leapt upon the running board of the car and killed both the Archduke and his wife. The floodtide of events that led to World War I had begun.

The world was shocked by the events in Sarajevo and mourned the death of the Archduke. The Emperor of Austria, Francis Joseph, longed to make Serbia pay for its involvement in the death of his heir. However, he realised that Serbia had a powerful friend in Russia and he would not move against Serbia without German support. On 5 July, the Kaiser eventually agreed to back any Austrian action against Serbia. It was the famous diplomatic 'blank cheque' that emboldened Austria to provocative action. Historians today debate the German motivation in issuing the 'blank cheque'. Some contend that it was a conscious effort on Germany's part to provoke a war aimed at continental domination. Others maintain that the Germans did not realise the dangers of their action and were simply wary of angering Austria, their only remaining stalwart ally. Regardless of motivation, the Austrians now had the support they needed to deal with the Serbian issue once and for all.

On 23 July Austria issued an ultimatum to Serbia. It contained 10 demands, some of which required Serbia to surrender aspects of its very sovereignty. They were designed to be so harsh that Serbia would refuse them, allowing for a war in which Austria seemed to

BELOW: WAR AGAINST SERBIA WAS WELCOMED IN AUSTRIA. HERE A CARDINAL BLESSES OFFICERS AT A MILITARY ACADEMY IN VIENNA BEFORE THEY PROCEED TO THE FRONT.

LEFT: FEW SOLDIERS IN EUROPE REALISED WHAT HORRORS AWAITED THEM IN THE NEXT FOUR YEARS. THESE AUSTRIAN RESERVISTS MAKE THEIR WAY TO THE FRONT JOYFULLY – ONE WONDERS HOW MANY SURVIVED TO SEE THE DEFEAT OF AUSTRIA IN 1918.

be the abused party, having sought just retribution for a heinous crime. Surprisingly, the Serbians agreed to most of the demands and asked to submit the remainder to an international tribunal. Thus the tables were turned on Austria. The British suggested a European conference to solve the problem, but both Austria and Germany refused to participate. Instead, Austria declared war on Serbia on 28 July 1914.

THE WAR SPREADS

At first sight, the war appeared to be limited to a minor confrontation between Serbia and Austria, but the entangling system of European alliances would soon convert the small war into a world war. Tsar Nicholas II of Russia found himself in quite a quandary. He was honour-bound to defend Serbia due to their military alliance, yet he realised full well that such a move on his part could lead to a European conflagration. The Russian leader chose honour over all else and began to mobilise the vast Russian army for war on 29 July. This second step towards world war caused a reaction in Germany.

At first sight, the war appeared to be limited to a minor confrontation between Serbia and Austria, but the entangling system of European alliances would soon convert the small war into a world war.

The alliance between France and Russia threatened Germany with a disastrous war on two fronts. However, Count Alfred von Schlieffen, the Chief of the German General Staff, had developed an ingenious plan to deal with such an eventuality. France was a small, modern country and could mobilise its army on virtually a moment's notice. Russia was vast and its communications poor. The Schlieffen Plan calculated that it would take the Russian Army some six weeks to prepare for war once their mobilisation process had begun. Thus Germany would enjoy six weeks in which it faced but one enemy: France. The plan stated that once Russia began to mobilise, Germany had to declare war on France and defeat her in the required six weeks. After that was accomplished, the German Army could then deal with the Russian threat at their leisure. On 29 July, upon the Russian mobilisation order, the six-week clock in Germany began to tick.

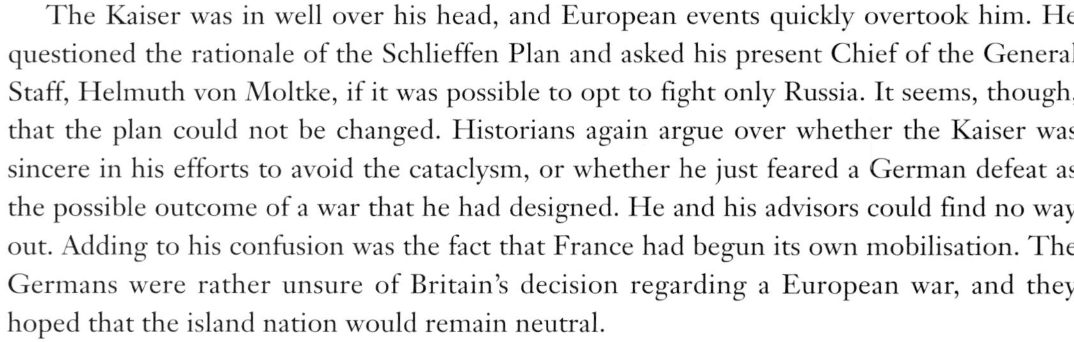

The Kaiser was in well over his head, and European events quickly overtook him. He questioned the rationale of the Schlieffen Plan and asked his present Chief of the General Staff, Helmuth von Moltke, if it was possible to opt to fight only Russia. It seems, though, that the plan could not be changed. Historians again argue over whether the Kaiser was sincere in his efforts to avoid the cataclysm, or whether he just feared a German defeat as the possible outcome of a war that he had designed. He and his advisors could find no way out. Adding to his confusion was the fact that France had begun its own mobilisation. The Germans were rather unsure of Britain's decision regarding a European war, and they hoped that the island nation would remain neutral.

BELOW: ALL ACROSS EUROPE MEN LEFT THEIR FAMILIES TO GO TO WAR. A GERMAN SOLDIER PASSES HIS CIVILIAN CLOTHES THROUGH THE BARRACKS GATE TO HIS MOTHER FOR SAFEKEEPING.

On 1 August Germany mobilised its armed forces. The very next day German forces moved into Luxembourg and demanded right of passage across neutral Belgium in their efforts to attack France. The Belgians refused and the Germans invaded the tiny country on 3 August.

The only major European powers outside the maelstrom were Italy and Britain. For their part, the Italians abandoned their alliance partners, whom they identified as the aggressors, and chose to remain neutral. Britain in form also had the choice to remain neutral, but in truth was irrevocably tied to France. Some historians invest Britain with some of the blame for the coming of the war, contending that Germany would not have moved so aggressively had Britain made its intentions to intervene on France's side clear. Britain, however, was side-tracked by problems of its own. The year 1914 would see the long-awaited implementation of Home Rule in Ireland and Protestants in northern Ireland and Catholics in southern Ireland had armed for civil war. Britain took its focus off of the impending bloodshed too late to have any impact on the rush towards war in Europe. The Government, led by Prime Minister Herbert Asquith and Foreign Minister Edward Grey, supported France, but it was the invasion of neutral Belgium that swayed the population to support the conflict. On 3 August Grey went before Parliament and made an impassioned speech in favour of entering the war in Europe to aid defenceless, brave Belgium. He reminded his countrymen that Britain had signed an agreement in the 1830s to defend the neutrality of Belgium and asked his people to honour it. His stirring speech won the day, leaving only the small Labour Party in opposition to the war.

Britain then issued an ultimatum to Germany, demanding that German troops leave Belgium and France, giving Germany 24 hours to comply before a formal declaration of war. When German Chancellor Bethmann-Hollweg received the news, he was livid. He had not expected Britain to enter the war, and found it impossible to believe that they would go to war over a rather old international agreement that he called a 'scrap of paper'. Britain's ultimatum had little effect, for Germany had no choice but to follow the path it had chosen.

In Britain the ultimatum would expire at midnight on 4 August. That evening, Edward Grey was in conference with John Redmond, a leader of the southern Irish Nationalists. The two men had often disagreed concerning the coming of Home Rule in Ireland and the impending unrest there. However, on this night both realised the importance of events as the minutes slowly ticked away, leading Britain into war. While the two leaders sat quietly pondering the moment, outside a man was snuffing out the gas lights along the street. It was midnight, and the British ultimatum was expiring. Grey stated prophetically to his guest, 'The lamps are going out all over Europe - we shall not see them lit again in our lifetime.' His prediction was all too accurate.

BELOW: RECRUITS QUEUEING TO ENLIST IN WHITEHALL, LONDON, IN 1914. MANY FEARED IT WOULD ALL BE OVER BEFORE THEY HAD A CHANCE TO SEE ACTION.

CHAPTER 2

Germany Strikes West

BELGIAN SOLDIERS ADVANCE TO MEET THE INVADING GERMANS IN 1914. BELGIUM WAS AN AFTERTHOUGHT IN THE GERMAN SCHLIEFFEN PLAN, WHICH AIMED TO DEFEAT FRANCE IN JUST SIX WEEKS. AS IT UNFOLDED THE PLAN LED TO A SERIES OF BATTLES THAT WOULD DECIDE THE FATE OF THE WESTERN FRONT.

A 'Cult of the Offensive' gripped the military machines of Europe. In reality, the new weaponry and the great industrial might of the belligerent nations would make offensives costly and futile, but military planners would cling to their offensive beliefs like grim death.

COMPETING PLANS

The Germans had invaded France, and risked British ire by violating Belgian neutrality, hoping to defeat France in six weeks. It seems that the Kaiser had good reason to expect a quick victory; after all, Germany had defeated France in a similar space of time in 1870. Most military thinkers in every country expected the war to be swift and decisive. The industrial revolution had provided the combatants with new weaponry that would make it so. Indeed a 'Cult of the Offensive' gripped the military machines of Europe. In reality, the new weaponry and the great industrial might of the belligerent nations would make offensives costly and futile, but military planners would cling to their offensive beliefs like grim death.

The French Army, numbering some two million men under the command of General Joseph Joffre, was thoroughly wedded to the idea of an audacious attack aimed at achieving a Napoleonic-style decisive victory. Their offensive scheme, dubbed Plan 17, called for a mass invasion of the German-held states of Alsace-Lorraine. Joffre and his generals believed that French fighting spirit, or èlan, would make up for what Plan 17 lacked in subtlety but the plan had several obvious weaknesses, including the fact that it left much of northern France thinly defended. Such details mattered little to the French, who planned to sweep forward so fast that any German riposte would come too late to stave off their inevitable defeat.

The British Expeditionary Force (BEF) numbered but 150,000 men under the command of Sir John French and they entered the French plans almost as an afterthought. The French expected their victory to be so swift that the BEF would barely have time to reach French soil before the war was over. As a result, Joffre relegated them to the northernmost

GENERAL HELMUTH VON MOLTKE.

MOLTKE

General Helmuth von Moltke, the nephew of the Field Marshal who had defeated France in the Franco-Prussian War, succeeded Schlieffen as Chief of the German General Staff in 1906. The younger Moltke saw fit to make several alterations to the Schlieffen Plan. Afraid of losing too much territory, he weakened the all-important right flank of the German advance and strengthened the defensive formations in Alsace-Lorraine. As the war began, the somewhat timid and nervous Moltke remained far behind the front lines and quickly lost touch with his advancing forces. As a result, he overestimated the success of the German advance. Adding to his difficulties was a Russian invasion on the Eastern Front and a British landing at Antwerp. The Schlieffen Plan called for German forces to ignore such distractions and to focus on the speedy defeat of France, but Moltke's confidence wavered. Frightened of the consequences, he removed troops from the right flank of the German advance to deal with the perceived threats. The delicate balance of the Schlieffen Plan was shattered. Furthermore, Moltke's mistakes helped lead to the critical Battle of the Marne. At this pivotal point, yet again, he lost contact with his advancing forces and sent Richard Hentsch, a mere colonel, to the front to deal with the strategic situation. His control lost, and his nerve broken, Moltke abandoned the offensive. Constant tinkering with the Schlieffen Plan and timidity had led German forces to a strategic defeat. This would help transform World War I into a gigantic stalemate. On 14 September 1914 the Kaiser relieved Moltke of his command.

Above: The Great War began the way most military experts expected – as a war of rapid movement, as evidenced by these Germans quickly fording a river with a field gun in the early days of the conflict.

portion of the line, farthest from Alsace-Lorraine and seemingly furthest from trouble. The Germans, too, paid the BEF little attention in their planning, the Kaiser even referring to the force as a 'contemptible little army' that would have scant impact on the outcome of the conflict. The original BEF, with customary aplomb, turned the pejorative term into a compliment and referred to themselves ever after as the 'Old Contemptibles'.

The German plan of action was developed by Alfred von Schlieffen. He realised that the French would probably attempt to seize their lost states of Alsace-Lorraine and he aimed to use such a predictable plan of action to his advantage. The 'Schlieffen Plan' called for a relatively small force to hold Alsace-Lorraine. The weakness of the defenders was designed to draw the attacking French further into a trap. While the French advanced into Alsace-Lorraine, five German armies would advance through Belgium into lightly defended northern France, before wheeling on the pivot of Alsace-Lorraine, rather like a great revolving door. The armies would capture Paris and then advance upon the attacking French from behind. While the French pushed on one part of the door in Alsace-Lorraine, the other part of the door would hit them in the back. It was to be a classic battle of envelopment, rather like Hannibal at Cannae. It would result in the destruction of the entire French Army in a *Kesselschlacht* (cauldron battle).

OVERVIEW

In 1914, following the dictates of the Schlieffen Plan, Germany attacked France, hoping to win a victory in the west in six weeks. German forces stampeded through neutral Belgium in a great wheeling motion designed to crush the French in a battle of envelopment. Initially the French played right into the German hand by attacking into Alsace-Lorraine. Such action allowed the Germans to advance in the north almost unopposed. Meanwhile, the British Expeditionary Force (BEF) landed in France and advanced to Mons, expecting to man a quiet sector of the line. Instead, they stumbled headlong into the path of the main German advance. After mounting a brave defence, the BEF retreated toward Paris. All seemed to be lost but the French reacted quickly to the disaster and rallied their troops for a successful battle on the Marne River at the very gates of Paris. The Germans were thrown back and their bid to win the war in six weeks had failed. Slowly World War I would engulf the entire length of France and would evolve into a trench war.

KING ALBERT OF BELGIUM.

KING ALBERT

After Germany invaded the tiny nation of Belgium, King Albert assumed command of the nation's small, but spirited army. He and his commanders hoped to make a gallant stand at the fortress city of Liege, but the speed of the German advance and the weight of German firepower forced the Belgians to retreat to and take refuge within the fortifications of the port of Antwerp within days. During the 'Race to the Sea' German forces once again pummelled the outmatched Belgians, forcing them to relinquish Antwerp and retreat further down the coast. Finally, after almost all of Belgium had fallen, in late October 1914 Albert's forces held firm at the Battle of the Yser, stemming the German advance partly by flooding the low-lying countryside and making it impassible to German troops; Belgian forces, led by their king, tenaciously held on to a tiny corner of their nation for the remainder of the war. Although Albert remained tied to the British and the French, relations between the erstwhile allies were often strained. King Albert distanced himself from most allied war aims, maintaining that he and his forces fought only for the freedom and independence of Belgium. Indeed, King Albert was often quite keen to pursue the notion of a compromise peace with the Germans, and his forces did not participate in many of the great Allied offensives in the west. By 1918, though, his position had modified and Albert personally led his army forward in the final Allied offensives that won the war.

Schlieffen realised that his plan had some weaknesses. The army on the German right flank would have to travel a tremendous distance to effect the capture of Paris and the envelopment of the French armies in the south. Success of his scheme was so important to Schlieffen that on his deathbed his final words were 'do not weaken the right flank'. He had also realised that to make such a massive military operation possible would require miracles of logistics. To that end, he meticulously worked out the supply of the advancing German forces. Even so, his plan was so delicately balanced that any alteration of the allocation of men or supplies would threaten to ruin the entire scheme.

General Helmuth von Moltke, in command of the German armed forces numbering over three million men, put the Schlieffen Plan into operation in 1914. Even before the outbreak of war, he had altered its very nature. His revised version placed more emphasis on the defence of Alsace-Lorraine which, as a result, weakened the all-important right flank. Once the battle had begun, it became apparent that Moltke was somewhat timid and made disastrous blunders that would doom the plan to failure.

Success of his scheme was so important to Schlieffen that on his deathbed his final words were 'do not weaken the right flank'. His plan was so delicately balanced that any alteration of the allocation of men or supplies would threaten to ruin the entire scheme.

GERMAN ADVANCE

The German First Army under General von Kluck occupied Schlieffen's beloved right flank position in 1914. To the immediate south, von Bulow, nominally von Kluck's superior, commanded the German Second Army. These two forces would have to achieve a seamless co-ordination of attack and advance to bring the Schlieffen Plan to a successful conclusion. Only moderately surprised that the Belgians chose to fight, the advancing Germans first had to overcome the obstacle of the Belgian fortress city of Liege. Military planners in Belgium and France saw Liege and other such Belgian fortresses as somewhat of a trump card. It was calculated that, as one of the strongest fortifications in the world,

THE GERMAN ATTACK IN AUGUST 1914

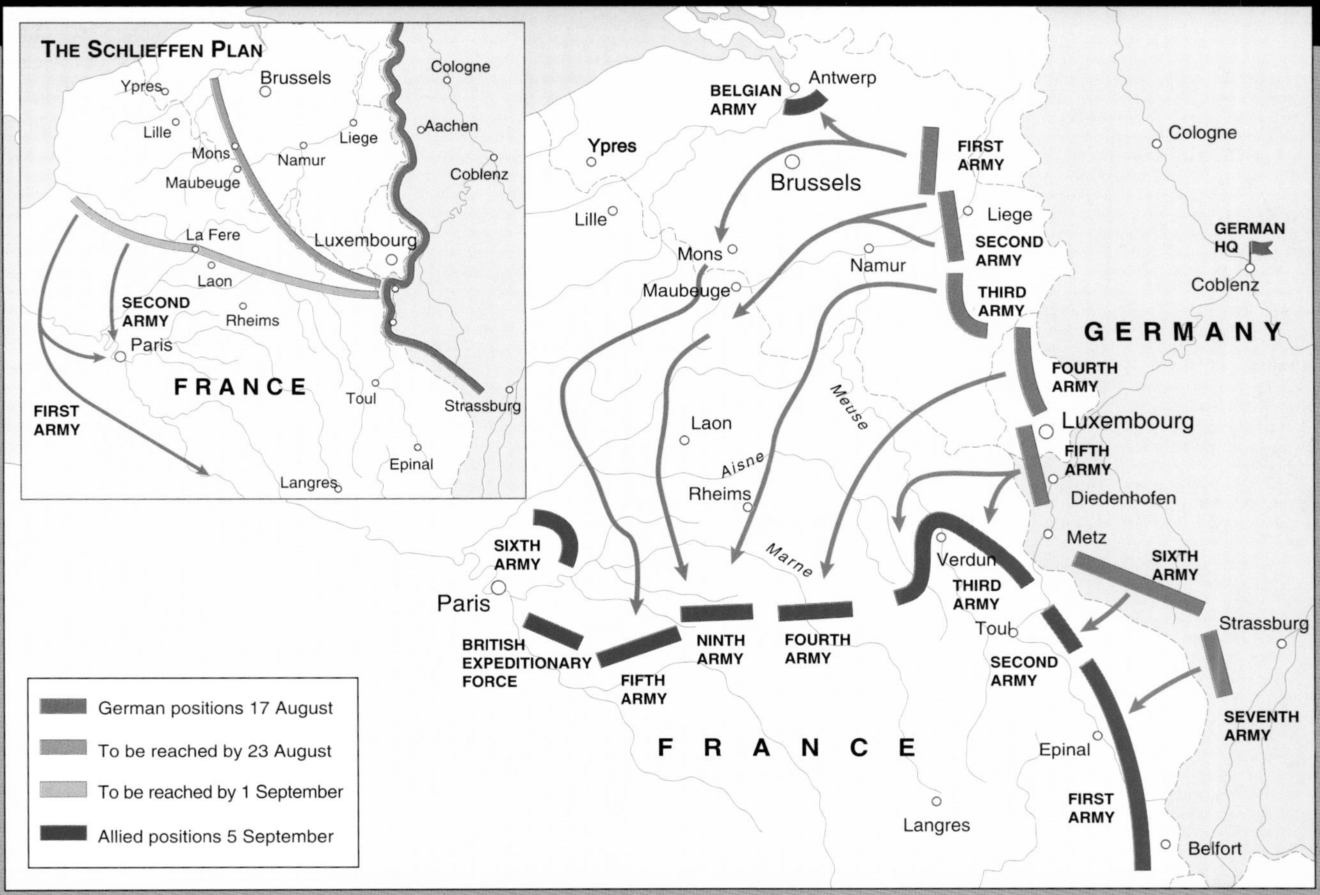

THE SCHLIEFFEN PLAN

- German positions 17 August
- To be reached by 23 August
- To be reached by 1 September
- Allied positions 5 September

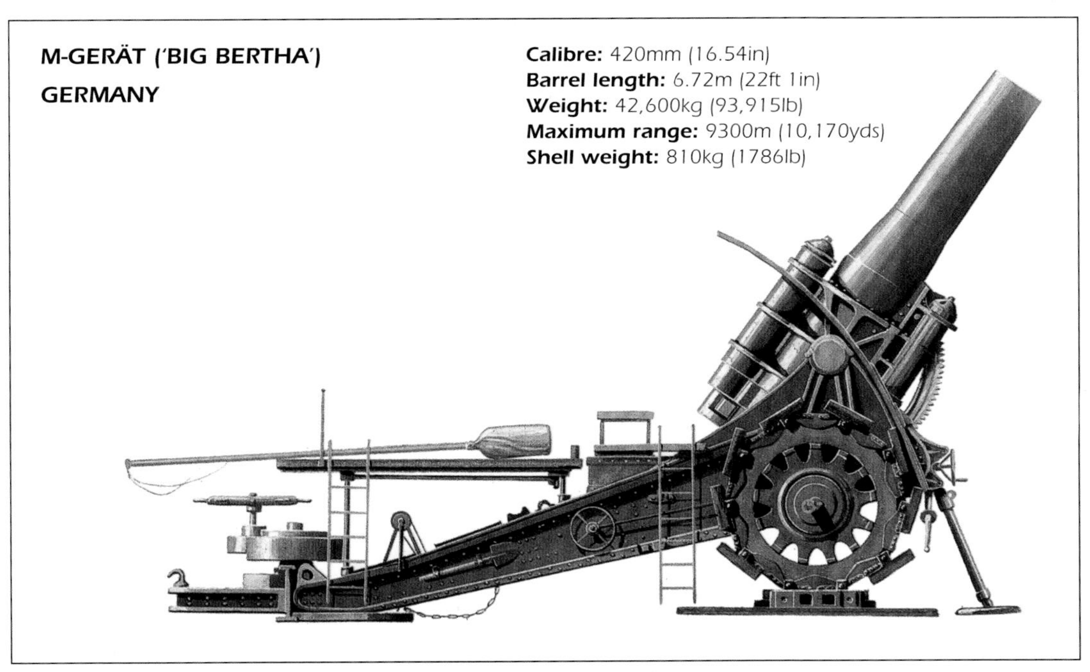

M-GERÄT ('BIG BERTHA')
GERMANY

Calibre: 420mm (16.54in)
Barrel length: 6.72m (22ft 1in)
Weight: 42,600kg (93,915lb)
Maximum range: 9300m (10,170yds)
Shell weight: 810kg (1786lb)

ABOVE:
MEN OF THE BRITISH EXPEDITIONARY FORCE ARRIVING IN LE HAVRE, FRANCE, ON 16 AUGUST 1914.

RIGHT:
OUTSIDE GERMAN HEADQUARTERS IN BRUSSELS IN 1914. GERMAN ACTIONS IN BELGIUM DURING THE COURSE OF THE WAR WOULD HELP TO ALIENATE NEUTRAL NATIONS, INCLUDING THE UNITED STATES.

Liege would halt any German advance for a great length of time. However, the Germans brought up massive 420mm (16.54in) siege howitzers to pound the fortress into submission, firing shells that weighed 810kg (1786lb), and laid waste to the Belgian defensive works, crushing the morale of the defenders. Mighty Liege held out for only one day. By 13 August the German forces had broken through all Belgium's defensive obstacles and into the open land beyond. The defeated Belgian forces, though they had fought gallantly against heavy odds, retreated north to Antwerp. German troops began to sweep into France.

The French had expected a German attack in the north, and had located powerful defensive forces in the neighbourhood of Metz to counter any such action. In reality, the focus of the German advance, however, lay much further to the north, shattering the French defensive scheme. Only the French Fifth Army, under General Lanrezac, stood in the way of the main German advance. As early as 14 August Lanrezac informed Joffre that he believed the main German advance would be on his front. Joffre, though, remained fixated on the French offensive of Plan 17.

While the Germans advanced through Belgium, the BEF, under the command of General Sir John French, disembarked in France. Though the Allies had discussed many possible options for the BEF, in the end it had been decided to add the force to the extreme northern section of the French line near the Belgian city of Mons. Here the British would be placated, and clear of any major action, as the French Army rolled to victory in the

ABOVE: THE NORTHUMBERLAND HUSSARS LEAVING NEWCASTLE IN SEPTEMBER.

BELOW: GERMAN SOLDIERS ADVANCE THROUGH A FIELD TOWARDS A CLASH WITH THE BEF AT MONS.

RIGHT: A POSED PHOTOGRAPH SHOWING GERMAN TROOPS ON THE ATTACK DURING THEIR ADVANCE THROUGH BELGIUM IN 1914 – NOTE THE BUGLER READY TO GIVE SIGNALS TO THE REST OF THE UNIT.

south. As the BEF began to reach its assigned position, expecting to occupy something of a quiet part of the line, von Kluck and von Bulow made a fateful decision. In an effort to narrow a gap that had developed between their forces, von Bulow instructed von Kluck to veer south. This meant that the powerful German First Army would advance through Mons and was on a direct collision course with the BEF. To make matters worse for the British, the French forces to their south, under the command of Lanrezac, had retreated in the face of the German advance, leaving the BEF alone and in danger of being surrounded and annihilated.

The powerful German First Army was on a direct collision course with the BEF. To make matters worse for the British, the French forces to their south had retreated, leaving the BEF alone and in danger of being surrounded and annihilated.

On 23 August the 170,000 strong German First Army slammed headlong into the 70,000-man BEF. In an epic battle the tiny British force defeated attack after attack, holding the superior numbers of Germans at bay. Some British soldiers contended that only divine intervention, symbolised by the benevolent 'Angels of Mons' kept destruction at arm's length. However, it was the discipline and marksmanship of the individual British soldier that won the day. Though small in numbers, the BEF ranked among the world's elite forces in terms of training. The Germans had not expected an encounter battle of this type at Mons, and for that reason their attacks on 23 August were rather poorly

co-ordinated. Even so, the BEF found itself in dire peril. One British soldier remembers his first taste of the terror of combat:

> I had been straining my eyes so for a moment I could not believe them ... A great grey mass of humanity was charging, running for all God would let them straight on to us not 50 yards off ... As I fired my rifle the rest all went off almost simultaneously. One saw the great mass of Germans quiver. In reality some fell, some fell over them, and others came on ... Then the whole lot came on again and it was the most critical moment of my life. Twenty yards more and they would have been over us in their thousands, but our rifle fire must have been fearful ... I don't think we could have missed at the distance and just for one short minute or two we poured the ammunition into them in boxfuls. My rifles were red hot at the finish.

The BEF had fought bravely, but General French knew that he could not persevere against such odds with two exposed flanks; such a course would doom the entire British force. As a result, on 24 August, even as von Kluck moved to surround Mons, the BEF began to retreat. Thus in the north, the 'Battle of the Frontiers' came to an end as a resounding German victory. Both the French and British forces in the area were in full retreat, and the Schlieffen Plan ground remorselessly on, somewhat ahead of schedule.

PLAN 17 AND THE FRENCH ADVANCE

On the southern part of the battle-front, General Joseph Joffre put into action the long-awaited French offensive, designed to seize the lost states of Alsace-Lorraine. On 14 August, even as the Germans moved into contact with Lanrezac in the north, the French First and Second Armies launched the main portion of Plan 17. The French found the going very difficult, partly because the rather timid Moltke had reinforced the German armies in the area and also because the German heavy artillery outranged the standard French 75mm artillery piece and thus rained death down on French units with relative impunity. Making matters worse, German commanders, most notably Prince Rupprecht of the German Sixth Army, placed pressure on Moltke to allow them to attack rather than

BELOW: BRITISH INFANTRY DURING THE LONG RETREAT AFTER THE BATTLE OF MONS. BITTER REARGUARD ACTIONS KEPT THEIR PURSUERS AT BAY.

defend. Here, Moltke's resolve crumbled in the face of such a royal request and he gave a German attack in Alsace-Lorraine his blessing. This fundamentally altered the Schlieffen Plan; French forces would not be enticed forward to their doom. Instead, on 20 August the German forces in Alsace-Lorraine rushed forward in a counter-attack, and by 22 August the French had been forced to relinquish all land that they had conquered in Plan 17. The result of Rupprecht's attack was a tactical victory, but a strategic defeat. French forces were back at their start line and, as a result, were able to react with sufficient speed once the nature of events in the north had been realised. If massive numbers of French troops were engaged deep within Alsace-Lorraine, far from adequate transport facilities, the outcome of the Schlieffen Plan might have been different.

On 23 August Joffre finally came to the belated realisation that his beloved Plan 17 was in a shambles and that the German advance to the north posed a threat to the very existence of France. Although Joffre can be blamed for continuing the attack after all hope of victory had faded, and of ignoring signs of danger in the north, he now emerged as the saviour of France. Generals up and down the line despaired of any chance to stand up to the German attack; it seemed to be the Franco-Prussian War all over again. Joffre, however, stood firm in his belief in ultimate victory. It was his calmness in the face of disaster

Below: BEF soldiers repair bicycles while under artillery fire in 1914 near the Aisne section of the front.

that eventually won the day for the Allies. Methodically, Joffre began the Herculean task of redeploying French forces northwards to meet the German offensive and defend Paris. He also worked very hard to halt the retreats of the French and British forces already in the area.

While Joffre calmly worked to overcome his initial errors, Moltke grew ever more frightened. He made several mistakes that would help ruin German chances for a quick victory in the west. In an effort to bolster their Belgian allies, the British had landed a small contingent of troops in Antwerp. Though the force posed little threat, Moltke chose to remove troops from the right flank of the advance to invest the Belgian fortress. Even worse, Moltke over-reacted to events on the Eastern Front. A Russian invasion of East Prussia caused Moltke great alarm, though the Schlieffen Plan warned to ignore the actions of the Russian Army until it had fully mobilised. Wary of the effects of losing German soil to the Russians, Moltke removed two army corps from the right flank of the advance in the west to aid forces fighting in the east. Thus, while the numbers of Allied troops in the critical area of the Western Front were on the increase, German forces were decreasing. Moltke had destroyed the delicate Schlieffen Plan, and initiative was shifting to the French side. Ironically the two corps that Moltke removed for use against the Russians were in transit across Germany when the battles in the east were won, and the battles in the west were lost.

BELOW: A NON-COMMISSIONED OFFICER OF THE BRITISH ROYAL HORSE ARTILLERY (RHA) AS SEEN IN FRANCE IN 1914. L BATTERY OF THE RHA WON THREE VICTORIA CROSSES AT NÉRY ON 1 SEPTEMBER 1914.

THE BALANCE BEGINS TO SHIFT

In the north, the German advance proceeded and nearly brought about the destruction of the BEF. During the retreat, Joffre was obliged to divide his forces to avoid passing through a large forest. As a result the British II Corps, under General Smith-Dorrien, veered north toward Le Cateau – and once again into the path of the German Army. Elements of von Kluck's forces struck the II Corps at Le Cateau on 26 August, and the situation for the British soon became desperate. Only a gallant defence and a hasty retreat under the cover of a determined rearguard saved II Corps from obliteration. It seemed that it would only be a matter of time before the BEF was destroyed and the relentless German advance reached Paris. Everything was going wrong for the Allies.

As the Germans moved through Le Cateau, Joffre redeployed his forces north to meet the coming threat. This enabled the French to create two new armies in the north, the Sixth and Ninth Armies, under the command of General Maunoury and General Foch respectively. In addition, the French were busy raising a force in Paris under the command of Gallieni. Joffre's quick thinking and his determination, coupled with Moltke's mismanagement, had begun to alter the balance of power in northern France. As September approached, the Allies had a total of 41 divisions in the north, as opposed to only 25 German divisions. The initiative had now passed to the Allies, who were afforded an opportunity to blunt the mighty German advance, now nearing the gates of Paris and possible victory.

THE FIRST BATTLE OF THE MARNE

On 31 August the Germans made a fateful decision that would alter the course of World War I. In an effort to pursue the supposedly beaten Allies more closely, von Kluck and von Bulow decided that German forces would wheel inside Paris rather than envelop and capture it.

On 31 August the Germans made a fateful decision that would alter the course of World War I. In an effort to pursue the supposedly beaten Allies more closely, and to shorten the ground to be covered by their tired and under-supplied armies, von Kluck and von Bulow decided that German forces would wheel inside Paris rather than envelop and capture it. But by wheeling inside Paris, the Germans would offer the Allies their flank and Joffre would be given an opportunity to counter-attack with his burgeoning forces. The French plan of action was simple and devastating. Maunoury and his newly-formed army would strike von Kluck's flank. Joffre hoped that von Kluck, seeing his vulnerable flank threatened, would turn his army to face Maunoury's assault. Such an action would create a considerable gap between von Kluck's and von Bulow's armies. Into this gap, the BEF would advance, threatening von Kluck with envelopment and destruction.

Though the British were initially reluctant to agree to such a daring and risky offensive scheme, the Allied counter-attack occurred on 6 September, beginning the First Battle of the Marne. As expected, von Kluck reacted to Maunoury's fierce attack by shifting troops from his left flank to meet the threat, creating a vulnerable gap in the German lines. The BEF, rather tentatively at first, advanced into the void between von Kluck's and von Bulow's forces, threatening the entire German position. However, a problem soon developed in the Allied assault. Von Kluck's forces fought with such ferocity that they

RIGHT: GERMAN SOLDIERS CROSS THE AISNE, BRINGING SUPPLIES TO THE FRONT IN AN EFFORT TO KEEP THE LOGISTICAL INFRASTRUCTURE OF THE SCHLIEFFEN PLAN INTACT.

threatened to throw the attacking French back into Paris; this would leave the BEF stranded between two superior German forces and facing annihilation. On 7 and 8 August the outcome of the First Battle of the Marne hung in the balance. At this point, Gallieni chose to intervene. Realising that the decisive moment was at hand, he sent some 6000 reinforcements to the hard-pressed Maunoury. The fresh troops sped to the front in some 600 taxicabs and buses, the fabled 'Taxis of the Marne'. Arriving in the nick of time, the reinforcements enabled Maunoury to hold the line and once again threaten the Germans with disaster.

The situation for the Germans was fast becoming desperate. Moltke, out of touch and losing his nerve in his distant headquarters in Luxembourg, had no true idea of the developing situation or how to control it. As a result, the now overmatched commander sent Richard Hentsch, a mere colonel, to investigate and take control of the situation on the battle-front. Hentsch, struggling to fulfill his overwhelming task, met with both von Bulow and von Kluck, and found that only von Kluck retained any confidence in victory at the Marne. On 9 September, after the frank discussions closed, Colonel Hentsch made the most important decision of his life, and ordered the German armies to retreat. The Battle of the Marne was over.

Above: General Joffre, here inspecting French troops, made a critical mistake by blindly following Plan 17 for too long. However, his confidence and calmness would allow him to save the situation and win the Battle of the Marne.

BELOW:
THE FABLED 'TAXIS OF THE MARNE' FERRY FRENCH TROOPS FORWARD INTO THE BATTLE THAT WOULD SAVE FRANCE FROM DEFEAT.

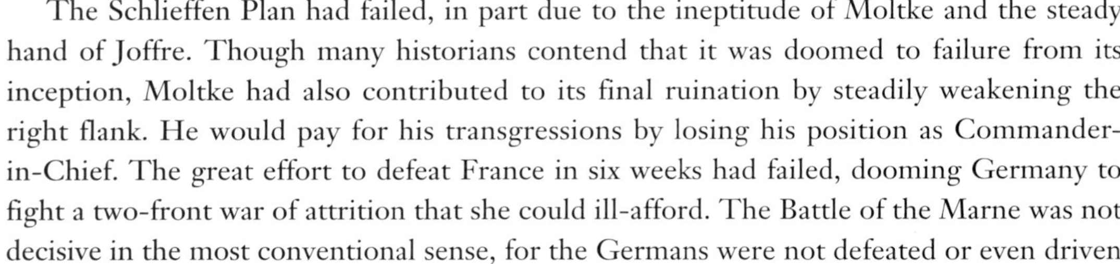

The Schlieffen Plan had failed, in part due to the ineptitude of Moltke and the steady hand of Joffre. Though many historians contend that it was doomed to failure from its inception, Moltke had also contributed to its final ruination by steadily weakening the right flank. He would pay for his transgressions by losing his position as Commander-in-Chief. The great effort to defeat France in six weeks had failed, dooming Germany to fight a two-front war of attrition that she could ill-afford. The Battle of the Marne was not decisive in the most conventional sense, for the Germans were not defeated or even driven from French soil. In some ways, though, it was one of the most decisive battles in history. It denied the Germans victory and forced them to fight a war that they could not win, a war that would soon settle down into a siege that ran the entire length of France.

RIGHT:
BRITISH ROYAL HORSE ARTILLERY ADVANCE INTO THE GAP BETWEEN THE ARMIES OF VON KLUCK AND VON BULOW AT THE BATTLE OF THE MARNE.

The Battle of the Marne was one of the most decisive battles in history. It denied the Germans victory and forced them to fight a war that they could not win, a war that would soon settle down into a siege that ran the entire length of France.

THE RACE TO THE SEA

After the ruination of the Schlieffen Plan, the Kaiser removed the over-matched Moltke and replaced him with General Erich von Falkenhayn. The new commander noticed, as did Joffre, that there remained to the north of the combatant forces an open flank – and the possibility of victory. Even as German forces near Paris fell back to the Aisne River, Falkenhayn began quickly to remove troops from Alsace-Lorraine in an effort to outflank the Allies in the north. Joffre, for his part, sought to press his advantage and launched an attack on the rudimentary German positions on the Aisne. On 14 November French forces attacked the German positions on the Chemin des Dames Ridge. Though the Germans had had little time to prepare their defences, they were able to call down withering fire upon the French attackers and succeeded in rebuffing the assault. The Battle of the Aisne was the first example of trench warfare on the Western Front and served as a portent of the future.

Above: German troops man rudimentary defences on the Aisne after the Battle of the Marne – foreshadowing the massive defensive networks to come.

Right: The shattered Belgian city of Ypres, which would be the scene of desperate fighting throughout World War I.

Below: British troops awaiting a German attack during the 'Race to the Sea'. At the First Battle of Ypres the BEF once again faced the brunt of the German advance and only escaped destruction by a narrow margin.

After this French failure, the Allies too began to shift forces to the north. As a result, both forces moved north at roughly the same speed. This phase of the war is often called 'The Race to the Sea'. Although several savage encounter battles raged during this period, neither side was able to turn the enemy's flank and gain a true strategic advantage. However, the Germans seized several important ports along the English Channel, including Antwerp and Zeebrugge. With few spoils from the 'Race to the Sea', Falkenhayn thought that he saw an important opportunity near the Belgian city of Ypres. Here the depleted and exhausted BEF held a very thinly defended portion of the Allied line. Falkenhayn hoped to mass troops in the area, break through the British lines and advance to the coast, possibly forcing the BEF to quit the war. After some rather inconclusive probing attacks, Falkenhayn unleashed the full weight of his offensive on 31 October.

The luck of the BEF held firm; once again, it found itself outnumbered and in danger of destruction. Some seven German divisions struck three under-strength divisions of the British I Corps under the command of General Douglas Haig. The Germans, making use of raw but enthusiastic recruits, came forward in human waves. German losses were incredible but the great wave of field grey rolled onward. The British line wavered and threatened to break under the tremendous stress but once again, the BEF relied on its discipline and controlled firepower to save the day. In the end, Haig had to call upon cooks and clerks to man the disintegrating defensive line. Against all odds, the beleaguered BEF held, repulsing the German advance.

Falkenhayn's forces tried one last time to achieve victory in a ferocious assault down the Menin Road toward Ypres on 11 November. Once again the BEF teetered on the brink of destruction before repulsing the German attacks. As had the Battle of the Aisne, the First Battle of Ypres demonstrated that an entrenched, inferior force could decimate an attacking force through effective use of the firepower of machine guns and artillery.

As the weather deteriorated and winter arrived in France, the war on the Western Front ground to a halt. Both the Allies and the Germans began to dig in, constructing a

Right: British soldiers shelter against the cold in late 1914.

Below: French prisoners being escorted to the rear by their German captors. As the weather worsened, the war settled down into a period of inactivity and both sides dug in.

system of trenches that ran from the English Channel in the north to Switzerland in the south. Never again would there be an open flank on the Western Front. The war of manoeuvre was over, and the war of attrition had begun. Undoubtedly the Germans had achieved the most success in the west in 1914. German forces were deep inside France and held the vast majority of Belgium. However, the Allies had survived. The Central Powers now faced the spectre of a prolonged war of attrition against a numerically and economically superior alliance. The future looked rather grim, and the cost of the

German soldiers decorate a Christmas tree.

THE CHRISTMAS TRUCE

As Christmas approached on the British sector of the Western Front, the weather turned clear and cold. Huddled in their trenches, the combatants – British and German alike – readied themselves for their first Christmas in the trenches. Late at night on 24 December, lighted Christmas trees began to appear in the German trenches. Men on both sides began to sing Christmas carols, and were stunned to find their enemies, dug in only a short distance away, joining in to sing the familiar songs. When morning came, nobody fired, lending the dawn an eerie calm. Men from both sides began to emerge from their trenches – under flags of truce – and made their way across No-Man's-Land to meet the enemy. All across the line fraternisation broke out among men who had recently been trying desperately to kill one another. Germans and British shook hands, exchanged gifts, sang songs, played football, took photographs and buried the dead. One British soldier remembers his experience:

> A German NCO with the Iron Cross ... started his fellows off on some marching tune. When they had done I set the note for 'The Boys of Bonnie Scotland, where the heather and the bluebells grow', and so we went on, singing everything from 'Good King Wenceslas' down to the ordinary Tommies' songs, and ending up with 'Auld Lang Syne', which we all, English, Scots, Irish, Prussian, Wurttembergers, etc. joined in. It was absolutely astounding, and if I had seen it on a cinematograph film I should have sworn that it was faked!

In some areas of the front, the Christmas truce never took hold, but in many areas it lasted for up to three days. It ended only when astounded officers ordered their men to recommence hostilities. Often the firing began again only after warnings and apologies were issued to the enemy. In the end, the Christmas truce did not hold and would not be repeated as the ferocity of the war grew apace. But for one brief moment, the common men in the trenches had bridged a growing gap of hatred to recognise each other's humanity.

success of 1914 was staggering. In the west, the Germans had lost some 120,000 casualties and the French had lost 65,000. But it was the BEF which suffered the worst fate by comparison. Of a force that numbered only some 70,000 at the outset of the war, the BEF had lost 55,000 casualties. Thus the original BEF that the Kaiser had derided as a 'contemptible little army' had been destroyed. But it had acquitted itself admirably. Three times the BEF faced the brunt of the main German advance and stood valiantly against all odds. It was the actions of the BEF that had tipped the delicate balance of war in favour of the Allies.

Left: As the war progressed men on both sides took part in a growing souvenir craze – collecting everything from weapons to shell-casings. Here a British soldier shows off a highly-prized souvenir – a German spiked helmet.

Chapter 3

The Eastern Front

In the east the Germans, including these men in East Prussia, were on the defensive in 1914, while they struggle to defeat France and Britain in the west. Ironically, though, it would be the war in the east that would bring the Central Powers their greatest success.

Danilov realised that of Russia's two opponents, Germany posed the greatest threat. The German Army was larger, more disciplined and better supplied than the army of Austria.

RUSSIAN AND GERMAN PLANNING

Like most other nations involved in World War I, the Russians had been constructing strategic plans for offensive operations for many years. The Russian Army, when fully mobilised, would be a juggernaut, numbering some 5.3 million men and dwarfing the combined armies of Austria and Germany. However, Russia was vast and had a very inefficient communications system and a poor industrial base. Thus it would take the Russians months fully to mobilise their mass army. During this time, supply of all wartime needs, from greatcoats to artillery pieces, would be strained to breaking point. In 1914, such considerations seemed almost irrelevant, for the war would be quick and decisive, ending before complete mobilisation could even take place. The Russian offensive scheme, developed by General Danilov, was dubbed Plan 19. It called for two simultaneous offensives, one aimed at Austria and the other at East Prussia. Danilov realised that of Russia's two opponents, Germany posed the greatest threat. The German Army was larger, more disciplined and better supplied than the army of Austria. But the Russians suspected that Germany would devote most of its military effort to a defeat of France, leaving behind only a covering force in the east, and this would provide Russian forces with an opportunity to shatter any German defensive forces and to seize the whole of East Prussia. Danilov hoped that all of this, plus a victorious offensive against a weak and distracted Austria, could be accomplished long before Russia had time even to mobilise its army fully.

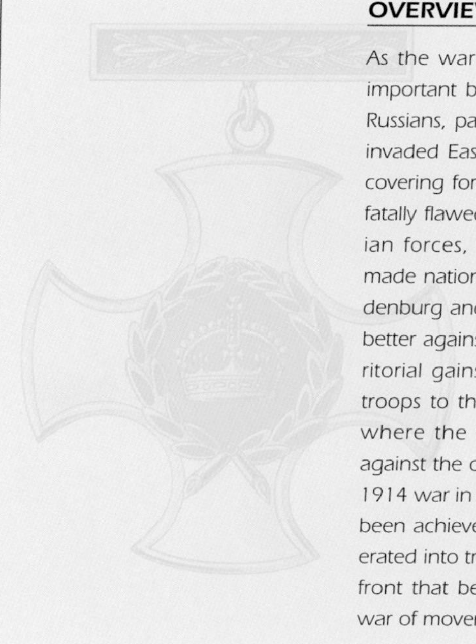

OVERVIEW

As the war in the west ground to an indecisive halt, important battles in the east raged on three fronts. The Russians, partly at the behest of the beleaguered French, invaded East Prussia, hoping to crush the small German covering force in the area. But the Russian offensive was fatally flawed, resulting in a crippling defeat for the Russian forces, whereas the unexpected German victory made national heroes out of the command team of Hindenburg and Ludendorff. Russian forces fared somewhat better against the inefficient Austrians and won great territorial gains in Galacia, forcing the Germans to send troops to the aid of their tottering ally. In the Balkans, where the war began, the Austrians achieved little against the outmatched Serbian Army. At the close of the 1914 war in the east, though no truly decisive victory had been achieved on any front, the conflict had not degenerated into trench war. This left the east as the only major front that belligerent nations could hope for a decisive war of movement in 1915.

In a sense, the Germans played into the hands of the Russians in the east. Following the dictates of the Schlieffen Plan, Germany chose to concentrate its efforts against France. The Schlieffen Plan predicted that a small covering force in East Prussia could hold the Russians at bay until the full weight of the Russian Army could be brought to bear. However, by that time Germany would have won in the west and would have transferred the bulk of her forces to the east. Initially, then, the defence of East Prussia was left in the hands of one single army, the German Eighth Army, under the command of General Prittwitz. He and his chief operations officer, General Hoffmann, were assigned the task of holding out in a defensive struggle against superior Russian forces, thus allowing the Schlieffen Plan to run its course in France.

In command of Russia's North-Western Front, and commanding the invasion of Germany, was General Zhilinsky. He had under his control some 650,000 men in comparison to the 135,000 German defenders in the area. The Russian forces were divided into the

TSAR NICHOLAS II, THE LAST TSAR OF RUSSIA.

TSAR NICHOLAS II

The Last Tsar of Russia, Nicholas II, presided over the end of a dynasty that had ruled supreme in the east for over 300 years. He led Russia to war in 1914 with a sense of foreboding that was, in the end, well-founded. While Russian armies foundered in the field, he stood firm against moderate political reform that could have saved his nation from the ravages of revolution. Making matters worse in September 1915, Nicholas II dismissed Grand Duke Nicholas and took over his position as commander-in-chief of Russian armies in the field. His absence from the capital left control of the government in the hands of incompetents. In addition, an increasing amount of authority fell into the hands of the unsavoury monk Rasputin, who wielded great influence with the Tsarina. As a military commander the Tsar proved to be a total failure. A contemporary quipped that he was 'incapable of command, yet would delegate it to no one else'. Henceforward the Russian Army drifted without a leader or a strategy, offering the Germans only the shadow of a threat. Bread riots broke out in St Petersburg in March 1917 and quickly led to the Tsar's abdication and arrest at his military headquarters. Had he been in the capital, he might have been able to affect the flow of events in the revolution. However, now he was but the prisoner of the Provisional Government. As revolution led to civil war, Nicholas fell into the hands of the Bolsheviks. In July 1918 the Bolsheviks executed the Tsar and his entire family. He had become a casualty of the war that he had helped to start.

Russian First Army under the command of General Rennenkampf, and the Russian Second Army under the command of General Samsonov. The choice of these two commanders to lead the Russian offensive was a titanic mistake; they had been rivals for years and thoroughly hated one another. Some historians even suspect that their hatred ran so deep that each hoped that the other would suffer a defeat at the hands of the Germans. Despite this, their plan was simple and tactically sound. Rennenkampf would lead an invasion of East Prussia directly from the east, locking the smaller German army into battle. As this was happening, Samsonov would lead his forces into East Prussia from Poland in the south. He would then swing behind the enmeshed Germans, envelop them and destroy them, ending all German resistance in East Prussia.

Several problems threatened to complicate the Russian plan. German and Russian railroads were of different gauges, leaving Russian rolling stock unable to operate within Germany and giving the Russian Army logistical problems. Communications also posed a serious problem; the armies of Rennenkampf and Samsonov were separated by hundreds of miles of inhospitable, enemy-held terrain. Both armies were to advance blindly, hoping that the other had been able to carry out its part of the scheme. Their limited communication took place over radio sets and was very inefficient. Making matters worse, the two Russian commanders committed a fatal blunder by failing to encode their radio communications, allowing German eavesdroppers to discern the location of the Russian forces at crucial junctures in the battle. A final problem was that the Germans had long ago wargamed possible scenarios in a war with Russia. They had come to the conclusion that the Russians would attempt an enveloping manoeuvre. Thus the Germans expected and were prepared for exactly what the Russians planned.

THE RUSSIAN ASSAULT

BELOW: THE MASSIVE IMPERIAL RUSSIAN ARMY BEGINS ITS SLOW MOBILISATION PROCESS IN 1914.

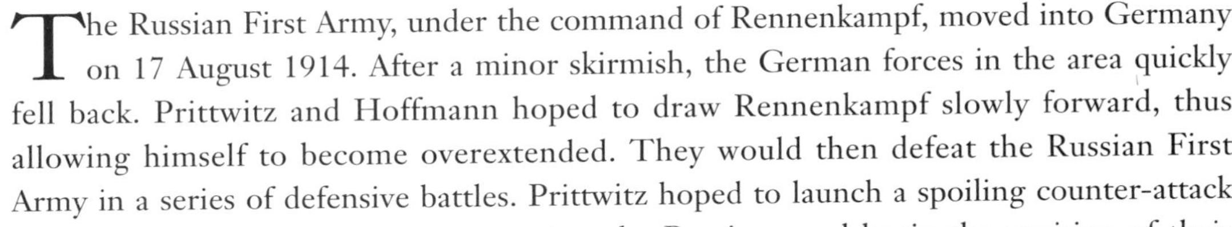

The Russian First Army, under the command of Rennenkampf, moved into Germany on 17 August 1914. After a minor skirmish, the German forces in the area quickly fell back. Prittwitz and Hoffmann hoped to draw Rennenkampf slowly forward, thus allowing himself to become overextended. They would then defeat the Russian First Army in a series of defensive battles. Prittwitz hoped to launch a spoiling counter-attack against the Russians, and begin the attrition of their forces near the village of Gumbinnen on 20 August. However, the German attack was poorly co-ordinated, leaving several German units to the mercy of the Russian artillery, and the German Eighth Army was forced to retreat.

Although his forces were victorious and had taken 6000 prisoners, Rennenkampf did not pursue the retreating Germans. His decision was partly due to his cautious nature, but he also realised that his job was to pin the Germans in place while awaiting Samsonov's advance from the south. If the Germans retreated too quickly, the Russian trap would not work.

ARTILLERY

Recent scientific advances, including recoil-absorbing devices and high-explosive shells, exponentially raised the lethality of artillery prior to World War I. Massive heavy artillery pieces could fire shells weighing over 454kg (1000lb) more than 16km (10 miles). High-explosive shells and airburst shrapnel shells could destroy any army caught in the open, long before that army could even come within sight of their attacker. Thus, deadly artillery barrages helped to make the defender dominant over the attacker during World War I. As the war progressed, both sides came to rely ever more heavily on great masses of artillery to move forward in the trench war. The Third Battle of Ypres in 1917 serves as an example. The battle began with a 19-day bombardment, using upwards of 4.2 milllion artillery shells. This represented a year's output for 55,000 munition workers, and was carried to the front in some 321 trains. To this day, every year Belgian farmers discover several tons of unexploded munitions in the area. However, the prodigious use of artillery had but little effect on the static nature of the war. Defenders constructed deep dugouts that were impervious to all but a direct hit. In addition, the artillery fire of the early stages of the war was notoriously inaccurate. Firing from such great distances at unseen targets required a level of communications and technical expertise that was lacking for most of the war. For the majority of the conflict artillery, although quite powerful, could not hit what it could not see. Defenders in their narrow trenches and underground bunkers were often quite shaken, but quite alive. Only in 1918 would scientific advances transform artillery to an offensive weapon with a war-winning capability.

BRITISH ARTILLERY IN ACTION ON THE WESTERN FRONT.

LEFT: GERMAN REFUGEES REPAIR A WAGON'S WHEEL DURING THEIR FLIGHT FROM THE RUSSIAN ADVANCE INTO EAST PRUSSIA.

Prittwitz judged the German defeat at the Battle of Gumbinnen to be nothing short of disastrous. Fueling his growing sense of panic was the news that the Russian Second Army under Samsonov had begun its advance from the south. Under the threat of seemingly imminent envelopment and destruction, he lost his nerve and asked Moltke, the overall German commander, for permission for the German Eighth Army to retreat more than 160km (100 miles) to defensive positions behind the Vistula River. Such an action would surrender the entirety of East Prussia to the invading Russians. Moltke, believing that the East Prussian front had to be held at all costs, decided to remove Prittwitz from command and replace him with the command team of General Paul von Hindenburg and his Chief of Staff, Erich von Ludendorff. In addition, the seemingly dire situation in East Prussia forced Moltke to make the disastrous decision to remove forces from the right flank of the invasion of France to bolster the Eastern Front.

Such a plan was fraught with great risk, for it involved dividing the German forces in East Prussia, leaving only a small covering force in Rennenkampf's path. If he ever discovered the plan, the lives of every German soldier in East Prussia would be forfeited.

THE BATTLE OF TANNENBERG

Even before the dismissal of Prittwitz, the chief operations officer of the German Eighth Army, Hoffmann, had seen that the Russian advance offered the Germans a chance for a great victory. He believed that the great distance separating the Russian armies gave a daring commander the opportunity to defeat both forces in order before they ever had the chance to unite. But such a plan was fraught with great risk, for it involved dividing the German forces in East Prussia, leaving only a small covering force in Rennenkampf's path. If he ever discovered the plan, the lives of every German soldier in East Prussia would be forfeited.

RIGHT:
GERMAN TROOPS SHARE A MEAL IN A CAMOUFLAGED DEFENSIVE EMPLACEMENT IN EAST PRUSSIA.

THE BATTLE OF TANNENBERG

THE EASTERN FRONT 1914–16

Baltic Sea
RUSSIA
Konigsberg
Gumbinnen
EAST PRUSSIA
Tannenberg
Warsaw
Brest-Litovsk
GERMANY
POLAND
Tarnow
Lemberg
Gorlice
Przemysl
AUSTRIA-HUNGARY

Baltic Sea
Labiau
Konigsberg
FIRST ARMY
EIGHTH ARMY HQ
Danzig
Korschen
Rastenburg
Marienburg
EAST PRUSSIA
Locken
Allenstein
Riesenburg
Rudczanny
Graudenz
Ortelsburg
Lobau
Neumark
Strasburg
Yanov
SECOND ARMY HQ
Lomza
Mlawa
Thorn
Ostrolenka
RUSSIA

Russian infantry
Russian cavalry
German infantry
German cavalry

FIELD MARSHAL PAUL VON HINDENBURG

After a fairly undistinguished career, Hindenburg had retired from the German Army in 1911. However, he was recalled to duty at a time of great national need: during the Russian invasion of East Prussia. With Erich von Ludendorff as his chief of staff, Hindenburg assumed command of the German Eighth Army with orders to halt the Russian steamroller in the east. Using plans devised by his predecessor, he scored a major victory at the Battle of Tannenberg, driving the Russians from German soil, and the victory catapulted him into the national spotlight. In November 1914 Hindenburg was appointed Field Marshal and took command of the entire Eastern Front. He then went on to enhance his reputation by scoring several tactical victories over the Russians in 1915. After the bloody failure at Verdun in 1916, he replaced Erich von Falkenhayn as commander of all German forces. He and Ludendorff chose to fall back to more defensible positions, known as the Hindenburg Line, in France, and concentrate on the destruction of Russia. This decision helped lead to the demise of Russia in 1917. As the war dragged on, and Hindenburg moved from victory to victory, his influence within Germany grew apace. By 1918 Hindenburg and Ludendorff easily dominated the outmatched Kaiser, and Germany became something of a military dictatorship under Hindenburg's control. With the demise of Russia, Hindenburg and Ludendorff chose to pursue total victory through a series of offensives in 1918 in France. Though victory seemed near at times for Germany, the Allies held and counterattacked with devastating force. Hindenburg advised the Kaiser to abdicate and sued the Allies for peace. He remained in command of the German Army until July 1919, and then retired as the greatest German hero of World War I. But his tremendous fame helped to call him back to duty as the President of the Weimar Republic. Aged and frail, the great commander found himself overtaken by a new force in Germany and in 1933 appointed Adolf Hitler as Chancellor of Germany.

FIELD MARSHAL HINDENBURG SURVEYS THE EASTERN FRONT.

ABOVE: MOLTKE MOVED TROOPS FROM THE WESTERN FRONT IN AN EFFORT TO SAVE THE SITUATION IN THE EAST.

Though Hoffmann developed the plan that brought German victory in the east, it was Hindenburg and Ludendorff who carried it out and reaped the rewards of victory. It called for an innovative use of lateral rail communications to carry out a lighting-fast transfer of German forces from north to south. Three German corps would make the journey south and lay in wait for the advance of the unknowing Russian Second Army under Samsonov. One German corps would engage Samsonov and lock his army into battle, while the other two corps would strike the Russian forces in the flanks, creating an envelopment. The German shift of forces began on 23 August, and relied on utter secrecy. If Samsonov caught wind of the German manoeuvre, his army could avoid the coming trap. If Rennenkampf discovered the ruse, however, matters would be undeniably worse.

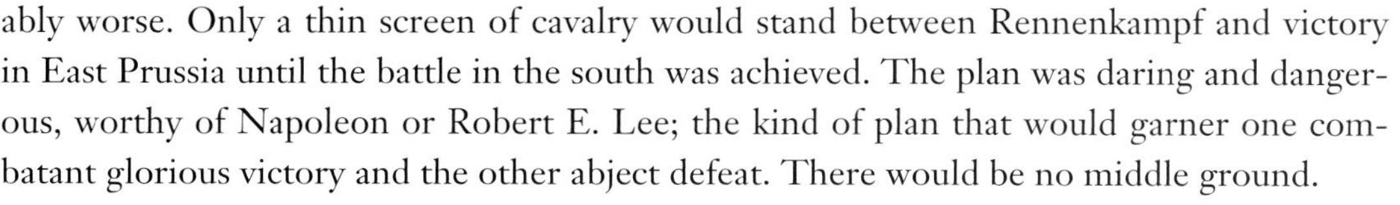

Only a thin screen of cavalry would stand between Rennenkampf and victory in East Prussia until the battle in the south was achieved. The plan was daring and dangerous, worthy of Napoleon or Robert E. Lee; the kind of plan that would garner one combatant glorious victory and the other abject defeat. There would be no middle ground.

Samsonov noted part of the German build-up on his front and informed Zhilinsky that a major battle was in the offing. Certain that it was nothing that he could not handle,

Above: German infantry advance at Tannenberg, only narrowly avoiding Russian artillery fire.

Samsonov ordered an advance on 26 August, the same day that the German forces in the area launched their envelopment manoeuvre. At first, Samsonov believed that the main German force was on his right flank and ordered an attack there. Although the Russian attack achieved some initial success, Samsonov was quite unnerved to discover German forces attacking his centre and his left flank. The scope of the German attack now became clear to the shocked Samsonov, and the dire nature of the situation even began to dawn on Zhilinsky in his headquarters far behind the front lines. The critical moment in the east had come: the entire Russian Second Army was in danger of destruction. But the situation could still be saved if Rennenkampf advanced south to strike the German forces from behind. Zhilinsky ordered the cautious Rennenkampf to move south, but whether his over-cautious nature, or his well-known hatred for his rival Samsonov motivated him, Rennenkampf plodded slowly westward, leaving the Russian Second Army to its fate.

To the south-west, the Battle of Tannenberg raged on. By 28 August the situation for the Russians had become critical, as both flanks began to collapse. Samsonov toured the front lines in an effort to raise the fighting spirit of his men, hoping that an advance from the Russian centre could yet save the day. However, the desperation that he saw on his tour forced him to realise that the battle was lost and that his army must retreat in order to survive.

The scope of the German attack now became clear to the shocked Samsonov, and the dire nature of the situation even began to dawn on Zhilinsky far behind the front lines. The critical moment in the east had come: the entire Russian Second Army was in danger.

LEFT: RUSSIAN TROOPS TAKING AND RETURNING FIRE DURING THE PIVOTAL BATTLE OF TANNENBERG IN EAST PRUSSIA.

GEWEHR 98
GERMANY

Calibre: 7.92mm (0.31in)
Length: 1255mm (49.5in)
Magazine: 5 round box

His decision came too late. On 29 August the German envelopment slammed shut behind the entrapped Russian Second Army, and the Battle of Tannenberg was over. For the Russians, Tannenberg was a debacle of epic proportions. The Russian Second Army lost some 125,000 men, while the Germans suffered only 15,000 casualties. After he realised the scale of the defeat, Samsonov committed suicide.

THE BATTLE OF MASURIAN LAKES

Flush with victory, the German Eighth Army, under the command of Hindenburg and Ludendorff, now began to redeploy northward to face Rennenkampf. The Germans, aware of Rennenkampf's exact location due to the interception of Russian radio messages, moved to strike the southern flank of the Russian First Army. Emboldening the German effort was the recent arrival of two corps that had been removed from the advance on the Western Front. On 7 September the reinforced Germans struck the Russian left flank, threatening to drive the Russian First Army into the sea. With the disaster of Tannenberg fresh in his mind, Rennenkampf feared that his forces would be

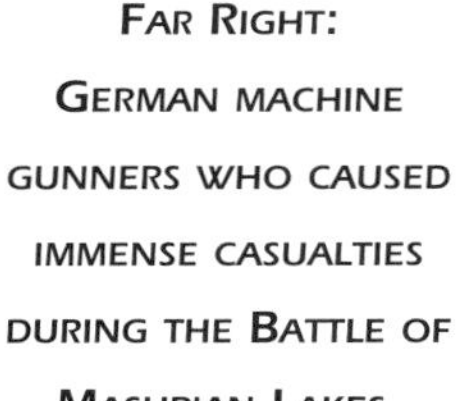

FAR RIGHT: GERMAN MACHINE GUNNERS WHO CAUSED IMMENSE CASUALTIES DURING THE BATTLE OF MASURIAN LAKES.

RIGHT: WORRIED STAFF OF GENERAL SAMSONOV DURING THE OFFENSIVE.

BELOW RIGHT: DEAD RUSSIANS LITTER THE LANDSCAPE IN THE WAKE OF THE RUSSIAN REARGUARD'S GALLANT STAND IN THE BATTLE OF MASURIAN LAKES.

For the Russians, Tannenberg was a debacle of epic proportions. The Russian Second Army lost some 125,000 men, while the Germans suffered only 15,000 casualties. After he realised the scale of the defeat, Samsonov committed suicide.

outflanked and destroyed, and he ordered a full retreat on 9 September. In an effort to stem the remorseless German advance so that the bulk of his forces could escape, he ordered two divisions to attack the German centre. It was to be a suicide mission for the brave Russian rearguard: the two divisions were totally wiped out. Each man sold his life dearly, holding the massive German force at bay for 48 hours, but many Russians had escaped due to the valour of their fallen comrades.

By 13 September all Russian forces had exited East Prussia. The Battle of Masurian Lakes was another disastrous Russian defeat. Some 120,000 Russians had been lost, compared to only 10,000 German casualties. Ultimately, the Russian effort to seize East Prussia had failed miserably. Zhilinsky was sacked, and Rennenkampf's reputation was destroyed. On the German side, both Hindenburg and Ludendorff became national heroes, though in many ways they had simply carried out Hoffman's masterful plan. The twin battles of Tannenberg and Masurian Lakes rank as among the most decisive in history. A German force, dwarfed by two invading Russian forces, enveloped and destroyed them both.

Hindenburg and Ludendorff would be quick to press their advantage and launch an invasion of Russian territory; the remainder of World War I in the east would be fought in

Below: The retreating Russians destroyed this bridge in East Prussia in a desperate attempt to slow the German advance. Indeed the Russians would never quite recover from the setbacks of 1914.

LEFT:
RUSSIAN SOLDIERS PAUSE FOR TEA AFTER THE FRONT STABILISED FOR WINTER.

Russia. Historians argue about the nature of the ill-fated Russian invasion of Germany in 1914. Russian command was inept at best, and the invasion was premature, launched as it was before the Russian armed forces were fully prepared. However, their sacrifice was not entirely in vain, for the Russian invasion forced Moltke to reduce critical forces in the west. This action helped the Germans to win the Battle of Masurian Lakes, but possibly partly caused the failure of the Schlieffen Plan, later dooming Germany to defeat in a war of attrition in the trenches.

Russian command was inept at best, and the invasion was premature, launched as it was before the Russian armed forces were fully prepared. However, their sacrifice was not entirely in vain, for the Russian invasion forced Moltke to reduce critical forces in the west.

AUSTRIAN PLANNING

The Dual Monarchy of Austria-Hungary boasted an army 800,000 men strong. Elderly Emperor Francis Joseph held nominal command over the Austrian Army, but wielded no real military power. It was Count Franz Conrad von Hotzendorf who controlled the military might of the Dual Monarchy. He was a supremely confident man, but is regarded by most historians as a bungler of the highest order. In addition, the instrument at his disposal, the Austrian armed forces, had several glaring faults. As a multi-national empire, Austria had to rely upon soldiers of dubious loyalty to the crown. Many fighting men of ethnic minorities eagerly awaited the coming battles as a chance to desert and fight against their Austrian masters. In addition, Austria's

ABOVE:
JUBILANT AUSTRIANS DURING THE FIRST WEEKS OF THE WAR, ON THEIR WAY TO THE FRONT.

RIGHT: SERB CIVILIAN MEN AND WOMEN HANGED BY THE AUSTRIANS FOR CIVIL DISOBEDIENCE IN MACVA IN 1914 ON THE ORDERS OF GENERAL POTIOREK.

BELOW: AN AUSTRO-HUNGARIAN PRIVATE IN 1914. THE AUSTRO-HUNGARIAN ARMY CONTAINED A BROAD ETHNIC MIX OF PEOPLES, REFLECTING THE NATURE OF THE AUSTRIAN EMPIRE.

transportation infrastructure was poor and the Austrian economy was ill-prepared to bear the strain of war.

Such problems were small considerations for Conrad in planning for the outbreak of war. He believed that the war would result in a quick destruction of Serbia and would be followed by a joint Austro-German campaign against Russia. However, fate intervened and did not allow Conrad such a clear path to victory. During war planning, it became clear that the Germans had decided to concentrate their forces on the defeat of France. Moltke, the German commander, pressed Conrad to agree to an Austrian offensive against Russia upon the outbreak of war. This offensive was designed to distract Russian forces from their planned invasion of East Prussia. Conrad agreed, but only after receiving assurances of a German attack in the north to coincide with the Austrian offensive. Thus 'Plan R', a joint Austro-German attack, was devised. Neither Conrad nor Moltke actually planned to honour their commitments. The Germans had no intention of launching an offensive in the east in 1914, and Conrad secretly schemed to launch an offensive against Serbia, not Russia. The Central Powers were thus destined to launch the war in the east based on a misunderstanding. The resulting Austrian debacle would strain relations between the two powers to breaking point.

THE ATTACK ON SERBIA

On the outbreak of war, Conrad chose to launch an offensive designed to crush the 'Serbian Menace' rather than honour his agreement with Moltke. The Austrians did not see their actions as a violation of the agreement with Germany, for Conrad expected a quick, decisive war against Serbia, allowing adequate time for a subsequent offensive into Russia. In their effort to defeat Serbia, the Austrians sent their Second Army, which formed their strategic reserve, to join two armies already along the Serbian border. It was thought that such a force, representing nearly half of Austria's military might, would easily be enough to deal with the little Balkan nation. Austrian forces in the area fell under the command of General Potiorek, the powerful governor of Bosnia-Herzegovina, whose importance allowed him to operate free of Conrad's oversight. Potiorek, although he felt somewhat responsible for the death of Francis Ferdinand, proved to be an incompetent military commander.

Serbia was much stronger than the Austrians had realised. The Serbian Army, once fully mobilised, numbered some 450,000 men under the very capable leadership of General Radomir Putnik. In addition, Serbian forces were battle tested, having fought in the recent Balkan wars, and could rely on mountainous terrain to help them in the defence of their homeland. On 12 August the Austrian forces attacked, forcing the Serbs to fall back to the Jadar River. All seemed to be going well for the Austrians, and they continued to believe that the war in the Balkans would be a short one. Putnik, though, launched a surprise counter-attack on 16 August, driving the Austrians back across the border. To make matters worse, the Serbs launched a brief invasion of Austria itself. The situation quickly stabilised and allowed for another Austrian invasion of Serbia in October, but this also failed with heavy losses.

Though his first attacks had failed, Potiorek remained confident. The Serbs, after all, could not hold out for long against Austrian might. It would only take one more push to make the entire Serbian edifice crumble. The Austrian Army launched its greatest offensive against Serbia in November, an offensive designed to destroy Serbia and save Potiorek's reputation. It began auspiciously with an Austrian victory near the Kolubara River. The sorely pressed Serbs chose to fall back into the rugged terrain in the centre of their nation and as a result, the Serbian capital of Belgrade fell on 2 December.

Though his first attacks had failed, Potiorek remained confident. The Serbs, after all, could not hold out for long against Austrian might. It would only take one more push to make the entire Serbian edifice crumble.

LEFT: SERBIAN GENERAL RADOMIR PUTNIK WITH HIS TROOPS DURING THE AUSTRIAN INVASION IN 1914. HIS COMMAND SKILLS FOILED AUSTRIAN ATTEMPTS TO CONQUER HIS NATION.

Right:
Serbian troops occupy rudimentary trenches during the height of the struggle against Austria in 1914.

The weather grew quite cold as winter began to set in, and the Austrian soldiers suffered greatly; they were only wearing summer uniforms. One Austrian soldier noted, 'The terrain is horrible, we have no reserves, the soldiers are thinking of suicide'.

However, Putnik saw a chance to steal victory from the jaws of defeat. He expected that the Austrian forces would have great difficulties in receiving supplies in the mountainous terrain. He was right. The weather grew quite cold as winter began to set in, and the Austrian soldiers suffered greatly; they were only wearing summer uniforms. Making matters worse, food and ammunition could not reach the Austrian front-line units due to the poor condition of Serbian roads. One Austrian soldier noted, 'The terrain is horrible, we have no reserves, the soldiers are thinking of suicide.' Having lured the Austrians into an over-extended and exposed position, Putnik launched a counter-attack on 4 December using the last of his reserves. Some 200,000 Serbs set upon 80,000 dispirited Austrians, forcing them to retreat back across the border. On 15 December Serb forces triumphantly recaptured Belgrade.

The Austrians had suffered a great defeat. The 'Serbian Menace' had not been crushed, and the outmatched Potiorek lost his command. Even worse, Austria had shown itself to be weak, unable even to defeat tiny Serbia. The Dual Monarchy now lost its status as a great power, and became ever-more reliant upon Germany.

The true test of the scope of the Austrian defeat in Serbia lies in simple numbers. In the campaign Potiorek had lost fully one half of his force: some 28,000 dead, 120,000 wounded and 75,000 prisoners. The Serbians too had suffered greatly, losing 22,000 dead, 91,000 wounded and 19,000 captured. The war was bitter, and both countries were exhausted. Even so, both nations remained committed to the other's destruction.

THE WAR AGAINST RUSSIA

Before the ultimate failure of the Serbian campaign, Austrian forces suffered an even greater defeat at the hands of the Russians in Galicia. When it had finally become clear to Conrad that Russia was a threat not to be ignored, the Austrian forces under his command belatedly put 'Plan R' into effect. The plan called for four Austrian armies to advance into Poland in an attempt to sever Russian lines of communication. It was hoped that such an action would help to blunt the Russian offensive into Germany, thus giving the Schlieffen Plan time to succeed. However, Conrad's own actions served to weaken the coming offensive. Pre-war planning had called for the Second Army to take part in the invasion of Poland, but it had been committed to the Serbian campaign. Thus the scale of Austrian operations in the east had to be reduced, offering the Russians a chance at victory.

On 22 August three Austrian armies invaded Poland. The Russians, expecting such a manoeuvre, had four armies, under the command of General Nicholas Ivanov, waiting in defence. Initially the Austrian advance went well, with a victory over the Russians at Krasnik that forced the Russian armies to fall back on Lublin. But the victory was to prove

BELOW: RUSSIAN TROOPS WEARING VARIOUS ITEMS OF UNIFORM OCCUPY TRENCHES AGAINST THE AUSTRIAN ADVANCE OF 1914.

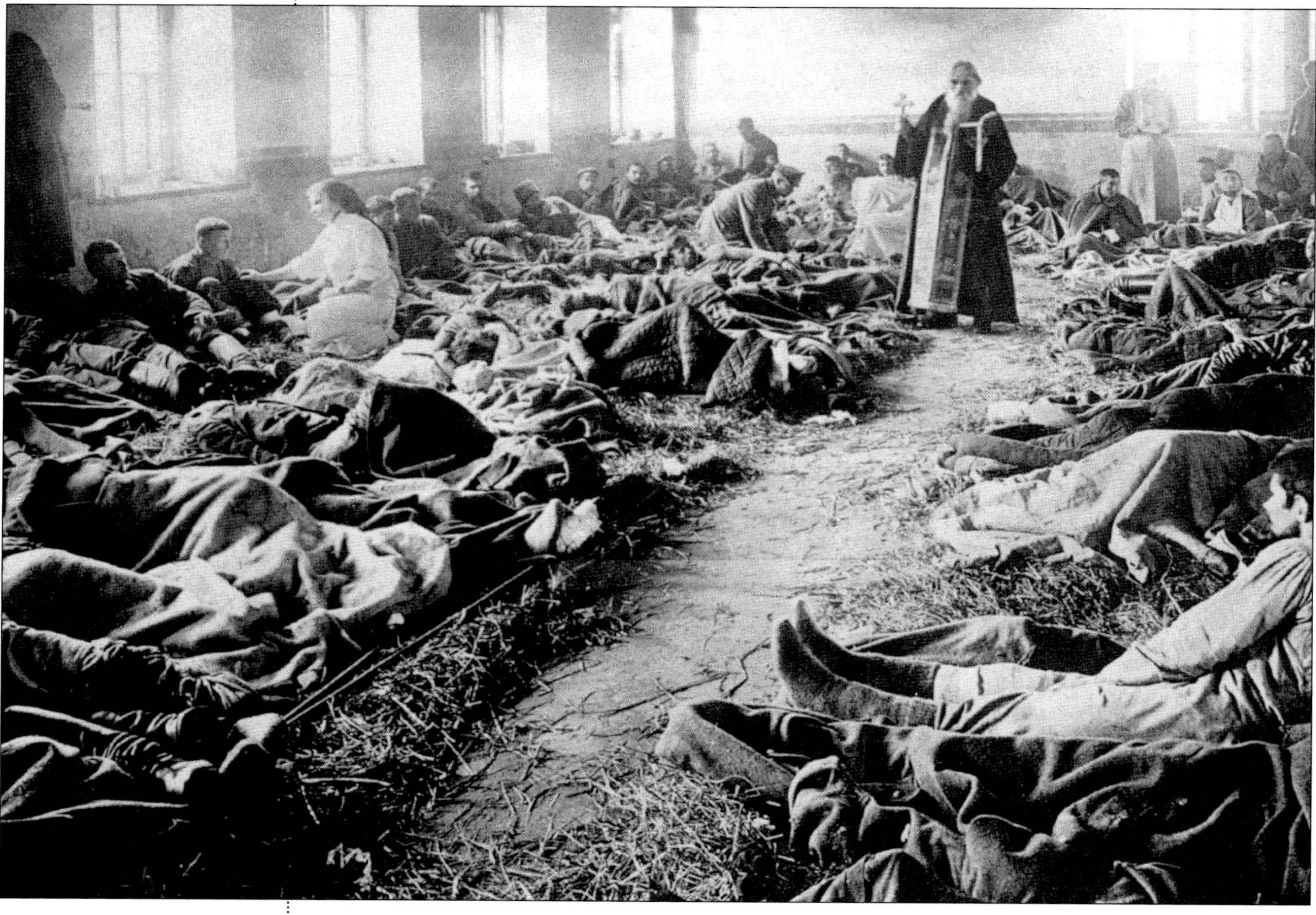

ABOVE: SOME OF THE MASSIVE NUMBER OF RUSSIAN WOUNDED RECEIVE BLESSINGS FROM AN ORTHODOX PRIEST IN A PRIMITIVE HOSPITAL AT SUVALKI ON THE EASTERN FRONT.

fleeting. Russian forces were too numerous, and communications between the widely separated Austrian forces were poor. Thus, while one Austrian army drove on toward Lublin, the Russians threatened to surround and annihilate the southernmost Austrian army under the command of General von Brudermann.

When Conrad learned of the impending disaster, he failed to grasp its true nature and succumbed to a fit of optimism. He ordered two of his armies to retreat to Lemberg and to stand fast there. All the while, the Austrian First Army, under the command of General von Dankl, pressed on toward Lublin. This action played into the Russian hands. The Russian Eighth Army, under General Brusilov, closed on the retreating Austrians at Lemberg and threatened to envelop them there. In the north, Dankl's continued advance opened both of his flanks to attack and his force too was threatened with destruction. The situation for the Austrians was dire indeed. The attack into Russia had been foolhardy and now threatened the Dual Monarchy with imminent defeat.

Conrad finally came to realise the dire nature of the situation. Aided in his decision by overhearing Russian radio traffic – which indicated that Russian forces were about to administer the death blow to the over-extended Austrian armies – Conrad ordered his forces to fall back to a line 225km (140 miles) west of Lemberg. The Austrian invasion of Russia had been crushed, and the tattered remains of the Austrian armies were in full

ABOVE: RUSSIAN TROOPS CELEBRATE THEIR VICTORY AT LEMBERG (NOW LVOV).

flight. Austrian forces surrendered most of Galicia to Russian control, leaving the Russians perilously close to breaking out of the mountainous country and into the Hungarian plain. In addition, Russian forces surrounded and laid siege to 150,000 Austrian troops in the fortress of Przemysl. The new defences in Galicia held, but Austria had suffered a catastrophic defeat, having lost 250,000 casualties and a further 100,000 men taken prisoner, nearly one half of the combat strength of the Austrian Army in the east.

GERMAN AID AND CONTINUED BATTLE

Austria's near collapse caused great consternation in Germany. Relations between the two allies became quite tense when Conrad warned the Germans that if they did not come to his aid, Austria might have to sue for a separate peace. Though fully involved on the Western Front, the Germans could not allow their tottering ally to fall so quickly and would have to send troops to the south to her aid. As the war progressed, it was only German military and economic aid that enabled the Dual Monarchy to survive. The ever-worsening situation caused the German ambassador in Vienna to remark, 'God preserve my poor fatherland from ever again making war with Austria as an ally.' For their part the Austrians came to view German aid and motives with suspicion and Conrad often referred to Germany as 'our secret enemy'.

The ever-worsening situation caused the German ambassador in Vienna to remark, 'God preserve my poor fatherland from ever again making war with Austria as an ally'. For their part the Austrians came to view German aid and motives with suspicion.

The Germans rushed a new army south, the Ninth – under the command of Hindenburg and Ludendorff – to join with the embattled Austrian forces in Galicia. When they arrived, the German command team was shocked to find that the Russians had 60 divisions in the area compared to only 18 for the combined Austro-German force. With such an advantage in numbers, Hindenburg and Ludendorff reasoned that the Russians would shortly launch a major offensive. The German commanders begged for reinforcements from the west to help stabilise the situation, but none were forthcoming. It seemed that there was little to do but sit and wait for disaster in the east.

The German commanders begged for reinforcements from the west to help stabilise the situation, but none were forthcoming. It seemed that there was little to do but sit and wait for disaster in the east.

However, Hindenburg and Ludendorff chose to launch an audacious attack, preferring a policy of action, which would make the duo legendary figures in Germany. Ludendorff reasoned that the German Ninth Army could strike before the Russians were ready, thus spoiling their attack. If all went well, he even hoped that Warsaw would fall to the force of German arms. On 28 September German and Austrian forces advanced, catching the Russians by surprise. As the Russians dissolved into frantic retreat, German forces reached the Vistula River south of Warsaw on 9 October. Further south, Austrian forces also enjoyed surprising success and relieved the beleaguered defenders of Przemysl. This rapid advance left the Ninth Army open to possible envelopment by the regrouping and numerically superior Russians. In an effort to avoid disaster, Ludendorff ordered a retreat. By the end of the month the Ninth Army had returned to its original positions.

The Germans learned, again through uncoded Russian radio messages, that the Russians planned to follow up their victory with an immediate invasion of the German region of Silesia. Once again Hindenburg and Ludendorff chose to launch a pre-emptive strike that would foil any Russian plan to launch an invasion of Germany. Utilising superior German rail communications, Ludendorff shifted German troops north and fell on the Russians from behind. Once again, German troops advanced to the Vistula before the surprised Russians could marshal their forces and threaten the isolated German Army with envelopment. Once the Russians brought their forces to bear, the Germans retreated to their original positions once again. In addition, Austrian forces in the south fell back, leaving Przemysl to its fate. Its defenders would hold out for another four months.

BELOW: GERMAN ARTILLERY IN ACTION ON THE EASTERN FRONT. THE GERMANS WERE ABLE TO CONCENTRATE MUCH MORE ARTILLERY ON THE BATTLEFIELD THAN WERE THE RUSSIANS – GIVING THEM AN EDGE IN THE BITTER CONFLICT.

As the winter struck the east, the front settled down until 1915. The bold attacks of Hindenburg and Ludendorff had not won a great victory. However, they had kept the Russians occupied and prevented a possibly disastrous Russian invasion. Thus for the Germans, 1914 in the east had been something of an unexpected victory. Inferior German forces had shattered every Russian attempt at invasion. However, for Austria, the battles of 1914 had been nearly fatal. Serbia had not been defeated, Galicia had been lost, nearly one half of the Austrian Army had been destroyed, and Austria had become reliant upon German support for her very survival. To the Russians, the results of the fighting of 1914 were somewhat mixed. There had been disaster in East Prussia, but victory in Galicia. Russia suffered crippling, hidden defeats during the opening months of World War I. Russian casualties had been prodigious, numbering over 1.5 million. Though mobilisation meant that the Russian Army still numbered over five million men, many of its best soldiers had been lost. All hope for a quick victory was gone by the end of the year, and Russia faced a war of attrition for which it was ill prepared. The stress placed upon the Russian economy by the war would be well-nigh unbearable. Finally, Russian actions in the east had an unintended and fatal effect: the threat on the Eastern Front had attracted Germany's military attention. In 1915 Germany would seek victory in the east, not the west.

ABOVE: AUSTRIAN AND GERMAN TROOPS ADVANCING TOGETHER AGAINST THE RUSSIANS. THEIR COMBINED ACTIONS WOULD EVENTUALLY BRING RUSSIA TO ITS KNEES.

CHAPTER 4

Stalemate in the Trenches

THE WORLD OF THE TRENCHES WAS ONE OF SQUALOR AND HARDSHIP AS DEPICTED BY THESE BRITISH SOLDIERS RESTING AMIDST THE LITTER OF WAR. AT ANY MOMENT THE TRENCH COULD BE SHELLED BY THE GERMAN GUNS, SENDING THE SOLDIERS SCURRYING TO THEIR DUG-OUTS.

STRATEGIC DEBATE

At the centre of the strategic debate was the advent of an unexpected new, attritional style of modern warfare. World War I had settled down into something that resembled a gigantic siege, a siege that many felt threatened to destroy the old world.

After failing to achieve victory at First Ypres, Falkenhayn had to attempt to come to terms with a two-front war. After much study, he concluded that the war in the west was a stalemate, and that in the east the Russians could give ground for an almost indeterminate length of time, denying German forces a meaningful victory. The German commander realised then that the war had degenerated into a war of attrition. Hindenburg and Ludendorff, the heroes of Tannenberg, did not agree. They argued that decisive victory beckoned in the east, if only Falkenhayn would transfer to them much-needed reinforcements. In the end, Falkenhayn agreed. The German offensive efforts of 1915 – with one notable exception – would be directed against Russia.

The Allies, too, had similar strategic problems. The French, led by Joffre, were quite certain that any Allied attack had to be made on the Western Front in order to expel the German Army from France. The British were not so certain. Several key British policymakers, including Winston Churchill, the First Lord of the Admiralty, and David Lloyd George, sought to circumvent the stalemated Western Front and attack elsewhere in Europe against less stalwart enemies. Thus dawned the 'Easterner-Westerner' debate that would haunt Allied planning for the rest of the war. Suggestions for an eastern alternative included landing British troops on the North German Plain as a direct threat to Berlin, landing troops in Greece to aid the Serbs, and landing troops at Gallipoli in an effort to defeat the newest German ally: Turkey. Most of the British military, including French and Haig, were vehemently opposed to any eastern strategy. They contended that Germany was the main enemy, and that striking Turkey would do little to help defeat the Germans. Though the debate in Britain raged on, in 1915 France remained the senior alliance partner. As the French were bearing the main burden of the war, they retained a firm control over Allied planning. As a result, the main Allied efforts of 1915 came on the Western Front. The only victory for the Easterners was in a seemingly rather minor naval assault on the Dardanelles.

OVERVIEW

After a great deal of strategic debate, the combatants in World War I decided to follow different roads to what they still hoped would be a quick victory in 1915. The Germans, under their new commander Erich von Falkenhayn, saw the Western Front as something of a stalemate and chose to make their main military efforts in the east in order to destroy Russia. However, the French and the British sought decisive battle in the west and hoped at least to drive the Germans from their gains of 1914. The result was the first year of true trench warfare on the Western Front, and both the Allies and the Central Powers struggled to come to grips with the dismal realities posed by a siege that extended from the English Channel to Switzerland. It was war on a scale never seen before, and a war that taxed the nations of Europe to the maximum. Even by the end of 1915, the strains of war were already becoming apparent across the continent.

TRENCH WARFARE

At the centre of the strategic debate was the advent of an unexpected new, attritional style of modern warfare. World War I had settled down into something that resembled a gigantic siege, a siege that many felt threatened to destroy the old world. As the Germans had fallen back from the Marne, they had dug in on the most defensible areas available, often behind rivers or on high ground. The pursuing Allies had also constructed trenches, but these were usually located on much less favourable ground. The Belgian city of Ypres serves as perhaps the most famous example of the advantage possessed by the Germans through locating their defensive works with great care. The British-held Ypres

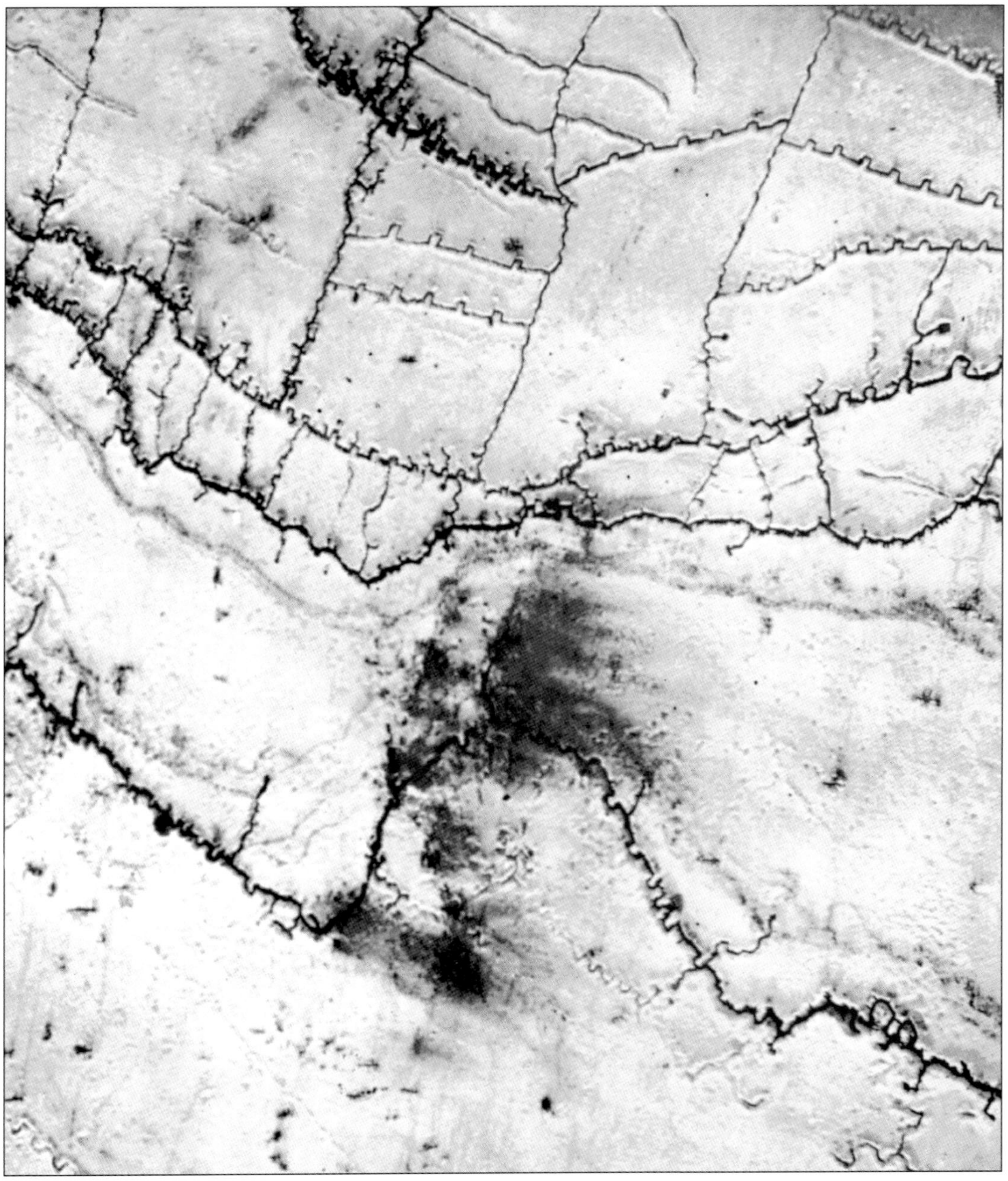

LEFT: THE TRENCHES FORMED SYSTEMS OF VAST COMPLEXITY, AS SHOWN BY THIS AERIAL PHOTOGRAPH, THAT DEFIED ATTACKERS' BEST EFFORTS TO ACHIEVE A DECISIVE BREAKTHROUGH.

lay in a salient jutting out into the German lines. The Germans had managed to seize a system of ridges that surrounded the British lines, and from there they could overlook the BEF, watching its every move. At a moment's notice, Germans could call down a hailstorm of fire upon any British activity in the entire sector. For this reason, the apex of the Ypres salient ranked as the most dangerous posting for the BEF and received the colourful name 'Hell-fire Corner'.

BELOW LEFT: GENERAL ERICH VON FALKENHAYN, THE ARCHITECT OF GERMAN STRATEGY IN 1915, WHO SAW THE WAR AS ONE OF ATTRITION.

Although the construction of trench systems would become more complex as the war dragged on, the trenches

GAS WARFARE

The Germans were the first to use deadly poisonous gas on a significant scale in the First Battle of Ypres in April 1915. In the attack, the Germans opened several cylinders of chlorine gas and allowed the clouds to drift into French and British lines. The Allied soldiers, not expecting the assault, had no respirators and suffered great losses as the chlorine slowly ate away the lungs of exposed troops, resulting in some 5000 grisly deaths. The use of gas resulted in the immediate introduction of counter measures, and by early 1916 the trademark box respirator was in widespread use. As the war progressed, both sides developed ever-more deadly types of gas and more effective delivery methods. In July 1915 the Germans began to enclose gas within artillery shells, and so no area of the Allied lines was immune from this dreadful form of attack. The most horrible type of gas was introduced by the Germans in July 1917 and became known as Mustard Gas. Odourless and colourless, it caused severe burning to the skin and the respiratory system. Although horrible, gas was never a war-winning weapon. Constantly updated defences meant that its use was often just a nuisance, forcing men to fight in their clumsy respirators. In total, during World War I, the use of gas caused one million casualties. The British poet Wilfrid Owen caught the terror of a gas attack in his poem *'Dulce et Decorum Est'* (*'Dulce et decorum est pro patria mori'* was a popular phrase on recruitment posters, meaning 'it is glorious to die for one's country'):

Gas! Gas! Quick boys! - an ecstasy of fumbling,
Fitting the clumsy helmets just in time;
But someone still was yelling out and stumbling,
And flound'ring like a man in fire or lime ...
Dim, through the misty panes and thick green light,
As under a green sea, I saw him drowning.
In all my dreams, before my helpless sight,
He plunges at me, guttering, choking, drowning.
If in some smothering dreams you too could pace
Behind the wagon that we flung him in,
And watch the white eyes writhing in his face,
His hanging face, like a devil's sick of sin;
If you could hear, at every jolt, the blood
Come gargling from the froth-corrupted lungs,
Obscene as cancer, bitter as the cud
Of vile, incurable sores on innocent tongues, -
My friend, you would not tell with such high zest
To children ardent for some desperate glory,
The old lie: *Dulce et decorum est*
Pro patria mori.

INDIAN TROOPS USE PRIMITIVE GAS MASKS ON THE WESTERN FRONT.

of 1915 were already formidable. They were usually 2.4m (8ft) deep, and were guarded by a parapet and row upon row of deadly barbed-wire entanglements. In better trench systems, the occupants constructed deep dug-outs beneath the trench proper, which protected them from all but a direct hit from a heavy artillery shell.

The trenches were constructed following a zig-zag pattern designed to limit the impact of shells and to prevent enemy flanking fire. Often front-line trench systems consisted of two trenches separated by 182m (200yds), but connected by communication trenches. Machine-gun nests interspersed in the front-line trenches provided tremendous additional firepower for the defenders. Behind the main trenches lurked several more defensive constructions, including additional machine-gun strongpoints, support trenches and artillery emplacements. The entire trench system amounted to a defensive belt often some 16km (10 miles) in depth, consisting of an unimaginable rabbit's warren of meandering trench lines. In all, the trench systems of the Western Front extended for a mind-boggling 8045km (5000 miles).

The trenches of World War I posed an insoluble problem for any attacker. Defenders could rely on the concentrated fire of machine guns and massed artillery pieces. Working in tandem, these weapons called down a deadly 'storm of steel' that could obliterate an attacking force if it was caught in the open in the area between the opposing trench systems. This open area became known as no-man's-land. In their attempt to overcome such daunting defences, attackers in World War I had relatively little in their arsenal. Infantry weapons and machine guns were useless against entrenched defenders. Artillery, with its plunging fire, seemed to be the only weapon that could destroy an entrenchment and evict its inhabitants. Only heavy artillery could accomplish such a task, but most combatant nations had far too few heavy artillery pieces available. As the war progressed, artillery and munitions became abundant and were used with great abandon. The British, for instance, fired off an amazing 1.5 million artillery shells in the preparatory bombardment for the Battle of the Somme. But artillery had a fatal weakness in the attack: inaccuracy. For the first time in military history artillery utilised indirect fire, meaning that the gunners could not see their targets and often fired from miles away. Achieving accuracy from such

BELOW: CONSTRUCTION AND MAINTENANCE OF THE TRENCH SYSTEMS ON THE WESTERN FRONT REQUIRED NEARLY CONSTANT, BACK-BREAKING PHYSICAL WORK. HERE BRITISH SOLDIERS BRING FORWARD SUPPORT MATERIAL FOR THEIR TRENCHES.

distances takes constant practice and consummate professionalism but the gunners of World War I had to undergo on-the-job training. As a result, from 100 shells fired at an unseen trench, only two would register direct hits. Taking production problems into consideration, chances were that one of the direct hits would be a dud. Artillery was masterful at destroying large targets – like an advancing army in no-man's-land – but was poor at hitting small targets, like a 0.6m (2ft) wide trench top. Thus artillery bombardments would be noisy and impressive, but often had little effect on an entrenched enemy. Only advances in technology would eventually come to alter the balance in 1918.

Finally, attacking forces in World War I lacked two essential things: communications and a weapon of exploitation. Before World War I, commanders had been able to see their battlefield and control it through the use of runners. For instance, the US Confederate commander, Robert E. Lee, could see almost the entire battlefield at Gettysburg and was able to issue instructions to his forces with relative ease. The Industrial Revolution, however, changed all of that. Battlefields were now vast, often covering hundreds of miles, but communications technology had not kept pace with these changes. World War II commanders could rely on radio communications to control their forces, but commanders in World War I did not have that luxury, for their radios were primitive and cumbersome. Once attacking forces left their trenches, commanders virtually lost all contact with their men, and thus all control of the battle.

Civil War and Napoleonic generals had a weapon that afforded the chance to convert victory into a rout: the cavalry. On the Western Front, though, cavalry was even more

Far Left: On an inspection tour a French general watches his men dig a trench. Officers on both sides in the war were roundly criticised for their failure to realise how bad the gruesome conditions were in which their men lived.

Below: Even during so-called rest periods soldiers on the Western Front were constantly at work. Here British soldiers manhandle their gun into a firing position.

ABOVE: TRENCHES WERE QUITE ILL-SUITED FOR EFFECTIVE USE OF CAVALRY – THOUGH COMMANDERS WERE SLOW TO LEARN THAT LESSON. HERE THE DECCAN HORSE ADVANCE AROUND THE TIME OF NEUVE CHAPELLE.

World War I was the single modern war that lacked a weapon of exploitation, that could utilise speed to transform a tactical victory into a strategic advance.

vulnerable than infantry when caught in the open. After World War I, generals could rely on the speed of armour to win lightning-quick victories over defending forces. Thus World War I was the single modern war that lacked a weapon of exploitation, that could utilise speed to transform a tactical victory into a strategic advance.

On the offensive, World War I generals were at a tremendous disadvantage in weaponry. Battles could not effectively be commanded due to a lack of communications and armies could only advance as fast as their feet allowed. However, defenders were able to make use of telegraph communications and rail transport behind the lines. This disparity meant that defenders always knew more about the battle than attackers and could rush reinforcements to the scene more quickly. The technological realities of the turn of the twentieth century thus dictated a defensive war. Defenders could out-shoot, out-think and out-manoeuvre attackers. However, wars are not often won on the defensive, and the military ethos of the time called for attack. Thus attack after attack went forward in abject futility and the war gained its well-earned reputation for horror.

NEUVE CHAPELLE

The French commander, Joffre, longed for a resumption of offensive action on the Western Front and called for a joint Franco-British assault designed to destroy the large German salient in central France. The plan involved a French offensive in Artois coupled with a British advance on the Aubers Ridge near the village of Neuve Chapelle.

However, Joffre's preparations for the offensive were delayed, and he decided on a postponement. General French, the commander of the BEF, did not agree with Joffre's reasoning and decided to go forward with the British portion of the offensive.

French entrusted the Neuve Chapelle offensive to Douglas Haig and his newly christened First Army. Detailed planning fell to the commander of IV Corps, General Henry Rawlinson. In his plan of attack, he chose to attempt only a short advance in order to seize the German front-line trenches, and then to defeat the inevitable German counter-attack. However, when Haig saw the plan, he altered it. He wanted a more meaningful advance, one designed to capture Aubers Ridge. Thus was born one of the great debates on the Western Front. Should offensives aim at short advances – termed 'Bite and Hold' offensives – or should one expect a breakthrough and a decisive victory? Haig often favoured the latter.

The BEF had gathered 340 artillery pieces to bombard a narrow attack frontage of only 1828m (2000yds), resulting in some 136kg (300lb) of shell crashing down on every yard of German trench. However, the preparatory bombardment was to be limited to a hurricane of fire for only 35 minutes. Rawlinson and Haig chose such a short bombardment partly out of a desire to retain surprise, and also because the BEF had very limited supplies of artillery shells to hand.

The assault rolled forward at 0730 hours on 10 March 1915. The Germans, partly due to British deception efforts, were quite surprised by the attack, for one of the few times of

Below: Combatants in the Great War relied, in the main, on horsed transport. Nations on both sides scoured the countryside to find the millions of horses needed to keep the massive armies in the field moving. Here a British Hotchkiss gun team practices before coming into action.

ABOVE: SOLDIERS WERE OFTEN LOADED-DOWN WITH HUGE PACKS THAT MADE ALREADY DIFFICULT FIGHTING CONDITIONS ALL THE MORE HARSH. HERE SEVERAL HEAVILY-LADEN FRENCH SOLDIERS DEFEND A SKETCHY POSITION AGAINST A GERMAN ATTACK.

FAR RIGHT: MASSED ARTILLERY CAME TO DOMINATE THE WAR. THE EVER-INCREASING NUMBERS OF GUNS, THOUGH, HAD AN INSATIABLE APPETITE FOR SHELLS – DRIVING COMBATANTS TO NEAR ECONOMIC RUIN.

the entire war. The surprise resulted in the BEF enjoying an initial numerical superiority of four to one. In the attack's centre, British troops, augmented by the Indian Corps, advanced quickly. They achieved their objectives with ease and pressed on past Neuve Chapelle. On the flanks of the advance, where the artillery bombardment had been less effective, both British and Indian troops ran into trouble. Here unbroken barbed-wire entanglements slowed their advance and they faced enfilade fire from German forces on their flank that had not been attacked.

Thus victory seemed to beckon in the centre while the flanks of the advance were engaged in bitter fighting. Haig and Rawlinson knew but little of the ongoing victories and defeats. Advancing troops had to communicate with their commanders through the use of runners or carrier pigeons; both methods were dangerous and took hours of valuable time. As a result, most information received at headquarters was badly out of date upon its arrival. Rawlinson chose to use his reserves, which were supposed to lead the assault on the Aubers Ridge, to aid in the faltering assaults on the British flanks. Rawlinson's critics contend that he could have achieved a great victory, if he had only reinforced the British and Indian troops in the centre of the advance, as they had nearly broken the German lines. Given the circumstances and the impenetrable 'fog of war' caused by lack of communications, Rawlinson's perceived mistakes are understandable.

Although they were surprised, the Germans reacted quickly to the threat at Neuve Chapelle and rushed some 16,000 reinforcements to the scene. Clearly, these fresh German forces would have dealt harshly with any British attempts to break through in the centre. On the second day of the offensive, the British forces had lost much of their initial

THE WESTERN FRONT IN 1915

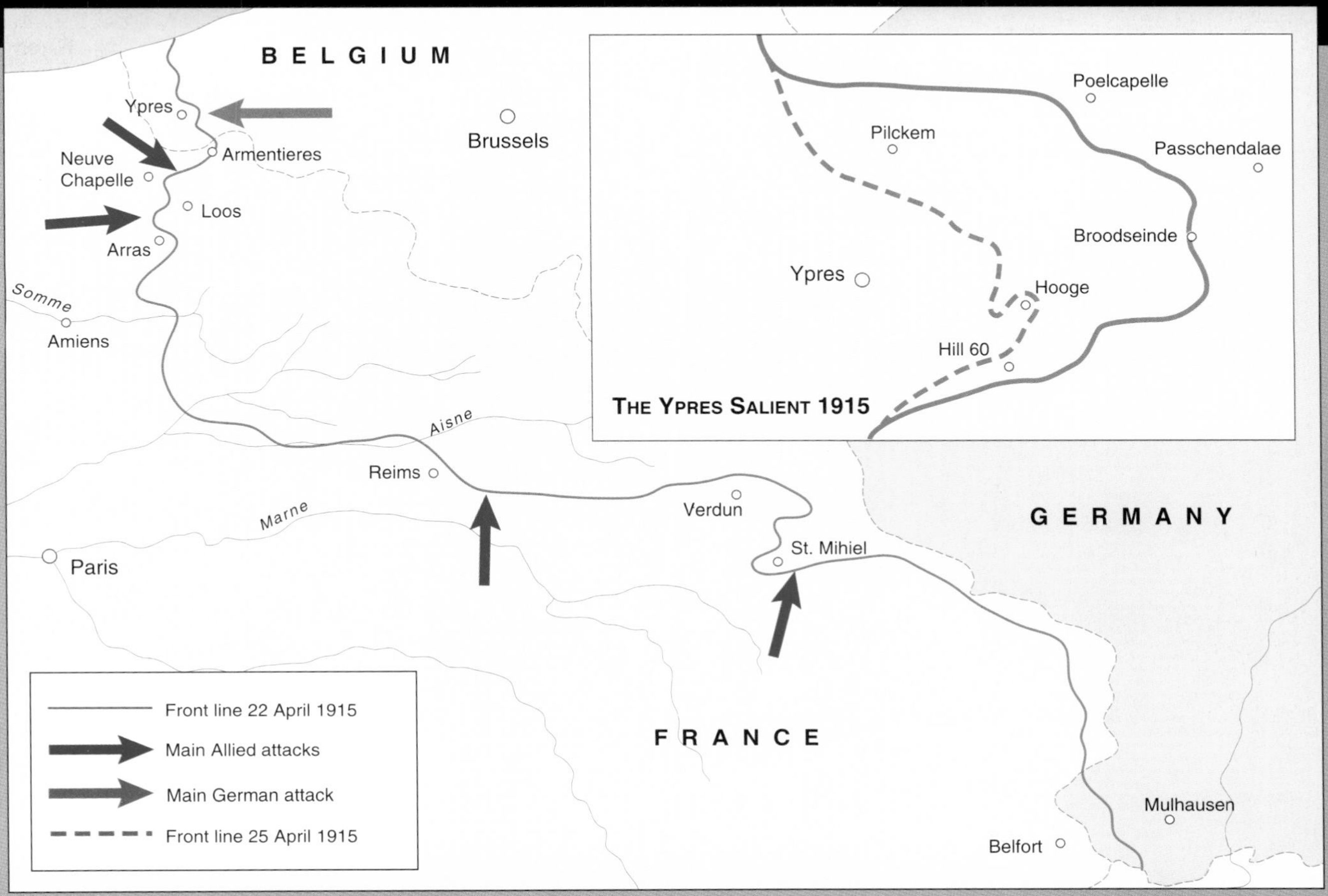

BELGIUM
Ypres
Neuve Chapelle
Armentieres
Loos
Arras
Brussels
Somme
Amiens
Aisne
Reims
Marne
Paris
Verdun
St. Mihiel
GERMANY
FRANCE
Mulhausen
Belfort

THE YPRES SALIENT 1915
Poelcapelle
Pilckem
Passchendalae
Broodseinde
Ypres
Hooge
Hill 60

Front line 22 April 1915
Main Allied attacks
Main German attack
Front line 25 April 1915

TRENCH LIFE

The men who lived in the trenches of the Western Front inhabited a troglodyte world that alternated between boredom and unimaginable horror. The men lived outside, or in small, often muddy dugouts, for months on end, enduring searing heat, bitter cold, drought and torrential rain. Food and sanitation were poor at best and non-existent at worst. In such unsanitary conditions, men quickly became covered in lice.

THE SQUALOR OF THE TRENCHES.

> We did not notice the lice so much when standing perished with cold on look-out. But when we got in our tiny dugouts, and our bodies began to get warm, then out would come the lice from their hiding places in our clothing ... Yes, they were our bosom companions and ... when utterly worn out, both physically and mentally, yet unable to sleep because of the lice, I have known men to actually cry and curse the lice and He who made them.

During prolonged periods of battle no-man's-land became an open graveyard, containing the broken bodies of several thousand people - both dead and dying - often in advanced states of decomposition.

> There we were entrenched within [457m] 500 yards of them [the Germans] and the whole ground between was full of dead which remained there, some being killed as early as 12 September and we did not leave until 13 October. You can imagine the stink. Besides this the whole place became a graveyard and mass of every sort of abomination.

Many of the dead and wounded, it should be remembered, were the dear friends of those who still lived in the trenches. To make matters worse, the survivors often had to watch as the swarms of rats that roamed the battlefield claimed the corpses of those once held dear.

> His body was decomposed. And it nearly made me sick ... he had been on the receiving end of something fairly big. And as I saw him I thought, 'Christ! We could bury him. We could cover him over' ... And this bloody great rat ran out of his arm here after supping up, he'd been feeding on his arm here, see. Bloody great thing ran out there, nearly made me sick.

Though veterans of World War I often recall good times spent with cherished comrades, all who spent battle tours in the trenches remember that part of their lives as having experienced Hell on Earth. The men who fought in the trenches lived through a soul-wrenching experience rarely equaled in the annals of warfare.

ROLLS-ROYCE ARMOURED CAR

Crew: 3 or 4
Armament: One Vickers 7.7mm (0.303in) machine gun

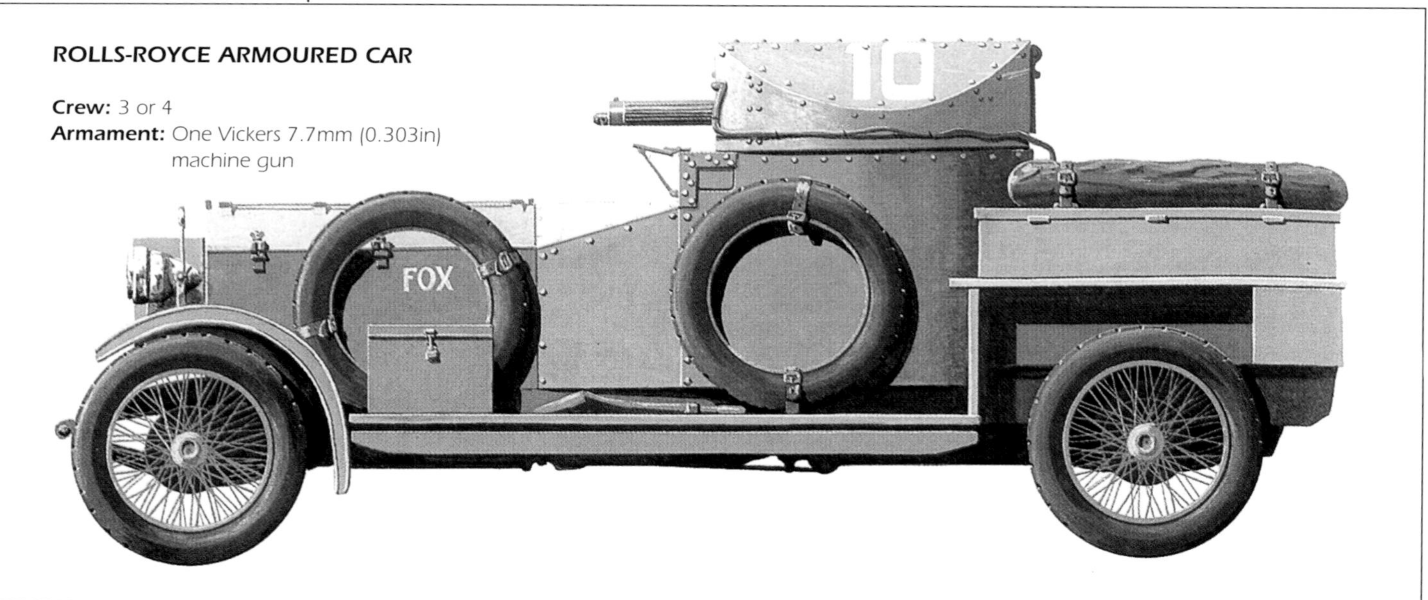

advantage. In addition, the preparatory bombardment was less heavy, less accurate and lasted only some 15 minutes, due to a shortage of artillery shells. Thus British and Indian forces assaulted a reinforced enemy in undamaged defences. All British attacks on the second day of Neuve Chapelle were repulsed with ease. On the third day of the offensive, German forces launched a counter-attack in an effort to take back their lost ground. But this was a mistake in German strategy. To this point the Germans, due to the dominance of the defensive, had suffered but one tenth of the total number of British casualties. However, in counter-attacking, the Germans left the relative safety of their trenches and took some 10,000 casualties.

Several lessons could have been learned from Neuve Chapelle. Surprise and an effective artillery bombardment had enabled the BEF to take a significant amount of ground on the first day of the offensive. However, the German quick reaction to the threat meant that a true breakthrough was never possible. On subsequent days, the balance of the battle had shifted to the defender, making further advance difficult, if not impossible. The Germans erred in their doctrine of counter-attack – thus making the total number of casualties at Neuve Chapelle nearly equal, with both sides suffering 13,000 total losses. Neuve Chapelle indicated that breakthrough was impossible and that offensives should aim at 'Bite-and-Hold' tactics. The battle also should have convinced the Germans that counter-attacks were wasteful. However, neither side had learned their lessons well.

Surprise and an effective artillery bombardment had enabled the BEF to take a significant amount of ground on the first day of the offensive. However, the German quick reaction to the threat meant that a true breakthrough was never possible.

THE SECOND BATTLE OF YPRES

Falkenhayn had planned to remain on the defensive in the west in 1915, but decided to carry out one offensive near Ypres in 1915, hoping to pre-empt any coming Franco-British attack in the west. He also agreed to test a new weapon in the attack: poison gas. At

ABOVE LEFT: THE CARNAGE OF THE WAR FORCED BRITAIN INTO A GREATER RELIANCE THAN EVER BEFORE UPON TROOPS FROM THE EMPIRE. HERE INDIAN SOLDIERS RIDE TOWARD THEIR REST IN A TRUCK – A RARE TREAT WHEN MOST SOLDIERS TRAVELLED ONLY ON FOOT.

ABOVE: PRIVATE HARRY CHANDLER OF 1/6TH NORTH STAFFORDSHIRES SEEN BEFORE THE BATTLE OF NEUVE CHAPELLE.

RIGHT: ALLIED VICTIMS OF A GAS ATTACK LIE IN THE TRENCH WHERE THEY FELL.

BELOW RIGHT: THE FRENCH, TOO, HAD TO RELY UPON THEIR COLONIAL FORCES, HERE RECEIVING ORDERS FROM A FRENCH OFFICER. ALGERIAN FORCES WERE THE FIRST TO FACE THE TEST OF GAS WARFARE AND FLED FROM THE NEW HORROR IN PANIC.

this early stage in the war, troops brought poison gas to the front lines in canisters. On the assigned day – if the wind was right – they would open nozzles on the canisters, allowing gas to escape and drift across no-man's-land to enemy lines. However, German troops almost gave away the surprise before the battle. The BEF, noticing the enemy movement, fired artillery barrages into the German front lines, and fearing that the canisters would break, several German soldiers ran screaming from their trenches. The British, although they noted the strange behaviour, did not realise what it meant.

On 20 April the Germans unleashed their preparatory bombardment, which lasted for two days and destroyed the beautiful medieval city of Ypres. On 22 April the barrage intensified and British soldiers began to notice a yellowish-green cloud rising above the German trenches. The ominous cloud drifted slowly across no-man's-land and hit to the left of the British lines. The poisonous chlorine gas struck French troops, mainly Algerian colonial forces, who were defenceless against the choking gas. Within minutes, the Algerians fled the battlefield, leaving a 6.4km (4 mile) gap in the Allied lines.

However, Falkenhayn had not expected as much from the gas assault and did not have sufficient reserves on hand to exploit his success. In addition, the German troops advancing into the gap quickly caught up to the slow-moving gas and, having no desire to enter the deadly cloud, halted their advance. Canadian forces on the fringe of the cloud held firm, often resorting to breathing through urine-soaked socks as a feeble form of defence. These brave men poured fire into the German flanks, while General Smith-Dorrien shifted his Second Army into the gap and launched counter-attacks to stabilise the situation. Although ultimate disaster had been averted, the Allied situation at Ypres remained very precarious.

On 24 May, after a month of continued fighting, Falkenhayn once again unleashed a major gas attack on Ypres. This time the gas struck Canadian forces holding the apex of the salient. Although they suffered horrific casualties, the Canadians held firm. The experiences of one soldier helps to illuminate the terror of gas warfare at the Second Battle of Ypres:

> [Upon reaching the front line trench] we found what was left of 'A' Company who had been holding this trench, lay in the bottom of it, overcome with gas. Black in the face, their tunics and shirt fronts torn open at the necks in their last desperate fight for breath, many of them lay quite still while others were still wriggling and kicking in the agonies of the most awful death I have ever seen. Some were wounded in the bargain, and their gaping wounds lay open, blood still oozing from them. One poor devil was tearing at his throat with his hands. I doubt if he knew, or felt, that he had only one hand, and that the other was just a stump where the hand should have been. This stump he worked around his throat as if the hand were still there, and the blood from it was streaming over his bluish-black face and neck ... What human being could have stood by and seen such sights without wanting to end the sufferings of such poor devils with a bullet?

LEFT: THE USE OF GAS QUICKLY BECAME COMMONPLACE IN WORLD WAR I. HERE THE INHABITANTS OF A TRENCH HAVE HUNG A SHELL-CASING THAT THEY WOULD STRIKE TO SERVE AS A WARNING BELL OF A GAS ATTACK.

Black in the face, their tunics and shirt fronts torn open at the necks in their last desperate fight for breath, many of them lay quite still while others were still wriggling and kicking in the agonies of the most awful death I have ever seen.

The failure of the German attack on 24 May brought the Second Battle of Ypres to an end. The Germans had succeeded in narrowing the Ypres salient, but had not achieved a great victory. The German failure was in part due to Falkenhayn's lack of faith in the abilities of gas as well as a staunch Allied defence. Second Ypres was the single time in World War I when the use of gas was so surprising that it could have resulted in a significant victory. The one chance had been wasted. The five-week battle was costly for both sides. The Germans lost nearly 40,000 men while the Allies suffered some 69,000 casualties. The stalemate continued.

ABOVE: INITIALLY METHODS OF PROTECTION AGAINST A GAS ATTACK WERE QUITE PRIMITIVE AND SOMEWHAT FUTILE. HERE MEN OF THE ARGYLL AND SUTHERLAND HIGHLANDERS MODEL THE VERY LATEST IN DEFENSIVE MEASURES ISSUED ON 3 MAY 1915 – GOGGLES TO PROTECT THE EYES AND CLOTH, USUALLY SOAKED IN URINE, IN AN ATTEMPT TO PROTECT THE LUNGS.

THE BATTLE OF ARTOIS

Even before the end of the Second Battle of Ypres, Joffre unleashed his long-awaited attack in Artois. His plan called for simultaneous French and British breakthrough attacks. He hoped that French forces in the south could gain Vimy Ridge, while British forces could gain Aubers Ridge. French forces, under the command of General Henri Petain, assaulted the 123m (400ft) Vimy Ridge on 9 May, following a punishing artillery barrage that lasted for five days. The French advance followed the pattern set by the British at Neuve Chapelle. Troops in the centre advanced quickly, to a depth of nearly 4.8km (3 miles) in the first 90 minutes of the offensive. At this point, the exhausted French soldiers met with unscathed German defences and fresh German reinforcements. A hail of machine-gun and artillery fire forced the French back before they had gained the crest of Vimy Ridge. The Germans had recovered from their initial shock by the second day of the battle, and so it dissolved into a costly battle of attrition lasting more than a month. French attacks after the first day gained little in the way of real estate, at a very high cost in human suffering. During the offensive the French lost some 100,000 men, while German casualties numbered 75,000.

In the north the British once again attacked in the area of Neuve Chapelle and aimed at capturing Aubers Ridge. However, due to a worsening shortage of artillery shells, the

British barrage was light and lasted only 40 minutes. The German defences in the area had been strengthened since the last battle, meaning that the BEF had little advantage over its determined enemy. Advancing British troops thus faced fierce resistance from Germans in undamaged defensive works. The attack went nowhere. The commander of the offensive, Douglas Haig, realised that due to lack of artillery support the assault was hopeless. As a result, to his credit he broke off the attack after only one day, having suffered some 11,000 casualties.

The first great effort to overthrow the German positions in France had failed. In each assault, Allied forces, through strength of artillery, had been able to pierce German front-line trenches. But exhausted soldiers

LEFT: FRENCH COLONIAL FORCES, UNUSED TO THE COLD, STAND WATCH FOR A GERMAN ATTACK.

BELOW: THE FIERCE FIGHTING OF 1915 HAD DEPLETED THE BRITISH SHELL RESERVES, RESULTING IN THE 'SHELL SCANDAL' AND THE EVENTUAL FALL OF THE BRITISH GOVERNMENT. HERE DAVID LLOYD GEORGE VISITS FRANCE TO DISCUSS THE SHORTAGE.

The Germans surprised the Russians by launching an attack during the height of a February blizzard. They succeeded in surrounding a bewildered Russian 10th Army achieving a great tactical victory.

could not carry their victories through to take successive German defensive lines. By then, the effectiveness of Allied artillery fire had waned, and the Germans had recovered from their initial shock. As a result, many French and British commanders began to see the conflict as one of attrition, while some leaders, most notably Haig, retained a stubborn belief that a great breakthrough victory could still be achieved.

THE RUSSIAN FRONT

The year 1915 began with mixed results on the Eastern Front. Conrad hoped to expel Russian forces from Galacia, while Hindenburg and Ludendorff longed for a massive offensive designed to surround and destroy Russian forces in Poland. Falkenhayn was more guarded in his expectations for the Eastern Front and never entirely met the massive troop demands made by Hindenburg. As a result, the offensives in the east were more limited in scope than Hindenburg had hoped. The Germans surprised the Russians by launching an attack east of the Masurian Lakes during the height of a February blizzard. They succeeded in surrounding a bewildered Russian 10th Army in the Augustow Forest, achieving a great tactical victory. Some 100,000 Russians were killed and an additional 90,000 taken prisoner. In the south, Austrian forces under Conrad attempted to emulate the German success. Conrad hoped to push the Russians out of the Carpathian Mountains

BELOW: A GERMAN CAVALRYMAN BECOMING THOROUGHLY BOGGED DOWN IN DEEP SNOW IN RUSSIA IN FEBRUARY 1915.

and relieve the besieged fortress of Przemysl but the Austrian offensive, fought in the mountains in the dead of winter, failed miserably. The 120,000-man Austrian garrison at Przemysl was forced to surrender and a Russian counter-attack inched ever closer to breaking out into the vulnerable Hungarian plain.

Although the Central Powers had achieved success in the north, the Austrian failure caused Falkenhayn great concern, and he approved the transfer of the German 11th Army, commanded by General Mackensen, to Galicia. The German move was made with the greatest secrecy, and Russian intelligence failed to discover the presence of the new German force. Falkenhayn had achieved a local superiority over the Russians. In addition, the Germans had amassed the greatest concentration of artillery yet seen on the Eastern Front to aid their coming offensive. On 2 May some 950 guns unleashed a preparatory barrage of hitherto-unseen ferocity, catching the Russian Third Army completely unawares. Shocked by the heavy shelling, several Russian units panicked and abandoned their positions. The Germans tore a gaping hole in the Russian lines between Tarnow and Gorlice and drove into Poland, their advance also threatening to flank the Russian forces further south in Galicia. As a result, the Russian forces there began to retreat and by mid-June the Austrians had retaken Lemberg. Austria was at last free from the threat of Russian invasion.

With the support of the Kaiser, Hindenburg continued his offensive actions in the east and ordered the German 11th Army to advance toward Brest-Litovsk in the south, while

BELOW: IN THE VASTNESS OF THE EAST THE GERMANS WERE OFTEN VICTORIOUS, BUT HAD THEIR LOGISTIC LINES STRETCHED TO THE LIMIT. HERE A UNIT IS INSPECTED BY PRINCE EITEL FRIEDRICH USING THE NORMAL MODE OF TRAVEL IN THE EAST – ITS OWN FEET.

Above: The vastness of the Eastern Front caused the Russians supply and logistical nightmares. The demands of war quickly swamped the inefficient Russian rail system and drove the economy into ruin.

Right: French soldiers attacking a German position in 1915.

the German 12th Army advanced to the north, east of Warsaw. The continued German offensive began in mid-July and made steady progress. Stavka, the Russian headquarters, realised that the dual German advance threatened to encircle all of the Russian armies currently located in the vast Polish salient. Leaving behind a rearguard of some 90,000 men, the Russians began to withdraw from their exposed positions. On 5 August the Germans took possession of Warsaw; by the end of the month they had reached as far as Brest-Litovsk, and the Polish salient had ceased to exist. The Russians had given up vast amounts of territory to the Central Powers, but had escaped with their army fundamentally intact. Although Falkenhayn's support for operations in the east began to wane, German forces there continued to advance, at a slower rate, until mid-September.

The German victories in the east in 1915 rank among the greatest of the entire war. Russian forces had been pushed back some 482km (300 miles). In addition, German and Austrian forces had killed 900,000 Russians and captured one million more. However, these gains came at a high cost, with the Central Powers suffering some 650,000 casualties. For Russia, 1915 had been disastrous but not fatal, but as the war dragged on, it became apparent that neither the Russian economy nor the Russian political system could stand the strain for much longer. Supplies for the armed forces were dwindling rapidly; many soldiers were without rifles. On the political front, Tsar Nicholas II made a titanic mistake. Blaming the Russian commander, Grand Duke Nicholas, for the recent defeats, the Tsar dismissed his cousin and took over personal command of the army. Although devoted, the Tsar was a miserable military commander. In addition, his absence from the capital left the floundering Russian political system in the hands of his wife, the Tsarina Alexandra, and her unstable advisor Rasputin.

Above: The famous recruiting poster by Leese depicting Kitchener calling on Britons to do their national duty.

FURTHER ASSAULTS

Undeterred by recent failures on the Western Front, Joffre scheduled a massive, combined Allied offensive. The main effort would be a French offensive in Champagne, aided by a secondary Franco-British attack in Artois. However, Falkenhayn was aware of the coming attacks and had strengthened his defences accordingly. The French Eighth Army Group in Champagne, under the command of General Castelnau, advanced between Verdun and Rheims on 25 September, following a massive, three-day bombardment. The infantry attacked in the midst of a heavy downpour that transformed the battlefield into a morass of mud. Despite this, Joffre still expected the spirit of his soldiers to lead to a breakthrough victory. Indeed, the advancing French soldiers were urged ever onwards by bands playing the *Marseillaise*. Although the attack carried the first line of German trenches, it inevitably lost its momentum in the maze of German second-line defences. At this point, Joffre became aware that no breakthrough was imminent and called a halt to the attack but predictably, the Germans counter-attacked and the battle raged until 4 November. Once

THE STERN PUBLIC FACE OF THE BRITISH MILITARY.

KITCHENER ARMY

In response to Kitchener's call for volunteers, in late 1914 hundreds of thousands of young Britons rushed to the colours. Millions of volunteers would form the 'Kitchener Army'. One private remembers getting caught up in the national excitement:

> I can remember that August of 1914 ... pretty warm it was, all those straw hats and the band in the park. I can remember the outbreak of war too, all the Union Jacks waving and the blokes lining up at the recruiting offices. Joined up myself I did. I was a bit young for the job, though, of course a lot of the blokes were ... I don't know what made me do such a thing. I wasn't brave, nothing like that.

One incentive in recruitment was that the government promised to allow soldiers to serve together who volunteered from the same town or locality. Thus many of the newly-raised units had a friendly, local feel and carried names like the Artists Rifles and the Public School Battalion. The best-known version of these units were the so-called 'Pals Battalions'. In some cases, almost the entire eligible male population of a small town joined and went off to war as one. Though the units were wonderful as a recruitment tool and fostered a sense of camaraderie, they had the horrific effect of localising the defeat of a major battle. The Barnsley Pals serve as an example. The small town of some 50,000 raised two battalions for the Kitchener Army. The Barnsley Pals saw heavy action during the first day of the Battle of the Somme and lost some 241 killed and nearly four times that number in wounded. Nearly everyone in Barnsley lost a friend or a loved one. Even now, citizens of Barnsley memorialise the loss that their battalion suffered over 80 years ago.

again the trench lines moved only a little – this time at the cost of 145,000 French and 75,000 German casualties.

In Artois the Allied offensive fared little better. The plan called for the French 10th Army to assault Vimy Ridge. Further north, the BEF was slated to attack toward the village of Loos. After breaking through, the two forces were to meet near the city of Lens, and work together to sever German communications in the area. The French assault proved disastrous. Once again French soldiers laboured nearly to the top of Vimy Ridge,

BELOW: ENGLISH RECRUITS LEAVING WHITEHALL, LONDON FOR FARNBOROUGH FOR THEIR ARMY TRAINING ON 1 NOVEMBER 1915.

having struggled through the German front-line defences, only to meet their doom at the hands of the German artillery.

In the Battle of Loos, the British met with more success. The offensive, commanded by Haig, caught the Germans somewhat by surprise; their attention was fixed on the French offensives further south. Aided by their first gas attack of the war, the centre of the British assault gained ground steadily; in fact, some soldiers reported breaking through the German second line of defences and looking upon open, undefended ground beyond. But the reserves to exploit such a success were nowhere to be seen. Against Haig's advice, General French, the Commander-in-Chief of the BEF, had placed the reserves so far behind the British lines that it took them an entire day to reach the battle lines. By that time, the fleeting opportunity was gone, for German reserves had been able to reach the scene first, and had quickly dug in, repaired the defences and awaited a new British assault. Thus Joffre's joint operation in the north had failed. Once again, the costs associated with failure were high. The French had suffered 190,000 casualties, the British 60,000 and the Germans 213,000. The war of attrition shambled forward.

BELOW: THIS 2ND LIEUTENANT OF THE ARTIST'S RIFLES CARRIES A FIELD SERVICE POCKET BOOK ISSUED TO ALL NEW OFFICERS DESTINED FOR THE FRONT LINE.

POLITICAL REPERCUSSIONS

Alone among the great powers, Britain had entered World War I without a mass army and conscription. At the beginning of the war, on the advice of Kitchener – who believed correctly that the war would be long and arduous – Britain embarked on the task of raising an army of millions. Still leery of the draft, Britain relied on a campaign of volunteerism – symbolised by a poster of a stern-faced Kitchener with the phrase **'Britons – Kitchener wants you'.**

The call for volunteers succeeded beyond the government's wildest dreams. Hundreds of thousands of young men flocked to the colours to join in the Great War. The numbers were so daunting that it was some time before the military establishment could find housing or weapons for the new soldiers. The new force, known as the 'Kitchener Army', represented the flower of British youth. Although these new recruits reached the trenches in dribs and drabs in 1915, most would not see action until the following year. Britain had never raised such a force before, and expectations for it would be high in 1916.

As the Kitchener Army readied for its climactic showdown with the Germans, the military failures of 1915 resulted in a command change for the BEF, for General French had fallen out of favour with the British Government. He had earned many enemies through his timidity early in the war, but it was his perceived failure to use reserves properly at the Battle of Loos that caused his downfall. French had failed to remain in close contact with Haig and had seemingly squandered a chance at a great victory. It also seems that Haig had a role to play in the downfall of his superior; there is little doubt that he wrote to King George V concerning French's shortcomings. However, Haig did not actually campaign for French's deposition. In December, French was removed from his position as Commander-in-Chief of the BEF, to be succeeded by Haig. The new commander would be tasked with leading the Kitchener Army to victory in 1916.

CHAPTER 5

The Widening War

WHAT STARTED AS A WAR BETWEEN AUSTRIA AND SERBIA SLOWLY TRANSFORMED INTO THE FIRST TRULY WORLD WAR, WITH FIGHTING TAKING PLACE ON THREE CONTINENTS – IN CONDITIONS RANGING FROM DESERTS TO THESE AUSTRIAN SOLDIERS FIGHTING IN THE HIGH ALPS.

Fighting in the searing heat, many Allied soldiers succumbed to native diseases, including malaria and dysentery. After suffering tremendous losses, the Allies finally reached Yaounde, only to find that the Germans had fled.

THE WAR IN AFRICA

Germany possessed four African colonies: Togoland, the Cameroons, German South West Africa on the Atlantic, and German East Africa on the Indian Ocean. Soon after the outbreak of war, the Allies decided to invade and conquer these valuable German colonial territories. The resulting African campaigns would be different from their European counterparts.

The small colony of Togoland was the first to succumb to an Allied offensive. The tiny German garrison there was beset by a French attack from Dahomey and a British attack from the Gold Coast, and by 26 August the Germans had surrendered. In the Cameroons, after a failed attack by British-led Askaris, British and French forces engaged in a combined offensive to overthrow the German garrison there. French native forces from Equatorial Africa, Belgian forces from the Congo and British native forces from Nigeria drove the German garrison of some 7000 men from the coast some 320km (200 miles) inland to the capital of Yaounde in 1915. To press their advantage, the 25,000 Allied soldiers had to struggle through almost impenetrable swamps and jungles. Fighting in the searing heat, many Allied soldiers succumbed to native diseases, including malaria and dysentery. After suffering tremendous losses, the Allies finally reached Yaounde in January 1916, only to find that the Germans had fled. The campaign had lasted 18 months but the Cameroons had fallen.

OVERVIEW

World War I was the world's first truly global conflict. From Africa to the Far East, the Allies sought to destroy vulnerable German colonies. These smaller conflicts imbedded within World War I involved African, Indian, Japanese, Arab, Turkish and Australian forces. In Europe itself the war widened to include new nations and new battlefronts – from Italy, through Bulgaria and into Turkey. In many ways, the war reached its greatest level of ferocity on a tiny peninsula guarding the strategic waterway that connected the Mediterranean and Black Seas: Gallipoli.

The conquest of the other two German colonies in Africa, however, was destined to be much more difficult. The British left the conquest of German South West Africa to the new dominion of the Union of South Africa, its forces under the ultimate command of Prime Minister Louis Botha, who had fought against the British in the recent Boer War. However, Botha could not begin his attempt to destroy the Germans in South West Africa immediately. Shortly after the outbreak of war in 1914, a revolution – prompted by the Germans – had broken out in South Africa among anti-British Boers.

In early 1915, once the Boer insurrection had been crushed, South African forces invaded German South West Africa; they also attacked from the sea. The campaign was fought in exceedingly difficult terrain, often in the blazing heat of the desert. As they did in the Boer War, the South African forces proved to be masters of cavalry tactics and outmanoeuvred the Germans at every turn. In addition, the South Africans were aided by a native uprising against the Germans. By July 1915 the campaign was over and German South West Africa had fallen.

The struggle for German East Africa was lengthy and dramatic. In that colony German forces, made up mainly of Askari soldiers, were commanded by the dashing Lt Colonel (later General) Paul von Lettow-Vorbeck. He led a small force that never numbered more than 3000 Germans and 11,000 native soldiers. At the beginning of the war, Vorbeck decided to make himself as much of a nuisance to the British as possible in an effort to occupy Allied forces. He proved to be a master of mobile, guerrilla warfare and in the end, his tiny command would pursue the war longer than Germany itself.

In 1914 and 1915 Vorbeck launched several raids into neighbouring Allied African colonies, and quickly attracted the attention of the British. In 1916 a South African force,

under the command of General Jan Smuts – now available due to the defeat of German South West Africa – reinforced the British forces in the area. He proposed a three-pronged offensive, using 300,000 Allied troops, to surround and destroy the troublesome Vorbeck. But Vorbeck quickly realised the impending danger and fled with his forces to the south, abandoning over half of German East Africa. During the prolonged campaign, the African climate and disease once again took their toll, decimating the ill-prepared South Africans and Europeans among the Allied force. As a result, Smuts chose to replace such troops with native forces, which proved to be much more resilient when, in 1917, the Allies launched another offensive. As a result, greater progress was made and the new South African commander, General van Deventer, captured a major German force and drove Vorbeck completely out of German East Africa and into Portuguese Mozambique.

ABOVE: THE WAR IN AFRICA WAS OFTEN AN IMPROVISED AFFAIR, AS SHOWN BY THESE PRO-GERMAN TROOPS RIDING CATTLE TO THE FRONT.

BELOW: GENERAL PAUL VON LETTOW-VORBECK, THORN IN THE ALLIES' SIDE.

It seemed that the war in Africa was over, but it lingered on, for although the German colony had fallen, Vorbeck chose to fight on. His dwindling force lived off of the land in Mozambique, using speed and daring to evade capture by the Allied forces. In this way, they continued to roam free and harried the Allies with guerrilla tactics until the end of war. They did not surrender until 23 November 1918, having received delayed news of the armistice.

The remarkable exploits of Vorbeck and his tiny force tied down several hundred thousand Allied soldiers for more than four years. He had led British, Belgian, Indian, South African and native forces on a chase of nearly 6436km (4000 miles) through the wilds of Africa. At the end of the campaign Vorbeck's force numbered only 4000 of his original 15,000 men. The Allies, especially South Africa, had devoted considerable resources to his destruction. Their losses were staggering: 80,000 British, South African and native soldiers lost their lives in the pursuit of Vorbeck. The Germans in Africa eventually succumbed to the Allied force, yet Vorbeck had succeeded beyond his wildest dreams.

THE AFRICAN NAVAL WAR

In 1915 British and German naval forces clashed on the inland lakes of east Africa. Initially German flotillas had the advantage in the small, but vicious struggle. To capture Lake Tanganyika, the British sent two armed launches from South Africa. These tiny vessels journeyed to the Congo and then proceeded up a series of rivers through swamps – sometimes being carried overland – covering a distance of 3860km (2400 miles), before they reached their goal. As a result of their epic journey, Lake Tanganyika fell to British control. More serious was the threat posed by the German light cruiser *Konigsberg*, which had fled up the Rufiji River in order to avoid contact with large British ships in the Indian Ocean. Although the river proved impassible to many of the heavy British warships, it was not impassable to all. Two aged British monitors slipped stealthily up the river system and caught the *Konigsberg* unaware. After a short battle, the German ship was destroyed and the threat it posed to British mastery of the African river systems was gone. The stirring exploits of the British naval units in east Africa inspired C.S. Forester to write his novel *The African Queen*. (The events became even more famous when Humphrey Bogart and Katherine Hepburn starred in the film of the same name.)

THE *KONIGSBERG* EVADING A BRITISH CRUISER IN THE INDIAN OCEAN.

THE WAR WIDENS

In the Far East, Germany was in possession of several colonies, ranging from the important port of Tsingtao on the coast of China, to a part of New Guinea and several island chains, including the Marianas and the Marshalls. But these Pacific colonies were virtually undefended as the German fleet remained in the North Sea. Japan, Britain's oldest ally, was under no obligation to enter the conflict because it had involved no direct German attack against British territory. Despite this, the British – seeking any aid in defeating Germany – requested Japan's entry into the war. Eager to gather up the German Pacific possessions, the Japanese obliged and joined the fray on 23 August 1914. The war in the Far East became a race as Japan, New Zealand and Australia rushed to be the first to claim choice parts of the German Empire. Australia seized New Guinea, New Zealand took over German holdings in Samoa and the Japanese took the Marianas and the Marshalls. The port of Tsingtao was the only fortified German colonial holding in the Far East, with a garrison of some 4000 men. With some British aid, the Japanese laid siege to the German defenders there and secured their surrender on 7 November 1914. Thus, with very few casualties, the war in the Pacific ended. During the short conflict, Japan had seized much important territory and had begun to construct an empire of its own. Continued efforts to expand this empire would help lead to the outbreak of World War II.

In the years leading up to World War I, Europe's great powers had been almost unanimous in their efforts to ignore the least of their number: Turkey, or the Ottoman Empire. Though the Turks had, perhaps, the closest economic ties to Germany, their leadership tried a number of gambits to form alliances with powers ranging from Russia to Britain. Only the Germans seemed to show a faint interest in an alliance with the Turks. In addition, one of the leading members of the Young Turk movement, the charismatic minister of war, General Enver Pasha, was decidedly pro-German. As a result, the two nations signed a rather half-hearted alliance on 2 August 1914.

The Turks were stunned to find themselves facing war within days of signing their pact with Germany. A strong faction within the Turkish Government still favoured the Allies, or neutrality, and thus the Turks bickered for months regarding their role in the European conflagration. The Germans pressed Turkey to enter the war to aid in their struggle with the Russians, but the Turks remained neutral.

Turkish relations with Britain had worsened when Churchill, the First Lord of the Admiralty, commandeered for the Royal Navy two Dreadnoughts being built in Britain for the Turkish Navy, causing vehement Turkish protests. Matters worsened for the Allies as the result of a crafty German diplomatic manoeuvre. The German battle cruisers *Goeben* and *Breslau* were fighting for their lives against superior Allied naval forces in the Mediterranean. Commanded by Admiral Wilhelm Souchon, they made for Turkey, eluding several powerful Allied flotillas along the way. Souchon sailed his ships into Constantinople and presented them to the Turkish Government. His sailors donned red fezzes, swapped their German uniforms for Turkish ones, and became members of the Turkish Navy while Souchon himself became the commander of the Turkish fleet. The Turks were now squarely in the German orbit and joined the war as one of the Central Powers on 31 October 1914.

Turkey boasted an armed force of some 800,000 men. However, the Turkish Government was wracked with turmoil, the Turkish economy and communications system were very poor, and ethnic strife haunted the fringes of the far-flung Ottoman Empire. Thus Turkey was among the least prepared of the European powers for the strains of modern war. In an attempt to strengthen their hand, the Turks called for a *jihad* (holy war) amongst their Muslim brethren against the Allies. Their call, however, fell upon deaf ears and the Turks quickly learned that the Arabs under their control were more apt to rise up against Turkish rule than side with their masters in war. Even without pronounced Arab aid, the Turks seized the offensive with abandon. One Turkish force struck at British control of the Suez Canal, but met with abject failure at the

Above: A German colonial soldier from an infantry company in East Africa in 1914.

Left: Native, or Askari, soldiers like these German troops bore the brunt of the fighting in Africa.

hands of the Australia and New Zealand Army Corps (ANZAC) defending the area. The British would not stand by and see the vital Suez Canal threatened, and made preparations for an offensive of their own into Palestine. However, the main Turkish offensive of the year came against the Russians in the Caucasus. Here Enver Pasha led nearly 95,000 Turkish troops on a winter campaign, beginning in December, although the bitter cold and snow of the high mountain passes soon took its toll. Furthermore, a Russian counter-attack forced the Turks back. A mere 18,000 Turks, including Enver Pasha, returned to their homeland alive.

Below: General Smuts, once an enemy of Britain fighting for the Boers, inspects British forces in East Africa.

Above: As the war worsened the need for colonial troops grew rapidly. Once raised, though, colonial forces – such as these Sudanese volunteers – needed intense training.

Although somewhat feeble, the Turkish attempts at offensives had caught the attention of the British. The first British counter-attack came in Mesopotamia and was designed, in large part, to protect vital oil-fields. The British, however, hoped for an even greater success against the Turks in 1915. Many Britons believed that an assault in the Dardanelles – the narrow straits that connect the Mediterranean Sea to the Black Sea – could cause the Ottoman Empire to crumble.

THE DARDANELLES OPERATION

Turkish entry into the conflict gave those Britain in favour of an Eastern offensive renewed hope that naval power, quite possibly augmented by an amphibious landing operation, could deal a quick and deadly blow to the weakest of the Central Powers. However, Kitchener and French were adamant that all available troops were needed on the Western Front. This dimmed the hopes of the Easterners, but only briefly.

In January 1915 Kitchener received news that the Russians had requested an Allied operation against the Turks to lessen pressure in the Caucasus. Failure to act would result in a reduction of Russian efforts on the battlefront against the Germans. Suddenly, in Kitchener's view, disaster loomed. Reduced Russian effort on the Eastern Front would allow the Germans to concentrate their forces in the west, causing untold damage to British and French offensive efforts there. At nearly the same time, Churchill received assurances from the naval commander on the scene, Admiral Sackville Carden, that naval

Mustapha Kemal (with binoculars) at Gallipoli.

MUSTAPHA KEMAL

In 1908 Mustapha Kemal (later Mustapha Kemal Ataturk) played a minor role in the Turkish revolution. Shortly thereafter he fell out of favour with the Turkish leadership and concentrated on his military career. He stood against Turkish entry into World War I on Germany's side, but once war was declared, devoted his considerable military powers to the aid of his country. Kemal became a national hero during the defence of the Gallipoli Peninsula. Twice during the campaign, only Kemal's actions saved the Turks from certain defeat. Promoted to corps commander after the close of the campaign, he was transferred to the Caucasus to try to retrieve the deteriorating situation there in the war against Russia. After the Russian Revolution, he moved to command the Turkish Seventh Army in Syria against advancing British forces. He quickly realised that the situation in Syria was hopeless and had to retreat to Aleppo to hold off the British there. Kemal was a man of vision who was destined to become the greatest Turkish hero of the conflict. Indeed, he was the only senior Turkish officer to never suffer a defeat during World War I. His hero status only increased as Turkey underwent serious periods of instability after the close of the conflict. His nation turned to him to retrieve the situation once again, and he served as the first president of the Turkish Republic.

power alone could force the Dardanelles, thus opening a supply route to Russia. British planners also hoped that a naval bombardment of Constantinople might cause the weak Turkish Government to fall and precipitate the Turks' withdrawal from the conflict. At last, the Easterners had exactly what they wanted: the Royal Navy alone could conquer one of the Central Powers. On 29 January 1915 the War Cabinet approved the attack on the Dardanelles.

The Dardanelles Operation began on 19 February when 12 battleships opened fire on Turkish forts guarding the entrance to the straits. Disappointment was almost immediate for the British because naval gunfire, with a rather flat shell trajectory, was of only limited use against the powerful forts, thus it took many days for the British fleet to begin its slow move up the straits toward Constantinople. During the operation it became clear that the Turks had several mobile batteries of guns that could fire down upon the British fleet and then move before the ships could launch their devastating reply. These guns could do but little against heavily armoured battleships but they could damage the all-important British minesweepers.

The British relied on North Sea fishing trawlers, and civilian crews to undertake minesweeping duties. On March 18, now under the command of Admiral de Roebeck (due to a mental collapse suffered by Carden), the fleet came under heavy fire from the Turkish mobile batteries. The frightened civilian minesweepers failed to detect a newly laid Turkish minefield and as a result, three Allied battleships were sunk. The price of forcing the Dardanelles had now become too high and so the naval effort was abandoned. British pride, however, was on the line, and operations against Turkey could not be entirely forsaken.

Above: General Enver Pasha, the pro-German Turkish commander-in-chief.

ABOVE: A TURKISH GUN OVERLOOKING THE DARDANELLES – NOTE THE NARROWNESS OF THE STRAITS.

GALLIPOLI

The British Government, with the support of Kitchener, decided to attempt an amphibious assault aimed at seizure of the Gallipoli Peninsula and the opening of the straits. For the effort, Kitchener gathered some 70,000 men: the British 29th Division and the Australia and New Zealand Army Corps (ANZAC) and placed the operation under the command of General Ian Hamilton. Although pitifully short on supplies and accurate maps of the area, Hamilton soon developed an invasion plan. The 29th Division, under the command of General Aylmer Hunter-Weston, would assault the tip of the peninsula, known as Cape Helles. Their objective was the seizure of Achi Baba, a dominating ridge located some 8km (5 miles) inland. Further north the ANZACs, under the command of General William Birdwood, would strike the western side of the peninsula near Gaba Tepe. Their task was the capture of the dominating heights of Chunuk Bair and then to move across the peninsula, thus surrounding Turkish forces in the south.

The British Government, with the support of Kitchener, decided to attempt an amphibious assault aimed at seizure of the Gallipoli Peninsula and the opening of the straits.

Originally the Turks had only one division located in the area. However, the delay between the end of the naval operation and the beginning of the invasion allowed them time to rush five reinforcing divisions to the scene. The Turks chose General Liman von Sanders, the head of the German military mission to Turkey, to command all forces on Gallipoli. In command of one of the Turkish divisions was Mustapha Kemal, destined to become the hero of the fighting on the peninsula.

ANZAC

As Britain went to war with the Central Powers in 1914, many independent dominion nations also chose to join the fray, including Australia and New Zealand. The Australia and New Zealand Army Corps (ANZAC) was formed in Egypt in 1914. Originally commanded by General Birdwood, the unit consisted of two New Zealand brigades and 20,000 Australian troops. It saw its first major action at Gallipoli on 25 April 1915 and fought on the peninsula for eight months. Here it became renowned for bravery and spirit. However, to the British, the Australians especially seemed a rather rowdy bunch who were bent on testing the limits of military propriety. ANZAC moved to the Western Front in 1916 and participated in most of the major attritional battles there, including the Battle of the Somme and the Third Battle of Ypres. In 1917 alone it suffered some 50,000 casualties, and by 1918 had earned a reputation as one of the most reliable Allied forces on the Western Front. As such, it played a pivotal role in the victorious attack at Amiens in August 1918 – an attack that in many ways won the war for the Allies. Later ANZAC forces were instrumental in the Allied breaking of the Hindenburg Line. By the close of the conflict, ANZAC, like many other units, was exhausted by the fighting it had seen – exhausted but victorious. For Australia and New Zealand, victory in World War I meant something more: the nations had come of age. In many ways, this war is still remembered in Australia and New Zealand, not least for being the first acts of new, great nations.

THE ANZACs IN ACTION AT GALLIPOLI.

ALLIED LANDINGS AT GALLIPOLI

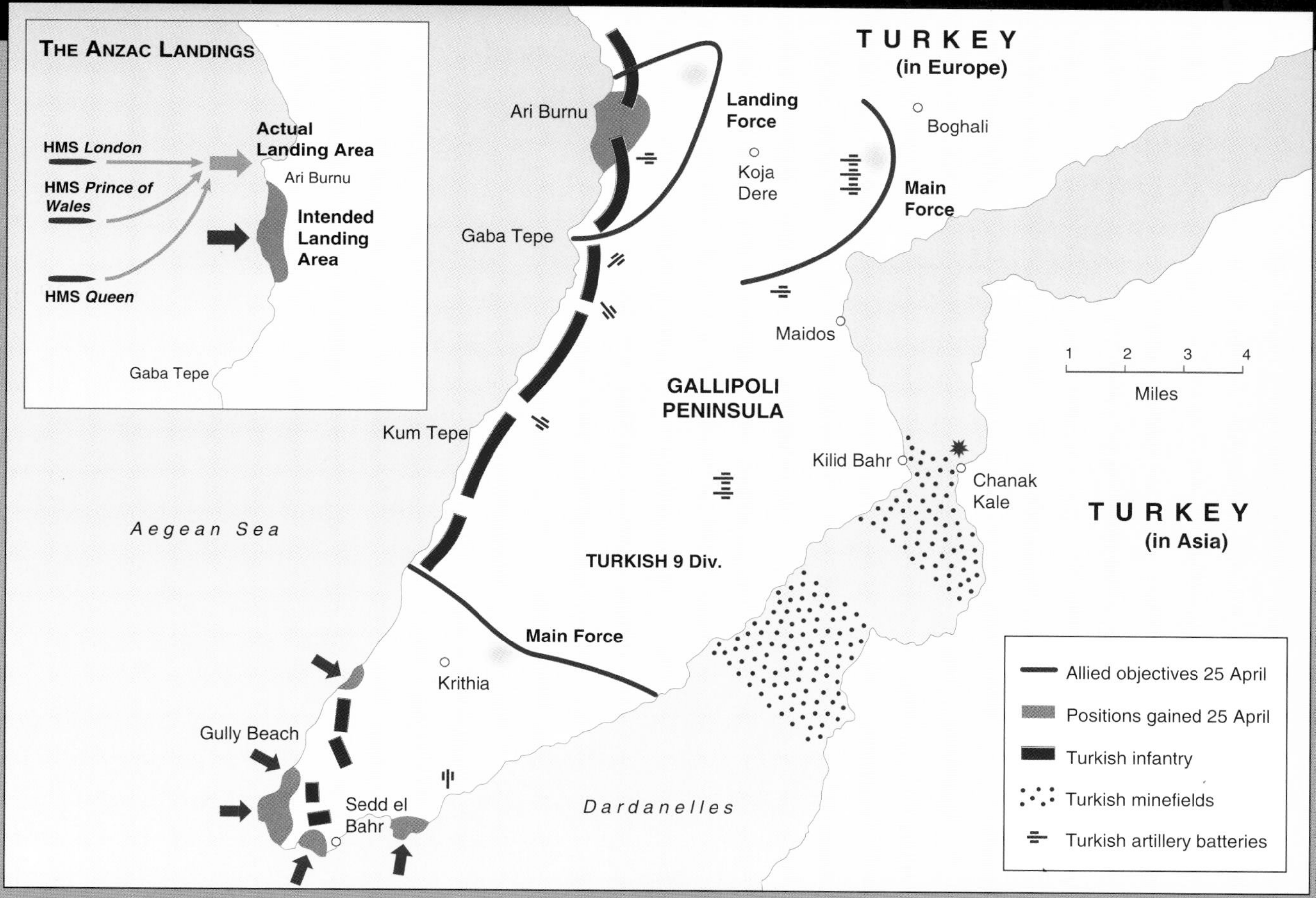

THE ANZAC LANDINGS

HMS *London*

HMS *Prince of Wales*

HMS *Queen*

Actual Landing Area

Ari Burnu

Intended Landing Area

Gaba Tepe

TURKEY (in Europe)

Ari Burnu

Landing Force

Boghali

Koja Dere

Main Force

Gaba Tepe

Maidos

GALLIPOLI PENINSULA

Kum Tepe

Kilid Bahr

Chanak Kale

TURKEY (in Asia)

1 2 3 4 Miles

Aegean Sea

TURKISH 9 Div.

Main Force

Krithia

Gully Beach

Sedd el Bahr

Dardanelles

Allied objectives 25 April

Positions gained 25 April

Turkish infantry

Turkish minefields

Turkish artillery batteries

RIGHT:
A TURKISH STEAMER UNDER ATTACK FROM A BRITISH SHIP AT GALLIPOLI.

BELOW:
TURKISH SOLDIERS LIE IN WAIT AT GALLIPOLI. THEIR WIDE FIELD OF FIRE OVERLOOKING THE BEACHES PROVIDED THEM WITH EVERY ADVANTAGE OVER THE BRITISH ATTACKERS.

The landings finally began on 25 April. The 29th Division had to land in five separate locations due to beach conditions at Cape Helles. The beaches received letter designations. The troops that landed on S and X beaches met only light resistance, while the men landing on Y beach met no resistance whatsoever. Tragically, the forces on these beaches – bewildered and poorly led – made no attempt to move inland. To the south, the forces landing at V and W beaches were not so lucky. On W beach men were faced with undamaged barbed-wire entanglements, both underwater and on the shore. Behind the wire lurked several well-placed Turkish machine-gun nests. Only with the greatest of bravery were the British soldiers able to get inland, where they halted to consolidate. Despite this, they suffered heavy losses. The 1st Battalion of the Lancashire Fusiliers began the day with a compliment of 957 officers and men. By its end, only 316 were not casualties.

The situation was much worse on V beach. Knowing the danger of opposed amphibious landings, the British experimented here. The main landing force approached the beach on board the *River Clyde*, a converted collier. Two holes, called sallyports, were cut into the side of the vessel for men to exit through, one at a time, and then run down a ramp formed by barges, and on to assault the beach. But the experiment failed, for the Turks had positioned several machine guns in the area. As the British soldiers began to emerge from the sallyports, the machine guns cut them apart, one by one. The results were devastating. One soldier remembers the scene as he exited the *River Clyde:*

> The sight that met our eyes was indescribable. The barges now linked together and more or less reaching the shore were piled high with mutilated bodies – and between the last barge and the shore was a pier formed by piles of dead men. It was impossible to reach the shore without treading on the dead, and the sea round the cove was red with blood.

ABOVE: **THE RATHER SPARTAN HEADQUARTERS OF GENERAL BIRDWOOD AT GALLIPOLI.**

BELOW: **GENERAL IAN HAMILTON, COMMANDER OF BRITISH FORCES AT GALLIPOLI.**

Eventually enough soldiers reached V beach to gain a footing. Everywhere, the advance had stalled. If only the forces at S, X, and Y beaches had moved forward, they would have struck the Turkish defenders from the rear. Blame for this failure must fall squarely on the shoulders of Hunter-Weston. He was a poor and overly cautious commander who was unable to seize the opportunity that beckoned.

Further north, the ANZAC forces, too, met with misfortune. A strong current pushed the landing 1.6km (1 mile) off course. Instead of landing on a rather broad beach, the forces landed on a very narrow one abutting a cliff (the tiny beach would become known as Anzac Cove). The undaunted forces scrambled through the rough terrain to their first goal of Chunuk Bair. However, Mustapha Kemal quickly realised the danger of the situation, and he and a battalion of Turkish forces rushed to the scene. Kemal's force reached undefended Chunuk Bair only shortly before the onrushing ANZACs. Heavily outnumbered, the Turks fought off several attempts to seize the heights, in brutal, often hand-to-hand fighting.

Although some 30,000 British and ANZAC forces had rushed ashore on that fateful day, the Turks held out, often by the narrowest of margins. Both sides began to dig in, and Gallipoli came to resemble the war of attrition on the Western Front. Conditions at Gallipoli, however, were much worse for the Allies. The Turks occupied the high ground everywhere – especially around Anzac Cove – and could pour withering fire into Allied trench systems. The Allies had failed to move far inland, meaning that in Gallipoli there were no 'safe areas' as there were in the rear areas on the Western Front. Men thus faced the constant threat of death even while resting behind the lines. The weather was often blazing hot, and the rocky, parched soil offered little in the way of water. All supplies had to be shipped in to the forces, straining the British logistic system to the point of collapse.

LEFT:
AUSTRALIAN SOLDIERS IN A RARE PEACEFUL MOMENT IN THE TRENCHES AT GALLIPOLI. THE TURKISH POSITIONS OVERLOOKED THE AUSTRALIAN TRENCHES – MEANING THAT THE AUSTRALIANS HAD TO BE VIGILANT AT ALL TIMES.

FAR LEFT TOP:
AUSTRALIAN TROOPS MAKING USE OF PERISCOPES TO WATCH FOR A TURKISH ATTACK. THE LEFT-HAND PERISCOPE HAS A RIFLE ATTACHED, ALLOWING THE SOLDIER TO SNIPE AT THE ENEMY FROM COVER.

FAR LEFT BELOW:
THE NARROW BEACH AT ANZAC COVE LED TO SUPPLY CHAOS. NOTE THAT THE PROXIMITY OF THE TURKISH-HELD CLIFFS MEANT THAT NO AREA IN ANZAC COVE WAS SAFE FROM ENEMY FIRE.

SUVLA BAY

In the succeeding months, the Allies tried several times to pierce the Turkish defences and capture the high ground. However, the assaults were bloody failures and attrition reigned supreme. Thereafter, British planners were determined to launch one great offensive in Gallipoli designed to break the stalemate and capture the entire peninsula. The plan called for two divisions to land on Gallipoli at a new site further north: Suvla Bay. It was hoped that this landing force would catch the Turks by surprise and move inland. Simultaneously, further south at Anzac Cove, three divisions would launch an assault on Chunuk Bair, rivetingTurkish attention, and adding to the surprise at Suvla. The two Allied forces would link up atop Chunuk Bair and then drive across the peninsula, thus surrounding the bulk of Turkish forces.

The plan, like that of the first day of the operation, was a good one. It would, however, rely upon surprise and daring. The planning went forward with such great secrecy that the Turks were indeed utterly surprised. However, poor command would once again plague British forces. General Frederick Stopford was chosen by Kitchener to command the landing at, and advance from, Suvla Bay. Stopford, however, was an overly cautious man who had retired from the military in 1909 due to ill health and who had never held a combat command in his life. His appointment was a tragic example of the tendency of the British military establishment to appoint commanders due to seniority rather than ability.

On 6 August the British and ANZAC forces launched their combined offensive. At Suvla Bay Stopford's force landed against no resistance: the surprise was complete. Speed was of the essence and British troops had to move forward to threaten the Turkish positions on Chunuk Bair and come to the aid of their ANZAC allies. But Stopford was overmatched. Instead of moving forward, he chose to dig in and avoid defeat. General Hamilton railed at his subordinate officer, demanding a forward movement. Only on 8 August did Stopford order the advance, and even then its pace was pitifully slow.

Further south, the ANZAC forces were fighting an epic battle, often hand-to-hand, along the rugged cliff-face. Miraculously, ANZAC forces succeeded in driving the Turks from the top of Chunuk Bair. Mustapha Kemal reacted with the speed that the British so sorely lacked: he rushed reinforcements to Suvla Bay, reaching the high ground there ahead of the slow-moving British force, thus ending any hope the ANZACs might have had for aid from the north. The Turks, under Kemal's direction, also launched fanatical counter- attacks on the ANZACs on top of Chunuk Bair, and fighting continued on the rugged hilltop for three days. Finally, exhausted and outnumbered, the ANZACs were driven back. One soldier recounts the sobering experience:

> Our scouts came in and said the Turks were coming up on all sides in thousands and before we had time to prepare to meet them we were under heavy fire with shrapnel and machineguns and the men began to fall ... A and C companies were nearly all done for in no time.

'Our scouts came in and said the Turks were coming up on all sides in thousands and before we had time to prepare to meet them we were under heavy fire with shrapnel and machineguns and the men began to fall ... A and C companies were nearly all done for in no time.'

A sense of betrayal pervaded the ANZAC units; they had achieved the impossible and had taken Chunuk Bair but their erstwhile allies had not supported their advance, leaving them to die. There is some bitterness to this day regarding events at Suvla Bay.

WITHDRAWAL

Though the fighting on Gallipoli dragged on for months, the failure of the Suvla Bay landings marked the end of any British hope for victory in the campaign. Defeat, however, was difficult to admit, and the war of attrition on the peninsula dragged on through the summer months. Heat, lack of supplies, and disease proved to be as formidable an enemy as the Turks during this time.

By October the weather had changed and the British commander, Hamilton, was sacked. His replacement, General Charles Monro, believed the battle to be lost and pressed for a withdrawal. His attitude caused Churchill caustically to remark, 'he came, he saw, he capitulated'. By mid-December, Monro had carried the day, and British and ANZAC forces began to depart from the dreary peninsula. Ironically enough, the withdrawal from Gallipoli was a dangerous operation carried out with consummate skill. The Allied forces proved to be adept at deception. Had the Turks discovered the growing weakness of the Allied lodgements, they could have wrought havoc on the entire operation, but they did not realise what was happening until it was too late. The last British forces left Cape Helles on 9 January 1916, bringing the Gallipoli campaign to a conclusion.

The failure at Gallipoli had repercussions within Great Britain. The Asquith government, weakened by a record of wartime failure, gave way to a coalition government. Churchill, perceived to be the author of the campaign, lost his seat in the Cabinet and even went to the Western Front for a time to try his hand at soldiering. In a military sense, Gallipoli represented a microcosm of what was wrong with the British armed forces. Planners had developed a good idea, although one that was limited by the defensive realities of World War I. British military leadership, however, represented by Hunter-Weston and Stopford, proved to be incapable of completing the task at hand. The war required professional, technologically sound officers, not well-meaning, nineteenth-century gentlemen.

BELOW: HMS *CORNWALLIS* FIRING AT THE TURKS AFTER THE EVACUATION OF ANZAC AND SUVLA BAY IN DECEMBER 1915. SHE WAS THE LAST SHIP TO LEAVE SUVLA BAY.

ITALY JOINS THE WAR

The Italians had not declared war as part of the Triple Alliance in 1914 on the grounds that the war was not defensive in nature. For the next nine months, the belligerent nations of Europe competed for Italian allegiance. As the price for entering the conflict, Italy demanded the land known as 'unredeemed Italy', including the city of Trieste and much of the Dalmatian coast, all part of the Austrian Empire. After overcoming Russian objections concerning ceding Slavic lands to Italy, the Allies promised to deliver these territories and colonial concessions to the Italians following victory in war. The Italian Government of Antonio Salandra agreed that the price was right, and Italy promised to join the conflict. Although supporters of neutrality nearly brought the Italian Government down with riots and protests after learning of the bargain, Italy declared war on Austria on 23 May 1915.

The Italian armed forces, although poorly led and backed by a weak economy, numbered some 875,000 men. The Austrians, involved as they were on two other fronts, could only dedicate 100,000 men to guard the border with Italy. This disparity of force led the Austrians to accept a defensive policy in the area. The mountainous terrain along the Austro-Italian border helped to make what should have been a military mismatch much more even. The Italians judged the area near to the Isonzo River to be the best for an offensive, but this was perfect for the Austrian defenders. The limestone ground is riddled with sinkholes, and these formed wonderful, ready-made entrenchments. In addition, the Austrians held the dominating high ground in this area that one observer called, 'a howling wilderness of stone sharp as knives'.

ABOVE:
ITALIAN SOLDIERS RUSH FORWARD IN FORBIDDING ALPINE TERRAIN.

FAR RIGHT:
AUSTRIAN SHARPSHOOTERS SNIPE AT ITALIAN SOLDIERS.

THE ITALIAN CAMPAIGN

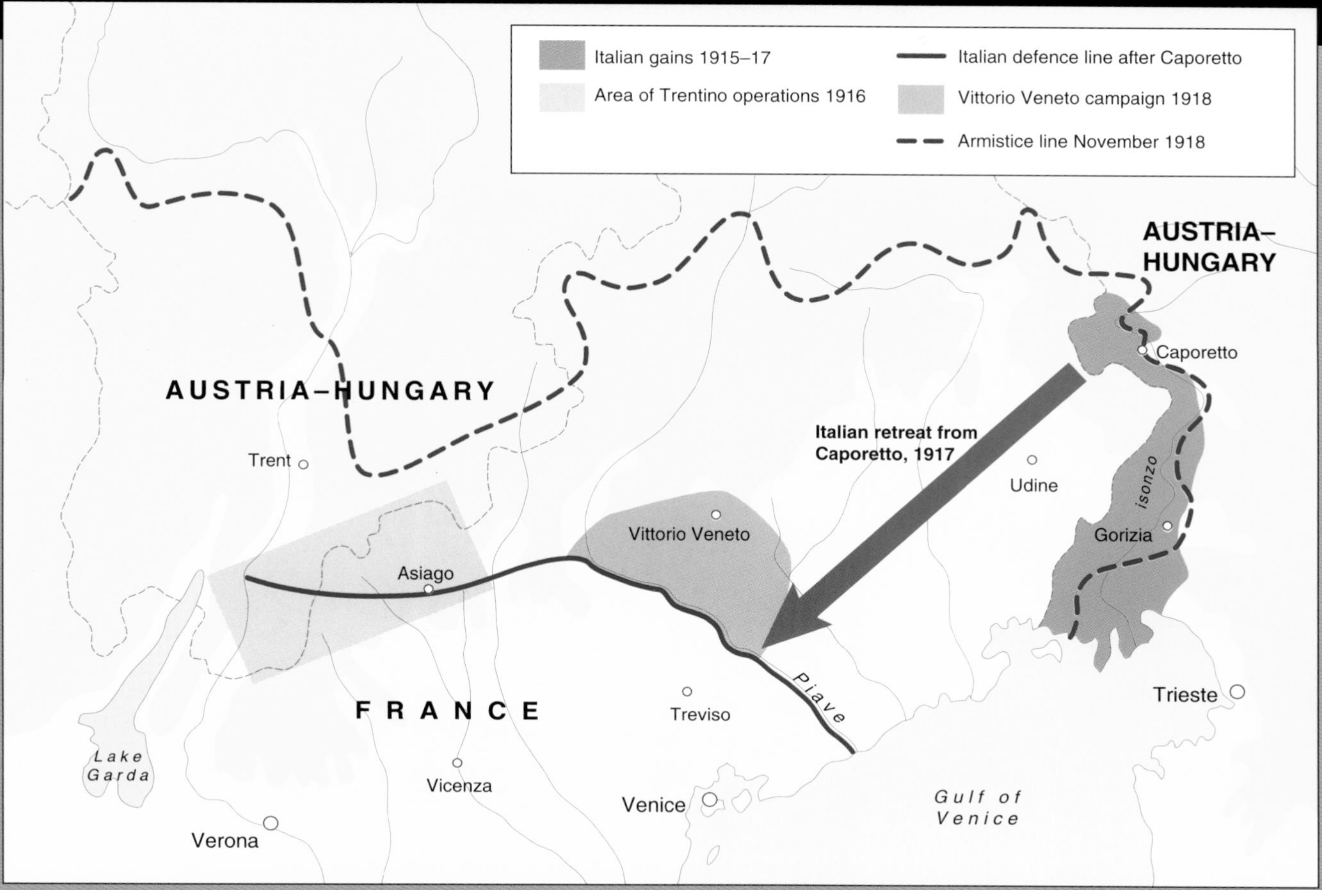

Italian gains 1915–17
Area of Trentino operations 1916
Italian defence line after Caporetto
Vittorio Veneto campaign 1918
Armistice line November 1918
AUSTRIA–HUNGARY
AUSTRIA–HUNGARY
Caporetto
Italian retreat from Caporetto, 1917
Trent
Udine
Isonzo
Gorizia
Vittorio Veneto
Asiago
Piave
Trieste
FRANCE
Treviso
Lake Garda
Vicenza
Venice
Gulf of Venice
Verona

The Italian forces were commanded by General Luigi Cadorna, who hoped to seize the heights near Gorizia before swinging south to take Trieste. Commanding the defending Austrian force was General Svetozar Boroevich von Bojna. On 23 June 1915 Italian forces moved forward into the First Battle of the Isonzo. With only minimal artillery support, they gallantly attempted to force their way up the steep, rocky hills in the face of heavy enemy fire. As Austrian artillery shells exploded, they shattered the sharp limestone of the region. As a result, shards of flying rock ripped many attackers to

Above: The Serbian Army was overwhelmed by the forces of Germany, Austria and Bulgaria.

> Italian soldiers, with a level of bravery that belies their military reputation, surged forward into a hail of fire, only to retreat. Austrian soldiers, often of Slavic background, fought doggedly in the defence, and the war became a stalemate.

shreds, and blinded others. Although they fought bravely, the Italians could not gain the Austrian lines in two weeks of heavy fighting. Despite this, Cadorna was not finished and launched three more offensives in the area during the remainder of the year. Each attack followed the pattern of the first. Italian soldiers, with a level of bravery that belies their military reputation, surged forward into a hail of fire, only to retreat. Austrian soldiers, often of Slavic background, fought doggedly in the defence, and the war became a stalemate. Once again attrition reigned supreme. During the first four battles of the Isonzo the Italians lost 250,000 men compared to 165,000 Austrian losses. Though the cost was high, and the gains minimal, in the coming years the Italians would launch seven more battles of the Isonzo.

SERBIAN DEFEAT

Like Italy, Bulgaria lurked on the sidelines of World War I, waiting to see who would emerge victorious and anticipating the best bid for her services. Unlike the Italian case, in this instance the Central Powers were in the best bargaining position. Recent successes in the war against Russia helped to convince King Ferdinand of Bulgaria that the Central Powers would emerge from the war victorious. In addition, Bulgaria was promised substantial slices of Serbia and even Greece for her participation in the

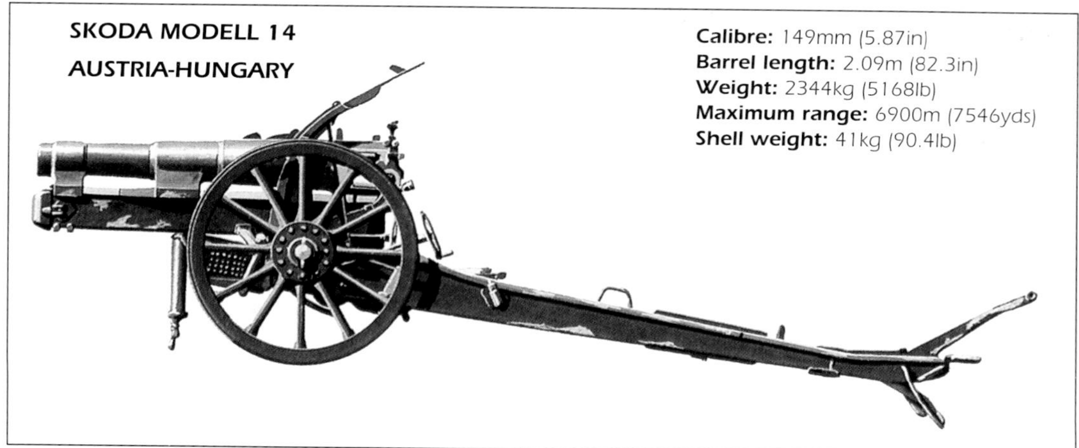

conflict. As a result, on 6 September 1915 Bulgaria signed a military alliance with the Central Powers.

The German diplomatic victory shocked the Allies, who believed the Bulgarian alliance portended a renewed assault on Serbia. To counter such a move, the Allies made plans to land an expeditionary force at the Greek port of Salonika. The Greeks were divided over which side to take in the growing conflict. In the end, they allowed an Allied force – initially numbering only one British and one French division – to land at Salonika. However, they informed the Germans that the Allied actions did not have their full support. Thus the Greeks walked the tightrope of neutrality.

The small Allied force proved to be of no help to Serbia. On 7 October an Austro-German force of 250,000 men, under the command of General von Mackensen, invaded Serbia from the north. Making lavish use of artillery, they soon had the outnumbered Serbians in full retreat. After only three days, the Serbian capital of Belgrade fell. On the following day, disaster struck yet again, as 250,000 Bulgarians invaded Serbia from the east.

RIGHT: AS THEY HAD IN RUSSIA, THE GERMANS CAME TO THE AID OF THEIR REELING AUSTRIAN ALLIES IN SERBIA – HERE GERMAN OFFICERS CROSS A RIVER DURING THE CENTRAL POWERS' VICTORIOUS CAMPAIGN.

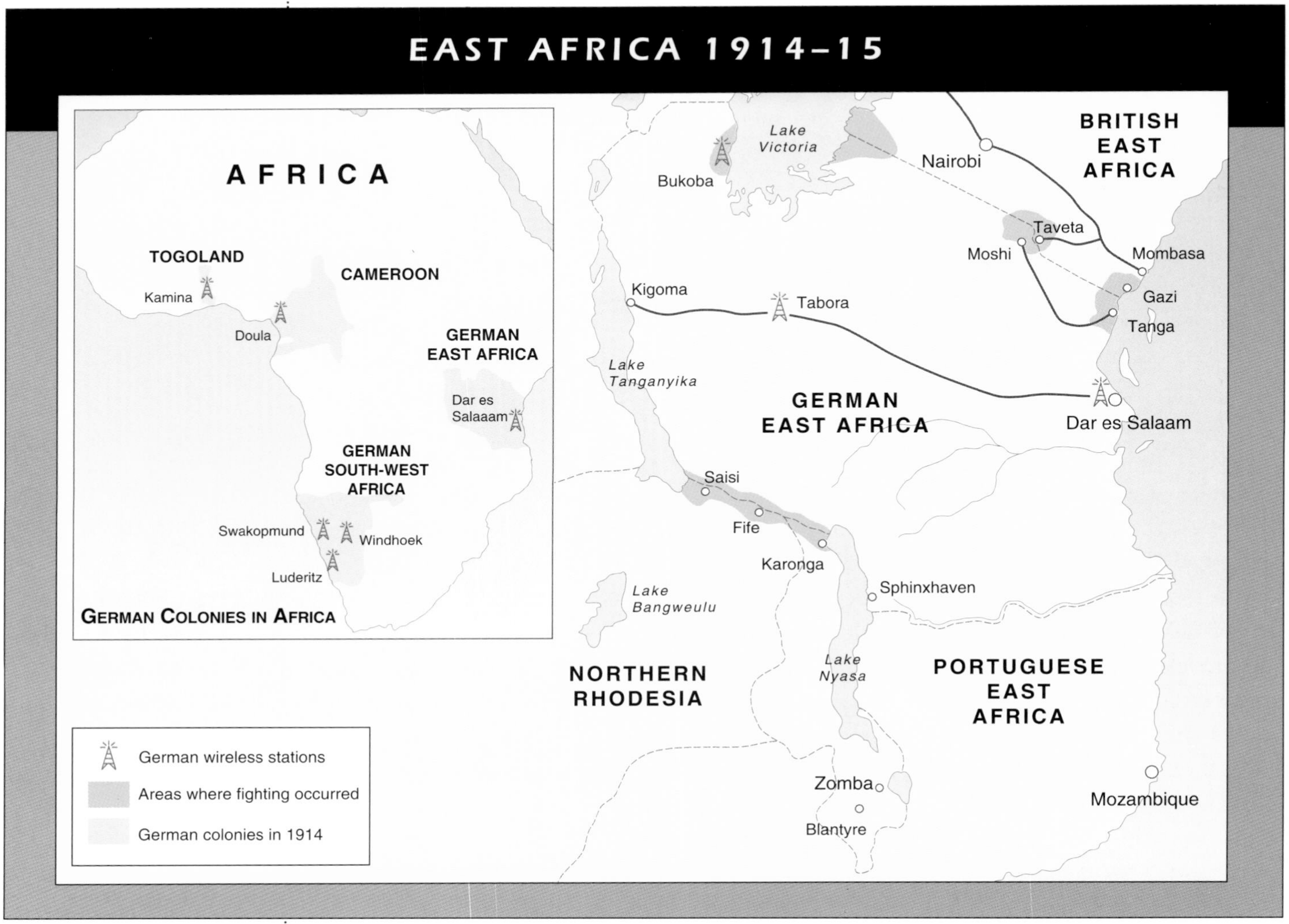

EAST AFRICA 1914–15

AFRICA
TOGOLAND
Kamina
Doula
CAMEROON
GERMAN EAST AFRICA
Dar es Salaaam
GERMAN SOUTH-WEST AFRICA
Swakopmund
Windhoek
Luderitz
GERMAN COLONIES IN AFRICA

Lake Victoria
Bukoba
Nairobi
BRITISH EAST AFRICA
Taveta
Moshi
Mombasa
Gazi
Tanga
Kigoma
Tabora
Lake Tanganyika
GERMAN EAST AFRICA
Dar es Salaam
Saisi
Fife
Karonga
Sphinxhaven
Lake Bangweulu
NORTHERN RHODESIA
Lake Nyasa
PORTUGUESE EAST AFRICA
Zomba
Blantyre
Mozambique

German wireless stations
Areas where fighting occurred
German colonies in 1914

RIGHT: A GERMAN SOLDIER ASKS FOR DIRECTIONS FROM A BULGARIAN RESERVIST ON SENTRY DUTY IN AN OCCUPIED SERBIAN TOWN.

The Serbian Army of only 200,000 was already falling back in the face of superior numbers, and was now threatened with envelopment and destruction. With the escape route to Salonika cut off by the Bulgarian advance, the Serbs fled through the mountains into Albania. The Serbian flight turned tragic as the advancing winter and the unforgiving terrain took the lives of nearly 75,000 men.

After reaching the safety of Albania, the Serbs boarded British ships and were transported to Salonika. The Allied force in Greece had played a small part in the war in Serbia, and now faced the superior forces of the Central Powers. To keep a close watch on the Allied force there, the Germans chose not to attack Salonika. Many Allied military leaders lobbied for the evacuation of Salonika, but the force remained and grew. Although it undertook no meaningful offensive action, by 1917 the Allied force in Greece numbered 600,000 men. The Germans were overjoyed to see such a misallocation of Allied force and referred to Salonika as 'the largest Allied internment camp'.

THE MESOPOTAMIAN CAMPAIGN

In November 1914 British and Indian troops landed at the head of the Persian Gulf in Mesopotamia; their goal was to protect British oil interests in the region. The Turks were unprepared for such an operation and by December the Allied forces had captured Basra and Qurna and the oil fields were safe. Having completed their main mission, the Allied force should have remained in defensive positions, holding the Turks at bay amid the harsh desert conditions. However, the commander of the British force, General John Nixon, and his superiors longed for a more meaningful victory in the region. Continued operations were risky at best, for the desert was unbelievably hot, sometimes reaching 48°C (120°F), and rife with disease. Supply lines were limited to vulnerable rivers. In addition, there was nothing in the area of strategic importance; there were only endless expanses of desert.

In March 1915, seemingly against all reason, the British forces advanced, pushing the Turks back some 112km (70 miles) along the Tigris and Euphrates Rivers. Once again the Allied force did not call a halt, but chose to advance 145km (90 miles) more to the town of Kut-el-Amara, preparatory to an attack on the city of Baghdad. On 26 September the Sixth Indian Division, commanded by General Charles Townshend, captured Kut after a

BELOW: A BRITISH 60-POUNDER ARTILLERY BATTERY BLAZING AWAY AMID THE INHOSPITABLE DESERT TERRAIN OF THE MESOPOTAMIAN CAMPAIGN.

RIGHT: GENERAL TOWNSHEND, THE BRITISH COMMANDER, MAKES HIS WAY INTO CAPTIVITY AFTER THE FALL OF KUT. NOTE THE GERMAN SOLDIER CARRYING THE DEFEATED GENERAL'S BAG.

three-day battle. Although Townshend was reticent to move further into hostile terrain, with ever-lengthening and increasingly vulnerable supply lines, Britain required a victory. Gallipoli had failed, and there were few gains on the Western Front, but if Townshend could seize Baghdad, it would be a propaganda coup of major proportions.

In November Townshend and his 12,000 men advanced north and faced a Turkish force located south of Baghdad. The battle, fought in terrible conditions, was costly to both sides. The Turks chose to fall back, but Townshend too had to retreat and returned to Kut. Sensing this weakness, the Turks followed and surrounded the Allied force at Kut. They then proceeded to lay siege to Kut for five months.

The Allied force, cut off from all resupply, only had enough rations for two months. By the end of the siege, they had been reduced to killing and eating their horses. Several British relief efforts failed to free the trapped defenders, and so Townshend surrendered his beleaguered garrison of 10,000 men to the Turks on 29 April 1916. For those soldiers, the worst was yet to come. Several of the starving men died in the horrible desert march to their prison camps. There, the survivors had to endure years in squalid, unsanitary conditions; only 3000 lived and returned home.

Townshend surrendered his beleaguered garrison on 29 April 1916. For those soldiers, the worst was yet to come. Only 3000 lived and returned home. The largest surrender to date in British history sent shock waves through Britain. Once again, British pride was on the line.

The largest surrender to date in British history sent shock waves through Britain. Once again, British pride was on the line. Nixon was replaced by General Stanley Maude and reinforcements were rushed to the area. By March 1917 the Allied force was ready to renew the offensive and by now the attackers significantly outnumbered the Turks and went on to capture Baghdad on 11 March 1917. Although the defeat at Kut had been avenged, the continued Mesopotamian Campaign represents a misallocation of Allied resources. The fall of Baghdad aided the Allied cause very little, yet by 1918, 450,000 Allied troops were located in that region. During the campaign, British and Indian forces suffered 92,000 casualties. Their sacrifice, though gallant, did little to sap the strength of the Central Powers.

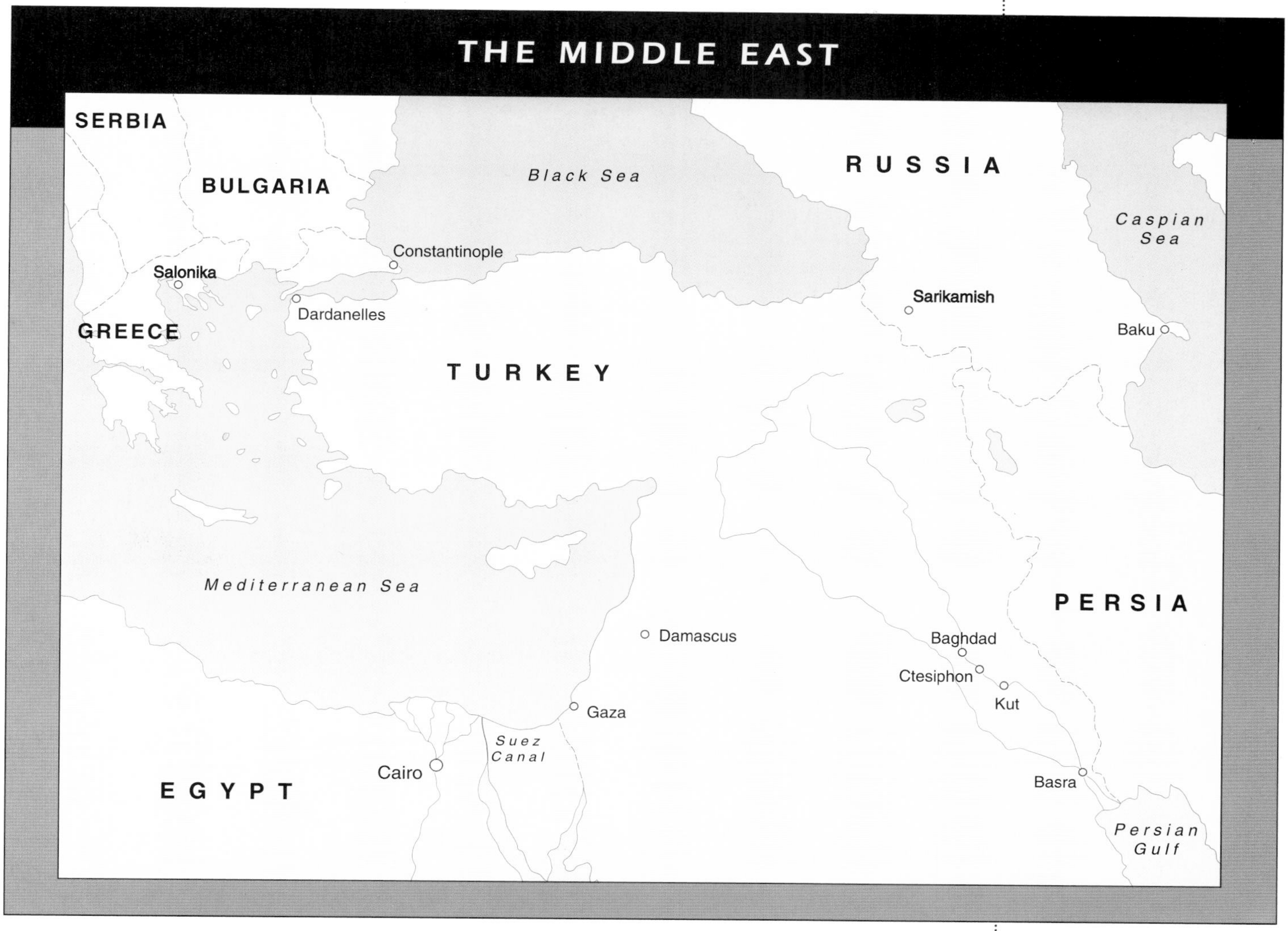

THE MIDDLE EAST

LEFT:
TURKISH FORCES RETREAT ACROSS THE DESERT, FLEEING FROM A RENEWED BRITISH ATTACK IN 1917. THE HARSH CLIMATE IN MESOPOTAMIA STRAINED LOGISTIC LINES ON BOTH SIDES AND MADE THE SUPPLY OF FRESH WATER CRITICAL TO SUCCESS.

CHAPTER 6

Slaughter in the West

IN AN ATTEMPT TO GAIN GERMAN PRISONERS TO INTERROGATE, CANADIAN TROOPS GO 'OVER THE TOP' ON A RAID DURING THE BATTLE OF THE SOMME IN 1916 – THE BATTLE AND THE YEAR THAT WOULD COME TO REPRESENT WORLD WAR I IN THE POPULAR IMAGINATION.

ALLIED AND GERMAN PLANNING

It was von Falkenhayn's plan to ring the exposed French salient with thousands of artillery pieces. He would then unleash unrelenting firepower upon French manpower. He never wanted to seize Verdun itself; his goal was to drag the French Army through a meat-grinder and 'bleed France white'.

Erich von Falkenhayn, eschewing a renewed offensive in the east, chose instead to try to win a climactic victory in the west. The German commander-in-chief still believed that a breakthrough on the Western Front was impossible. He had, however, developed a horribly simple solution for victory against the French. In his planning for the German attack in the west, he boiled war down into its essence: attrition. He chose to assault the historic French city of Verdun because of its defensive liabilities. Although ringed by an impressive series of forts and entrenchments, Verdun lay in a narrow, exposed salient, surrounded on three sides by German firepower. In addition, only one sub-standard road led into the city, thus impairing French logistics. Finally, the city was of great historic significance to France, meaning that Joffre would opt to defend it, no matter what the cost. It was von Falkenhayn's plan to ring the exposed French salient with thousands of artillery pieces. He would then unleash unrelenting firepower upon French manpower. He never wanted to seize the fortress of Verdun itself; his goal was to drag the French Army through a meat-grinder and 'bleed France white'.

OVERVIEW

In many ways 1916 is the defining year of World War I. During that year, both the Germans and the British made concerted efforts to end the war through offensives on the Western Front, resulting in the twin tragedies of Verdun and the Somme. While the Germans resorted to a war of attrition in an effort to 'bleed France white', the British aimed at a decisive breakthrough. Both offensives failed to achieve their goals and led to a year of unrelenting, epic slaughter that would come to haunt an entire generation. Events in the east and on more peripheral fronts seemed to offer no more hope to the belligerents. The year ended with the onset of a terrible winter, one that saw many of the combatant nations question their ability to prosecute the war for another year.

The attack on Verdun caught the French unaware, partly due to the strength of the fortress city. Verdun had long occupied an important position along a traditional German invasion route. For

RIGHT: THE SEEMING GOAL OF THE GERMAN ATTACK IN 1916, AND THE CENTRE OF FRENCH RESISTANCE – THE CITY OF VERDUN ITSELF.

DOUAUMONT

The mighty Fort Douaumont was the lynchpin of the Verdun defensive system. The huge fort, which began construction in 1885, measured some 400m (437yds) across. It was surrounded by 27m (30yds) of barbed wire entanglements and a 7m (24ft) deep moat flanked by machine-gun galleries. The walls of the fort were made of 2.4m (8ft) thick reinforced concrete covered in a protective shield of earth. On 25 May 1916 the Germans called off a massive attack scheduled to strike the formidable fort and its 400-man garrison, but a single engineering section seemingly did not receive the orders to stand down. Nine men, led by Sergeant Kunze, made their way toward the imposing fort. Having reached the moat without incident – it seems the French defenders outside the fort thought

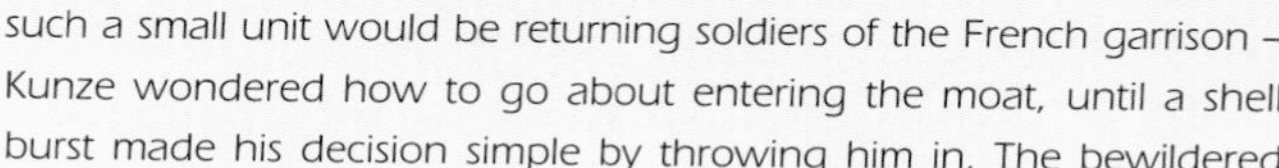

such a small unit would be returning soldiers of the French garrison – Kunze wondered how to go about entering the moat, until a shell burst made his decision simple by throwing him in. The bewildered Germans still met no resistance and made their way to the menacing machine-gun galleries. In a semi-comic episode, they formed a human pyramid to gain entrance to the machine-gun apertures 3.6m (12ft) above ground. After some failures, resulting in German soldiers tumbling all over the moat, Kunze and a few of his men made it inside the fort. Kunze pulled his pistol and wandered around Douaumont yelling, 'Hands up' at every corner and room entrance. The brave German sergeant rounded up only small groups of French soldiers until he discovered several men of the garrison lurking in the basement, sheltering from the incessant German shell fire above. Ironically, a French communications error had kept the majority of the garrison from entering the fort until it was too late.

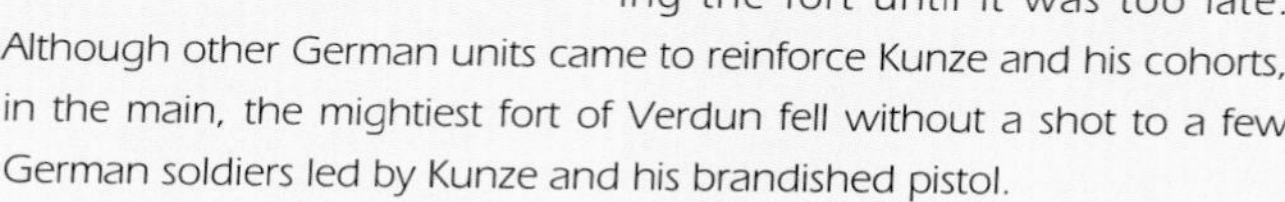

Although other German units came to reinforce Kunze and his cohorts, in the main, the mightiest fort of Verdun fell without a shot to a few German soldiers led by Kunze and his brandished pistol.

AN AERIAL VIEW OF ONE OF THE FORTS RINGING VERDUN.

this reason, the French had constructed a series of impressive forts and defensive works – some 60 forts arranged in three concentric circles – around the city, making it the most defensible place on earth. Joffre simply could not believe that the Germans would attack such a formidable obstacle, and had denuded many of the defensive fortifications around Verdun of their artillery and garrisons to add their weight to his own proposed offensive for 1916. This played right into German hands, and instead of being strong, the defences of Verdun were weak indeed when they finally struck.

Falkenhayn entrusted his ambitious plan to the German Fifth Army under the command of Crown Prince William. His attacking force numbered some five corps, which had entered the line around Verdun without alerting the defending French. However, numbers of men meant comparatively little to Falkenhayn; he hoped to 'bleed the French white' through the use of artillery, while saving German manpower. Towards this end, the Germans had ringed the French fortress with 1200 artillery pieces, including 650 'heavies'. Falkenhayn hoped that such a concentration of firepower would attrit the defenders in a contest between steel and flesh.

VERDUN

At 0715 hours on 21 February 1916, the Germans unleashed their bombardment, firing one million shells into an area of the French line of only 31 sq.km (12 sq.miles). Only the strength of modern industry made such a horror possible. At a very important point in

Above: 'Big Bertha', a 420mm (16.54in) German artillery piece, fires at French positions at Verdun. The Germans hoped that heavy use of artillery would 'bleed the French army white'.

the French defences near the Bois de Caures, the Germans concentrated 80,000 shells upon an area of the French line only 457m (500yd) by 914m (1000yd). One French defender in the area said that the German artillery fire was 'a storm, a hurricane, a tempest growing ever stronger, where it was raining nothing but paving stones'. The slaughter was prodigious, but some defenders remained. When the Germans came forward in the Bois de Caures, 800 dazed defenders under the command of Colonel Driant manned their machine guns and took a fearsome toll upon the advancing mass of German infantry, killing 4000, and checking their advance for two days. Driant only gave the order to retire after he had been flanked and his ammunition had run low. However, during the retreat, Driant was fatally wounded. Such incidents were repeated up and down the line, and the German advance was disappointingly slow.

Joffre was slow to react to the danger posed by the German attack, for he still harboured hopes for a grand French offensive. While he vacillated, the German offensive ground on, advancing on the city of Verdun itself. The German forward movement illustrates a mistake made by von Falkenhayn. His original plan had called for a struggle between German steel and French flesh. However, the pressures of war were too great, and Falkenhayn decided, partly due to the insistence of the Crown Prince, to seize the city of Verdun itself. In so doing, Falkenhayn doomed his own offensive, for all of the tactical advantages in World War I lay with the defender. Slowly, the Germans inched forward against stubborn French resistance. Falkenhayn made some fantastic gains, including the seizure of the main French fort defending Verdun, Fort Douaumont.

Joffre finally noticed the serious nature of the German effort and rushed reinforcements to the scene under the command of General Henri Petain, who succeeded in revitalising the French defensive forces and began to repair and augment the one road leading into Verdun so that more supplies and munitions could reach the stricken city. The road soon became known as *la Voie Sacrée* (the sacred way). Under his command, and with an infusion of fresh troops, the French Army stood firm at Verdun, and by 28 February had checked the German advance.

The Germans hoped to seize the important high ground of the aptly-named *le Mort Homme* ('the dead man'). Having taken this ground, the Germans would dominate much of the area and Verdun would be vulnerable.

RENEWED GERMAN ADVANCE

After the failure of his initial attack, Falkenhayn, under pressure from the Crown Prince and his chief of staff General Knobelsdorf, shifted the emphasis of operations to the west bank of the Meuse River. Here the Germans hoped to seize the important high ground of the aptly-named *le Mort Homme* ('the dead man'). Having taken this ground, the Germans would dominate much of the area and Verdun would be vulnerable. On 6 March, following a punishing bombardment, the Germans advanced against weak French resistance. However, the defenders stiffened as the Germans made for the all-important heights. In the face of determined resistance, the initial German attack failed, and led to a

LEFT: FRENCH SOLDIERS TAKE A BRIEF REST FROM THE FIGHTING AT VERDUN AS THE BOMBARDMENT CONTINUES ALL AROUND AND OVER THEM.

three-month struggle for *le Mort Homme*. The battle for the hill of death would be one of the most ferocious ever fought on the Western Front, involving nearly constant shelling and brutal hand-to-hand fighting. The artillery fire in the area was so intense that nearby hill 304 had its top shorn away, losing some 7.6m (25ft) of elevation during the battle. The battlefield was a wilderness of shell holes, shattered trees and broken bodies. Finally, in late May the Germans took possession of the hill of death, only to find that ownership of the heights made little difference to the overall battle. During the struggle for the hill the French had lost 89,000 casualties to the Germans' 82,000. The battle had formed the most concentrated killing field of the Western Front. Both sides were bleeding profusely – and Falkenhayn's grand scheme was failing.

ABOVE: FRENCH REINFORCEMENTS TRUDGE TOWARD VERDUN ALONG *LA VOIE SACRÉE* (THE SACRED WAY).

BELOW: THE BITTER FIGHTING AROUND VERDUN LED TO TACTICAL INNOVATIONS – SUCH AS AN INCREASED RELIANCE ON SMALL, MOBILE INFANTRY FORMATIONS, AS EVIDENCED BY THIS GERMAN ASSAULT GROUP PREPARING FOR ITS ROLE IN THE ATTACK.

After the horror of *le Mort Homme*, Falkenhayn gathered his forces for one last attempt to overthrow Verdun, his previous notion of using artillery to attrit the French now a distant memory. In an effort to augment his defences in the area, Joffre had sent reinforcements under the command of General Robert Nivelle. Once again, heralded by an intense barrage, on 1 June the Germans moved towards their goal of Fort Vaux. Here a meagre 600 defenders, under the command of Major Sylvain-Eugene Raynal, fought a bitter, underground war against the German attackers. Using both gas and the newly invented flame-thrower, the Germans pressed the embattled French ever deeper into the recesses of the fort. Amid the stench of rotting bodies, the French fought on. Only after his water ran out did Raynal and his force surrender, having inflicted some 3000 casualties upon the Germans.

VERDUN DRAWS TO A CLOSE

However, even with this victory, the German offensive at Verdun slowly dragged to a halt. Coming to the aid of their embattled ally, on 1 July the British launched their own offensive on the Somme. Now involved in two massive battles on the Western Front, the Germans shifted to the defensive in both in order to husband their resources and survive. In August, displeased with the turn of events, Kaiser William II dismissed Falkenhayn and replaced him with the successful command team of Hindenburg and Ludendorff. They chose to remain on the defensive in the west against unified Allied action.

The Battle of Verdun, however, was not over, for now the French attempted to retake the ground they had lost from the Germans. In preparation for their offensive, under the direction of Nivelle, they perfected the 'Creeping Barrage', a risky artillery technique that called for infantry to advance right behind a rolling, protective curtain of artillery fire. Such techniques allowed French attackers to reach German trenches before the defenders had the chance to emerge from their defensive dugouts. On 19 October Nivelle's men struck the surprised Germans and recaptured Fort Douaumont before struggling forward to seize Fort Vaux. In mid-December, a renewed French offensive pushed

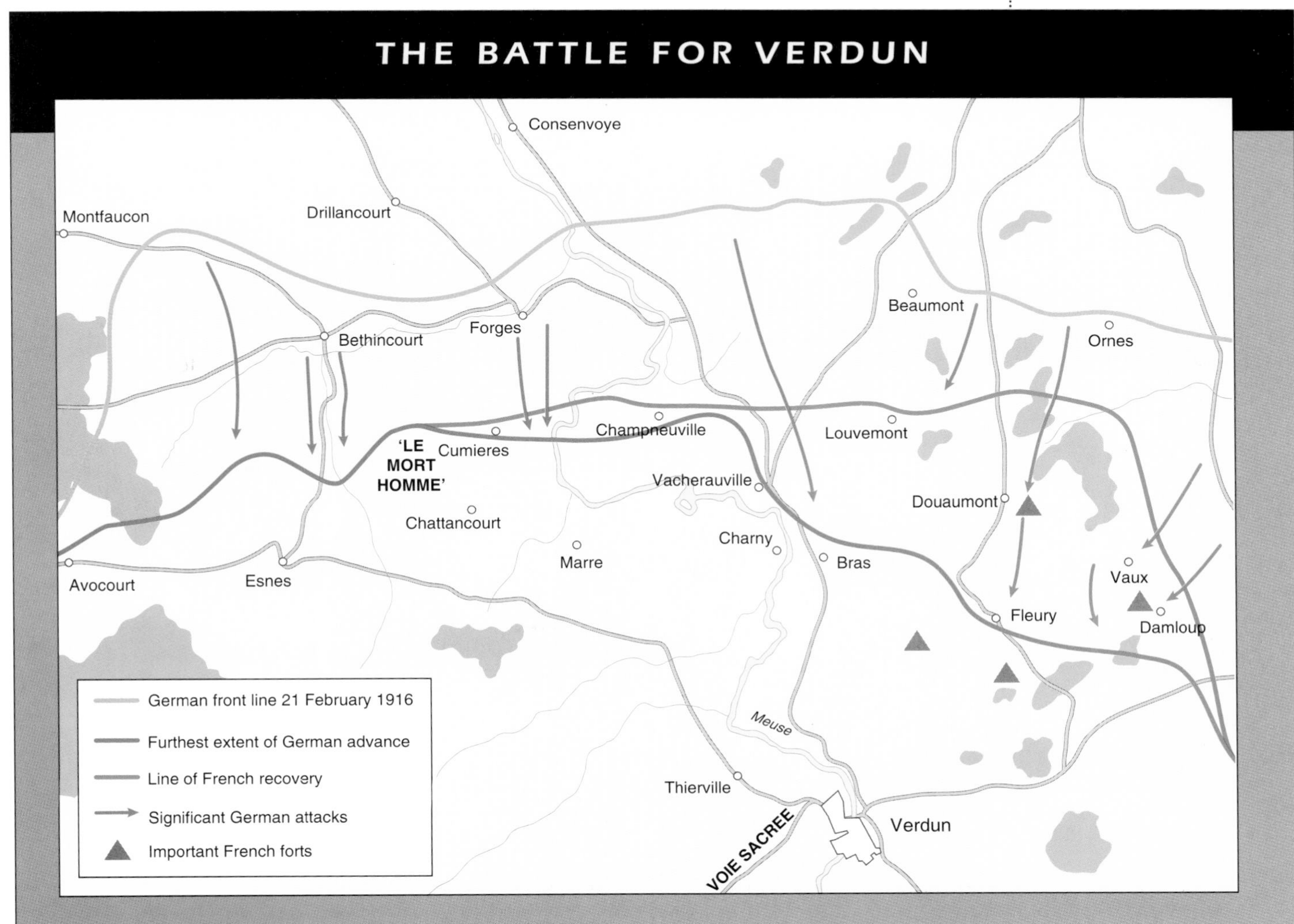

RIGHT:
THE FRENCH PERFORMED A MIRACLE OF LOGISTICS AT VERDUN – SUPPLYING THE NEEDS OF A MASS ARMY THROUGH THE USE, IN THE MAIN, OF ONE SMALL ROAD, *LA VOIE SACRÉE*.

BELOW:
IN EVERY NATION SCIENTISTS ATTEMPTED TO DEVISE NEW WEAPONRY TO AID THE ARMIES IN THE FIELD – HERE THE GERMANS UNLEASH THE FURY OF A FLAMETHROWER, ONE OF THE NEWEST WEAPONS OF THE WAR, UPON FRENCH LINES AT VERDUN.

the Germans some 3.2km (2 miles) beyond Douaumont: nearly back to their original start line.

The Battle of Verdun had finally come to a close, after almost 10 months of intense struggle. For the French Government, the slaughter was too much to bear, and Joffre was removed from command and replaced by Nivelle. The human cost of the battle was mind-numbing. The French lost nearly 400,000 casualties, some 160,000 of which were fatal. The Germans lost 350,000 casualties, nearly 100,000 fatal. The landscape around Verdun was destroyed – and has yet to recover. The men who fought at Verdun – French and German alike – exhibited wonderful bravery and courage, persevering in the face of disaster. These men fought through hellish conditions in a battle the very name of which has become synonymous with futility.

THE SOMME

As Verdun lumbered on to its horrible conclusion, the BEF made ready to launch its own massive offensive further north in the vicinity of the Somme River. Partly in response to desperate French appeals for aid, Haig chose to launch his attack by July. The volunteers of 1914 had reached the line and the Kitchener Army stood ready to prove itself in battle. It was to be the greatest military effort to that point in British history, and a uniquely British tragedy.

In his Somme planning, Haig followed a different path towards victory from Falkenhayn at Verdun. A commander from the old school,

Haig longed for open warfare and decisive battles. He realised that the infantry, with its low offensive capabilities, could not achieve such results, and so the artillery was again to be the main weapon. The BEF would simply amass so much artillery and then shell the battlefield so lavishly that no German could survive. They would then walk across and occupy the trenches full of German dead. If all went well, the cavalry would gallop through the infantry and unhinge the entire German position.

Haig entrusted his offensive to the British Fourth Army under the command of General Henry Rawlinson. Aided by French troops to the south, Rawlinson planned to attack the Germans near the French town of Albert. In that area, the Allies gathered 23 divisions to only six German divisions. The plan called for using the numerical superiority to achieve a breakthrough assault made possible by the artillery's destruction of the German defensive positions. Toward this end, the BEF amassed over 1400 artillery pieces for the bombardment. On 24 June 1916, these guns opened up with a hurricane of fire on the German defensive emplacements. For a week, it continued, and a total of 1.5 million shells rained down upon the Germans on a front line of less than 40km (25 miles). As the attack neared, the bombardment increased in intensity and the guns fired at a rate of 3500 shells per minute, but impressive as it was, it was doomed to failure.

Of the British artillery pieces, 1000 were field guns. These guns were light and mobile, but could not fire shells large enough to destroy the German trenches, or far enough to duel with German artillery. To make matters worse, of the 1.5 million shells fired in the preliminary bombardment, 1 million were shrapnel shells, which burst in the air and peppered the landscape with small lead pellets. Again such shells could devastate an army in the open, but did precious little to the Germans sheltering in their deep dugouts. The main use of shrapnel in the offensive was the destruction of barbed wire. Even in this task, however, the field guns firing shrapnel were of little effective use.

ABOVE: A MEMBER OF THE FRENCH 116TH INFANTRY REGIMENT.

LEFT: AT THE BATTLE OF THE SOMME THE BRITISH HOPED TO UNLEASH SUCH A HEAVY ARTILLERY BOMBARDMENT UPON THE GERMANS THAT NO ONE COULD SURVIVE. HERE A BRITISH 234MM (9.2IN) GUN TAKES PART IN THE SOMME BOMBARDMENT ON 1 JULY 1916.

RIGHT: .
BRITISH TROOPS ADVANCE THROUGH BARBED WIRE ENTANGLEMENTS ON THE FIRST DAY OF THE SOMME.

BELOW:
THE BRITISH BOMBARDMENT, THOUGH, HAD FAILED TO CUT THE WIRE OR KILL THE ENEMY – AND THE GERMANS MANNED THEIR MACHINE GUNS TO MOW DOWN THE WAVES OF BRITISH INFANTRY ADVANCING AT WALKING PACE.

These figures mean that some 400 artillery pieces firing some 500,000 high-explosive shells had to do the bulk of the real work. But the problems did not stop there. The manufacture of high explosive is difficult and very exacting. British industry had only recently been put to the task, and it had been fairly inefficient. As many as 30 per cent of British shells fired during the bombardment were duds, and others did not explode at the required time. Some shells even mistook the shock of firing for impact and exploded in the barrels of the British guns. Finally, much of the British bombardment was hopelessly inaccurate. As a result, on 1 July 1916 when the British went over the top to face the foe, the Germans, though dazed by the intense bombardment, were quite alive.

The British attackers, certain that nothing could have survived the inferno of artillery fire, left their trenches, dressed their lines and began to walk across no-man's-land toward the German lines, sometimes even kicking footballs toward the enemy. The German defenders, given ample warning by the long barrage, poured forth from their dugouts, mounted their machine guns, called down their shrapnel and cut down the British infantry in swathes. The British fought gallantly and in the south, where the bombardment was the most effective, achieved most of their initial objectives. In the north, however, especially near Thiepval and Gommecourt, the artillery barrage had failed and British troops faced intact barbed-wire entanglements and well-placed machine guns. Although brave British

ABOVE: SOME OF THE 57,000 BRITISH CASUALTIES ON THE FIRST DAY OF THE SOMME IN A CRAMPED AND UNHYGENIC FIRST AID POST.

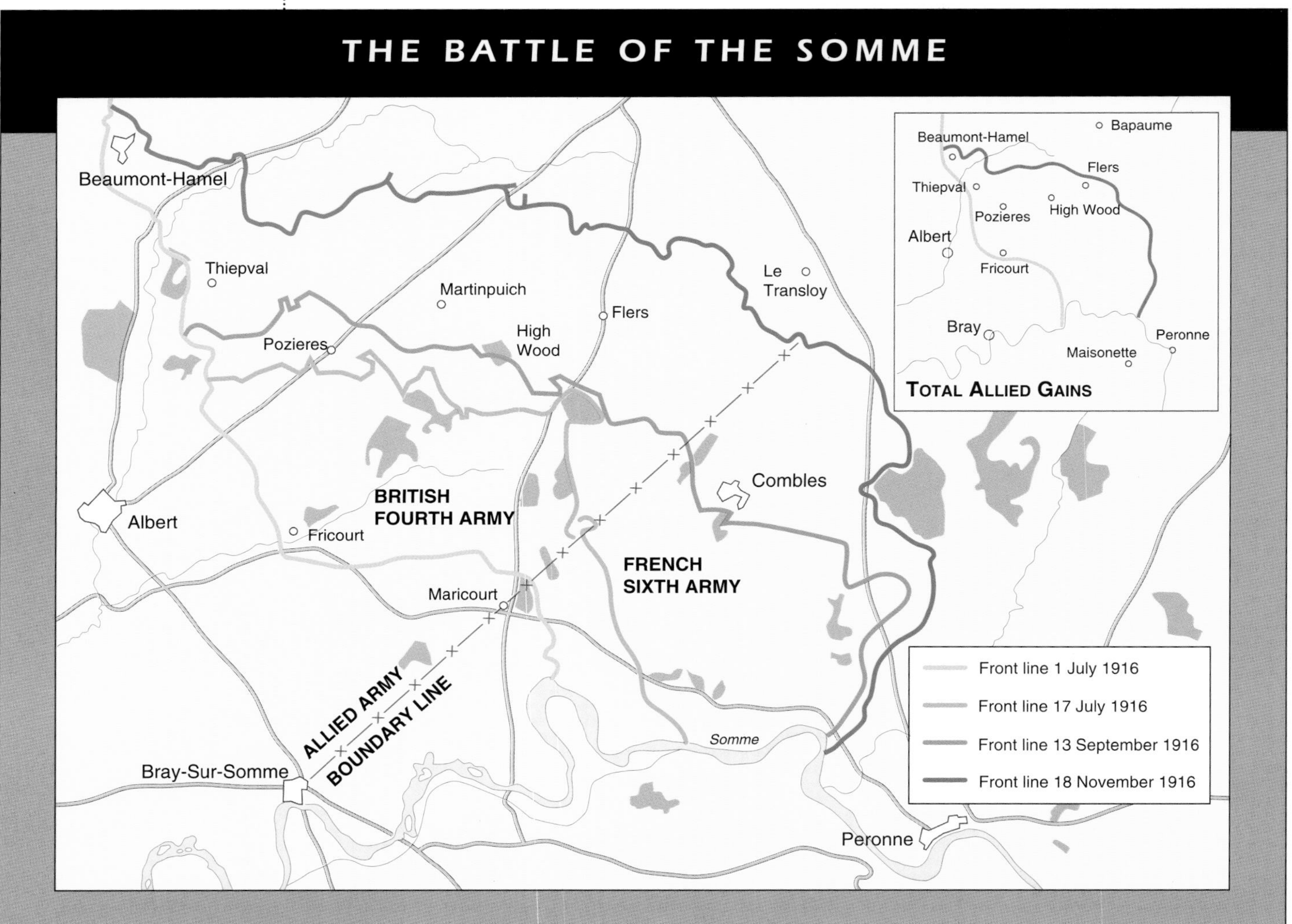

soldiers clawed and fought their way through such obstacles, at times even reaching the German trenches, in most areas in the north they did not even dent the German front-line trenches, much less effect a breakthrough. In what was possibly the worst single day of World War I, the BEF had gained but 4.8 sq.km (3 sq.miles) of territory at the cost of over 57,000 casualties. One British soldier recalls his experiences that fateful day:

> Went over top at 7:30 a.m. after what seemed an interminable period of terrible apprehension ... The din was deafening ... I was momentarily expecting to be blown to pieces ... Suddenly however an appalling rifle and machine gun fire opened against us and my men commenced to fall. I shouted 'down' but most of those that were still not hit had already taken what cover they could find. I dropped in a shell hole and occasionally attempted to move to my right and left but bullets were forming an impenetrable barrier and exposure of the head meant certain death. None of our men was visible but in all directions came pitiful groans and cries of pain ... I finally decided to wait till dusk ... [and crawl back to my trenches] flat on my stomach ... At last I reached the parapet and fell over into our trench now full of dead and wounded. I found a few of my men but the majority were still out and most were dead.

THE OFFENSIVE CONTINUES

Although the first day of the Somme was a failure, like the Germans at Verdun, the British at the Somme remained on the offensive. Haig harboured continued hope that his hammer blows might force the Germans to break and restore a war of movement. However, the British Commander-in-Chief began to move more toward attrition as the answer. If he could not break the German lines, he would use British firepower which, in conjunction with the losses at Verdun, would force the Germans to give way. Haig's continued attacks never did force a breach in the German lines, but they did have an effect on German strategy. The Germans, once again using the advantages of the defensive, rushed reinforcements to the scene. However, their offensive efforts at Verdun limited their forces to a dangerously low level. As a result, the Germans adopted a defensive posture in both battles, putting an end to their effort to 'bleed France white'.

The British slowly learned and drew lessons from their mistakes on the first day of the Somme. Infantry tactics, almost ignored on 1 July, once again became important. In the next major action, launched on 14 July, the infantry attacked from prearranged positions in no-man's-land at night. Rawlinson had chosen to attack an area considerably smaller than that of 1 July (5486m (6000yds) compared to 20,117m (22,000 yards)) but the BEF pummelled the German lines with the same amount of artillery, resulting in a barrage some five times stronger than that of 1 July. As the punishing barrage lifted, the dazed German

BELOW: MEMBERS OF THE 13TH ROYAL FUSILIERS REST AFTER AN ATTACK ON LA BOISSELLE ON 7 JULY 1916 NEAR ALBERT.

Above: Canadians go 'over the top' in the latter stages of the Somme offensive in October 1916.

defenders, already confused by a night attack, were shocked to find the British attackers upon them so quickly. From Bazentin le Grand Wood in the north, to Trones Wood in the south, soldiers of the BEF quickly over-ran the German front line and support systems with slight losses. Once again, although Rawlinson toyed with the idea of committing cavalry to the battle, the forward movement had not resulted in a major breakthrough. The attack lost its impetus in the maze of German defensive works, and the defenders were quick to rush reinforcements to the scene to stop the British advance. The attack degenerated into an attritional slogging match.

Heartened by the results of 14 July, Haig and Rawlinson planned one more great assault, timed for September. However, much preparation and 'line-straightening' had to be done in the meantime. Thus the next two months were dominated by small-scale attacks, and consequently have come to be known as the period of the 'forgotten battles'. The BEF launched 90 minor offensives along the Somme front during this time, and were met by 75 German counter-attacks. In many ways, this period marked the worst time at the Somme for the BEF. In total, 80,000 British became casualties for the gain of a mere 5 sq.km (2 sq.miles) of territory; worse results by far than the better-known futility of 1 July.

As Haig readied for the renewal of a major offensive, science and technology provided him with a new weapon: the tank. Developed in part by Winston Churchill and the Admiralty, the tank would eventually revolutionise warfare, but not in 1916. The British Mark I tank was available in too few numbers to make a true difference at the Somme, with only 32 reaching the assembly point for the offensive. In addition, the tank, which came in a 'male' version with a cannon and a 'female' version with machine guns, only had a top speed of 4.8kph (3mph). Its lack of speed, poor armour and minimal firepower made it a cumbersome and vulnerable weapon. Finally, the tank was prone to breakdown, leaving only nine to advance with the British forces in the coming attack. Thus it was no war-winning weapon yet, but it did have its uses against German machine-gun nests and as an infantry shield.

On 15 September the BEF once again undertook a major offensive at the Somme. This time, the infantry was guarded by a creeping barrage and by the few available tanks, which caused terror among the German defenders. A single tank attacked a trench and captured 300 prisoners, while four others conquered a highly defended village. The tanks, however, were too few in number and the German defences were battered but remained intact. The BEF had seized 9.6km (6 miles) of territory at a cost of 30,000 casualties. Once again, results were better than those in the past, but came nowhere near achieving Haig's beloved breakthrough.

Although the major British efforts at a decisive victory had ended, the battle of attrition dragged on until November. In nearly five months of fighting, the British and French had succeeded only in making a dent in the German lines some 48km (30 miles) long and 11km (7 miles) deep at its deepest point. The cost for such meagre gains was staggering: the BEF lost 420,000 casualties, the French lost 200,000 and the Germans 450,000. The seeming futility of the battle shocked many in Britain. The Kitchener Army had taken the field with high expectations, but those hopes had been dashed on the killing fields of the Somme. To the Germans also, the battle was something of a revelation. The new command team of Hindenburg and Ludendorff were aghast at the pounding that the proud German Army had taken at Verdun and the Somme. Indeed, the generals wondered if Germany could stand losses on such a scale for much longer. As a result, they made an astounding decision: they chose to abandon much of their gains on the Western Front and retreat to a pre-prepared defensive position that came to be known as the Hindenburg Line.

The cost for such meagre gains was staggering: the BEF lost 420,000 casualties, the French lost 200,000 and the Germans 450,000. The seeming futility of the battle shocked many in Britain. The Kitchener Army had taken the field with high expectations, but those hopes had been dashed on the killing fields of the Somme.

LEFT: THE SOMME MARKS A QUANTUM LEAP FORWARD IN MODERN WAR, FOR IT WAS IN THIS BATTLE THAT THE TANK, LIKE THE ONE PICTURED AT LEFT, FIRST SAW WARTIME ACTION.

EVENTS ON THE SOUTHERN FRONT

BELOW: THE WOUNDED IN NO-MAN'S-LAND DEPENDED ON STRETCHER BEARERS SUCH AS THESE NEAR THIEPVAL.

As the great battles of attrition raged on the Western Front, both Austria and Italy sought decisive battle in their southern conflict. Conrad, having recovered from the gloom of 1915, decided to use an Austrian Army brimming with new recruits to launch an attack against Italy in the Trentino. If only the Austrian troops could advance out of the Alpine zone and into the Italian plain, a forward movement of only 65km (40 miles) through Padua would succeed in surrounding the entire Italian Army based at the Isonzo. For their part, the Italians persevered in their plan of attack along the Isonzo River, aiming at a breakthrough into 'unredeemed Italy'.

The Italians struck first, rushing their offensive to aid the French at Verdun. General Cadorna sent his army into the Fifth Battle of the Isonzo on 11 March 1916, but made few gains against stubborn Austrian resistance. Meanwhile, Conrad gathered troops in the Trentino for his offensive. Cadorna, however, knew full well the Austrian plans and warned the commander in the area, General Roberto Brusati, to be ready. The vain Brusati was indignant that Cadorna had intervened in his affairs and chose to ignore the warning. Thus when Conrad opened his Trentino offensive on 15 May the Italians were caught unaware. A short but intense Aus-

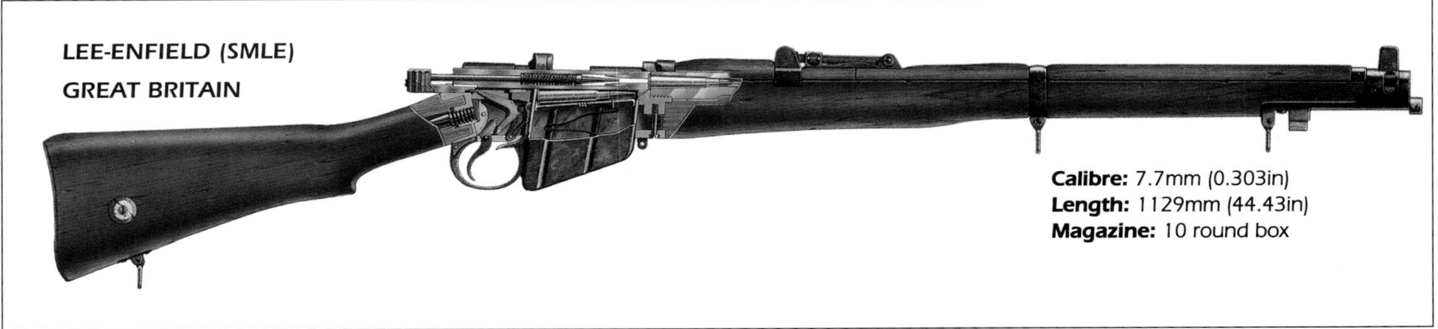

LEE-ENFIELD (SMLE) GREAT BRITAIN

Calibre: 7.7mm (0.303in)
Length: 1129mm (44.43in)
Magazine: 10 round box

trian bombardment dislodged large sections of the Alpine peaks, causing massive avalanches that destroyed Italian defences and entombed the defenders. Fighting hard through difficult terrain, the Austrians nearly broke out into the Italian plain, but fierce Italian resistance and reinforcements from the Isonzo front won the day. By mid-June, partly due to a renewed Russian offensive further east, Conrad was forced to abandon his Trentino offensive. Once again casualties were high in fierce fighting; the Austrians lost 81,000 men as compared to 147,000 Italian losses.

While the Austrians were involved in the Trentino and against the Russians, Cadorna sought to press his advantage on the Isonzo front. Using rail communications to shift his forces quickly back to the Isonzo, he was hoping to catch the Austrians by surprise. Italian forces opened the Sixth Battle of the Isonzo on 6 August and were met with only light Austrian resistance. Even so, the Italians were only able to move forward some 4.8km (3 miles) in the inhospitable terrain, creating a vulnerable salient into the Austrian lines. During the remainder of the year, Cadorna launched the Seventh, Eighth and Ninth Battles of the Isonzo in order to strengthen the newly won Italian positions. When winter finally put an end to the fighting, the Italians had lost 126,000 more casualties and the Austrians 103,000. All the Italians had to show for their sacrifice was a few more miles of desolate limestone hillsides. The troubles of 1916 destroyed the career of Italian Prime Minister Salandra, the man who had taken Italy into World War I.

Below: The shattered village and wood of Beaumont-Hamel attacked on the first day of the Somme by the Newfoundland Regiment, which lost over 700 men (or 91 per cent of its total strength) in mere minutes. It was finally taken by the British in November 1916.

THE RUSSIAN FRONT

In the east the Russians, too, heeded the calls of the beleaguered French and launched an offensive which was designed, in part, to take pressure off Verdun. The first Russian offensive was a poorly run affair, commanded by General Alexei Evert in March near Lake Naroch. After the costly and futile attack, the Russian military command decided to remain on the defensive. Only General Alexei Brusilov believed that an effective Russian attack was still possible. He advocated a simultaneous attack along three portions of the front that would keep the Germans from rushing reinforcements to any one area. One of the main attacks would fall in the south, against the Austrians under his direction. In this offensive, he proposed a radical shift in the use of infantry. Instead of advancing in waves, he would send his men forward as infiltration troops. Their task was to penetrate the enemy's first position, while a second echelon of troops moved through the gap to exploit any success. The Germans would notice the renewed danger to Austria and send reinforcements from their front. Then Evert would attack the weakened German positions using the same techniques, thus winning a great victory. The Tsar was so taken with the plan that it received his immediate approval.

BELOW: ON THE SOUTHERN FRONT MEN, INCLUDING THESE ITALIAN TROOPS WHO ARE SEEN HAULING A 75MM (2.95IN) ARTILLERY PIECE UP A SHEER CLIFF, FACED ALMOST INSURMOUNTABLE PROBLEMS DUE TO THE MOUNTAINOUS TERRAIN.

The Brusilov Offensive opened on 4 June against the Austrians with great success. In the first day of the offensive, the Russian Eighth Army smashed its way through all Austrian defensive positions and opened a gap in the Austrian lines 32km (20 miles) wide. Several Austrian units panicked and fled, while some Czech units surrendered without firing a single shot. Within two weeks, the entire Austrian front had collapsed and Brusilov's forces had advanced 40km (25 miles), capturing nearly 200,000 prisoners. Conrad, rightly sensing disaster, recalled

Conrad, sensing disaster, recalled several units from the Italian front and called for help from his German allies. Falkenhayn obliged and sent the beleaguered Austrians reinforcements from the German portion of the front in the east. His move played right into Brusilov's hands.

LEFT: AUSTRIAN SHARP SHOOTERS IN ACTION IN THE TYROL ON THE SOUTHERN FRONT IN EARLY 1916.

several units from the Italian front and called for help from his German allies. Falkenhayn obliged and sent the beleaguered Austrians reinforcements from the German portion of the front in the east. His move played right into Brusilov's hands.

Evert in the north was supposed to advance on 14 June against the weakened German front, sealing a major Russian victory. However, the timid general was still smarting from the defeat he had suffered in March. As a result, he did not advance until 3 July, and then moved very slowly, even though he enjoyed a large numerical superiority over the

Above: Russian troops on the move in Kiev readying for the next attack. The Brusilov offensive gave the Central Powers some concern, but put great stress on the Russian economy.

Germans. Evert's inaction enabled the Germans to concentrate their efforts against Brusilov in the south, unafraid of swift Russian action in the north. Though Brusilov had received reinforcements, he was unable to make his way through the mountains against the strengthening defensive forces of the Central Powers. By October, all forward movement had ceased.

Although the Brusilov offensive had gained an impressive amount of territory, it had done so at great cost. The Germans had suffered 350,000 casualties and the Austrians nearly 750,000. However, the Russians had lost over one million men in the campaign. Such heavy losses placed an almost unbearable burden on the Russian people. In addition, the weakness of the Russian economy was beginning to show. Strained to the limit by war, the economy had faltered, leading to several shortages in Russia. Losses were mounting, starvation haunted the countryside, and faith in victory was fading. Russia had begun its downward spiral into revolution.

ROMANIA

The initial success of the Brusilov offensive also had an unforeseen consequence: it convinced Romania that the Allies were poised to win the war. Romania, like Italy, sat on the sidelines of the war, closely watching its shifting balance and waiting for the best deal for entry. By 1916, the offer made by the Allies had come to include the entirety of Transylvania and additional land to the south. Even so, the Romanian Government of King Ferdinand was not convinced of the wisdom of becoming a belligerent; that is, not until Brusilov's army crashed through the Austrian lines. Romania declared war on the Central Powers on 27 August 1916.

LEFT: GENERAL BRUSILOV, THE RUSSIAN ARCHITECT OF NEW TACTICS THAT WOULD COME TO DEFINE MODERN WARFARE. IT WAS THE APPARENT SUCCESS OF HIS OFFENSIVE IN 1916 THAT ENCOURAGED THE ROMANIANS TO ENTER THE WAR ON THE SIDE OF THE ALLIES.

The timing of the Romanian declaration could not have been worse, for Brusilov's offensive had just bogged down. In addition, the Central Powers decided that they quickly had to eliminate the Romanian threat, which could disrupt the entire war effort on the eastern and southern fronts. Toward this end, Germany appointed Falkenhayn, recently removed from overall command of the German Army, to lead an offensive against Romania. Thus Romania, with only a tiny army, faced invasion from two fronts. In September, a Bulgarian force struck across the border and advanced toward the port city of Constanta. A few days later, Falkenhayn's Austro-German force invaded from Transylvania. The huge

IRELAND

Ireland, which had been on the verge of civil war over Home Rule, initially rallied behind the cause of Great Britain in World War I. In 1914, Irish volunteers, both Protestant and Catholic, rushed to the colours. After the initial war euphoria wore off, recruitment fell off in the southern part of Ireland, for many there saw Britain's difficulty as Ireland's opportunity. The nationalist group Sinn Fein especially saw World War I as a time to push for Irish independence and planned an urban uprising in Dublin. One of the leaders of the plot was Roger Casement who went to Germany in an effort to raise Irish volunteers from among the various German prisoner-of-war camps. He hoped to return, with German help, at the head of an Irish legion to overthrow British rule on the island. However, his hopes were dashed, and he returned to Ireland via U-boat in early 1916, being captured soon after he set foot on his home soil. His return, although inglorious, was the signal for 1500 Sinn Fein volunteers, led by Patrick Pearse, to begin an uprising in Dublin. On Easter Monday 1916 the rebels took control of several strategic points in the city, hoping that the Irish population would rise up, following their brave example. The population did not answer their call, and a massive infusion of British troops defeated the uprising with great violence. However, it was the brutal nature of this British reprisal which exacerbated the situation in Ireland and helped to create a public backlash against British rule. For the remainder of the conflict, the British had to station nearly 50,000 troops in Ireland to keep order there. Once the war concluded, the Irish troubles which had begun in the Easter Rebellion would only worsen.

BRITISH TROOPS SUPPRESSING THE EASTER RISING IN DUBLIN.

pincer movement threatened the Romanian Army with envelopment and destruction, and the only solution was retreat. On 5 December the Romanian capital, Bucharest, fell to the invaders, but still the retreat continued. Finally, after losing most of their country to the Central Powers, the Romanian Army held in the remote mountains of Moldavia. The tiny nation had lost 350,000 casualties and had virtually ceased to exist. The swift, victorious campaign was to be one of the Central Powers' greatest successes, and conversely one of the greatest allied defeats, of 1916. In addition, the disgraced Falkenhayn had exacted a measure of revenge and had retrieved his career.

ACTIONS IN THE MIDDLE EAST

In the Middle East, the main initial allied concern was the defence of the Suez Canal. After repulsing Turkish efforts to capture the canal in 1915, the British military began to consider operations to make the canal safe from future assaults. General Archibald Murray was assigned the task of strengthening the British presence there and decided to use his scant forces to push the British perimeter around the canal well into the inhospitable Sinai Desert. His original plan called for British troops to advance through the desert some 145km (90 miles) to El Arish, nearly to the Palestinian border. Even though the Turks, who were sorely pressed elsewhere, could do little to stop Murray's advance, British troops only inched forward. Due to the desert terrain, the British had to construct railroads and water pipelines as they advanced in order to keep their army alive. Thus it took all of 1916 to reach El Arish, but at least the Suez Canal was now safe from attack.

In 1917 Murray attempted to overthrow the Turkish defensive lines near Gaza as the first step toward a drive to Jerusalem. British and ANZAC forces, including cavalry units, moved forward on 26 March and seemed poised to crush the Turkish defenders. However, due to a communications breakdown the nearly victorious British cavalry retreated at the critical moment and the defences held. Three weeks later, Murray tried once again to break the

BELOW: AUSTRIAN TROOPS TRAIN IN EVACUATION TECHNIQUES FROM A MINE WHILE WEARING NEW GAS MASKS.

Turkish lines, but failed miserably. As a result, the new British Prime Minister, David Lloyd George, replaced Murray with General Edmund Allenby. Realising that Britain needed a victory to help raise morale, Lloyd George implored Allenby to capture Jerusalem as a Christmas present for the British people. The general assured Lloyd George that he would not be disappointed.

ABOVE: ROMANIAN INFANTRY IN DRESS UNIFORMS MARCHING THROUGH BUCHAREST, THEIR CAPITAL, ON THE DAY WAR WAS DECLARED.

THE ARAB REVOLT

In Arabia, the Turkish call for a *jihad* against the Allies had fallen on deaf ears. Although they shared the same religion, to the Arabs, the Turks were imperial overlords. A war in which Turkey was sorely pressed represented an opportunity not to be missed to gain Arab freedom. Hussein ibn-Ali, the grand sharif of Mecca, ruled the Hejaz, a narrow strip of land along the Red Sea, and was an important religious figure in the Arab world, as well as the most important Arab leader of his region. The British, realising the trouble that an Arab revolt could cause for the Turks, pledged Hussein their support for Arab independence. The British offer, combined with Turkish provocation, caused Hussein to proclaim an Arab revolt on 5 June 1916. Another front had been opened against the Central Powers.

The Turks quickly launched an offensive from their garrison in Medina upon the outgunned and undersupplied Arabs. Aided by British artillery and machine guns, the Arab force launched guerrilla attacks on the Turks, forcing them back into Medina, and then laid siege to the city in late 1916. In January Hussein sent an army, under the leadership of his son Emir Faisal, northwards along the Red Sea and captured the important city of Wejh. From here, the Arabs could launch attacks into Turkish-held northern Arabia and aid the British efforts in Palestine. Noting the importance of the fledgling Arab military effort, the British sent a liaison officer to Faisal's army: T.E. Lawrence, the famed 'Lawrence of Arabia'.

The dashing and self-publicising Lawrence had gained intimate knowledge of the Arab people and their customs while travelling on foot throughout the region undertaking research for his B.A. thesis at Oxford. At the beginning of the conflict, due to his fluency in Arabic he became a member of the British intelligence service in Egypt. Once at Faisal's side, he helped to raise

BELOW: A BULGARIAN, GERMAN AND TURKISH SOLDIER POSE FOR A PHOTOGRAPH IN OCCUPIED ROMANIA.

Above: Australian Light Horse riding their horses in the edge of the Mediterranean near the Suez Canal in Egypt in 1916.

Right: T.E. Lawrence, pictured before his transfer to Arabia, who did much to spark the Arab revolt against the Turks.

the Arab revolt to new heights. Wearing traditional Arab garb, and fighting on camel back, he proved to be an inspiration to the Arabs. Together Faisal and Lawrence convinced several of the tribes of northern Arabia to join the revolt. With this renewed strength, Lawrence accompanied the Arab forces on an epic march through the desert waste toward the port city of Aquaba on the Sinai Peninsula. The city's Turkish defenders believed the desert to be impassable until the Arabs came thundering out of it on their camels in July 1917. It was to be the most important battle of Lawrence's career, but he missed it. Just before the final charge, he accidentally shot his own camel and was knocked unconscious by the beast's fall. However, the attack on Aquaba was a smashing success and Lawrence, despite his mishap, became a British national hero.

From here, Arab raids would support British advances into Palestine, and guerrilla attacks would help to sever the Turkish supply line in the area. Lawrence later publicised his exploits in his *The Seven Pillars of Wisdom* and his fame widened, but what made him a hero was that his victory, however small, came close on the heels of a year of stalemate and slaughter, a year in which Britain lost its national innocence on the killing fields of the Somme: the year 1916.

ARTHUR BALFOUR, BRITISH SUPPORTER OF ZIONISM.

PALESTINE

In its efforts to win a victory in World War I, Britain made several promises that helped to muddle the situation in the volatile Middle East. In an effort to hasten the outbreak of the Arab revolt, in early 1916 British representatives promised to support the establishment of an independent Arab state after the conflict had ended. T.E. Lawrence, often known as 'Lawrence of Arabia' negotiated with Arab leaders in good faith, believing in the promise of independence, and pressing the Arabs to ever-greater military efforts against the Turks. However, in May 1916 the French and British negotiated the Sykes-Picot agreement which promised to carve most of the Arab world up into British and French colonial mandates. Unsure of which agreement would rule the day, the Arabs battled on against their Turkish overlords. Worse was yet to come. In November 1917, in what is sometimes seen as an effort to gain much-needed wartime capital, British Foreign Secretary Arthur Balfour announced what would become known as the Balfour Declaration. He stated that Britain would 'view with favour the establishment in Palestine of a national home for the Jewish people', and would help to 'facilitate the achievement of this object'. Thus Britain had promised the Arabs an independent state, the French slices of that state as colonial possessions, and Palestine to the Jewish people. The three goals were simply not compatible. The Arabs, often weakened by fighting among themselves, proved to be quite restless under Western colonial rule. Even worse was the implementation of the Balfour Declaration. Under British protection, Jews began to move back to their ancestral homeland; the Zionists' dream was finally coming true. However, the Arabs in the area were unhappy with this development and conflict ensued, a conflict that still plagues the world today.

LEFT:
FAISAL AND HIS AGAYL BODYGUARD ADVANCE THROUGH THE DESERT ON CAMELBACK.

CHAPTER 7

The Fight for Naval Mastery

A SQUADRON OF THE GERMAN HIGH SEAS FLEET, CONSTRUCTED SPECIFICALLY BY ADMIRAL TIRPITZ TO CONTEST BRITISH CONTROL OF THE SEAS AROUND EUROPE, STEAMS THROUGH THE BALTIC SEA BEFORE THE OUTBREAK OF WAR IN 1914.

Through their constant prodding, the High Seas Fleet would undertake limited actions in the North Sea in an attempt to lure isolated units of the Royal Navy into a trap.

NAVAL FORCES AND PLANNING

On the outbreak of war in 1914 the British Grand Fleet was still considerably larger in size than the High Seas Fleet of Germany. The Admiralty chose to locate most of the fleet's strength in the anchorage at Scapa Flow in the Orkney Islands off the northern coast of Scotland. Admiral John Jellicoe was chosen to command its 21 Dreadnoughts, 8 pre-Dreadnoughts and 80 cruisers and destroyers. Somewhat cautious, Jellicoe was offset to a certain degree by his dashing and flamboyant subordinate, Admiral David Beatty, who commanded the British battlecruiser squadron. The Admiralty did not plan to seek decisive battle against the smaller German fleet, but instead chose to enforce a blockade of Germany, in which ships patrolled the English Channel and the 320km (200 mile) gap between Scotland and Norway, thus denying German ships access to the Atlantic Ocean and the world's trade.

The German High Seas Fleet, consisting of 13 Dreadnoughts, 16 pre-Dreadnoughts and 40 cruisers and destroyers, and based mainly at the port of Wilhelmshaven, was commanded by Admiral Friedrich von Ingenohl. In many ways the construction of the High Seas Fleet had helped to cause the war. However, once the war started, neither Ingenohl nor the Kaiser, who was personally involved in naval planning, chose to risk the fleet in pitched battle with the Royal Navy. Thus the High Seas Fleet remained inactive, only pursuing operations in the protected Baltic Sea. It was quite a poor return on a fleet that had cost Germany so much in terms of both money and international goodwill. Tirpitz, the architect of the German Navy, and other admirals pressed for a more active role in the naval war. Through their constant prodding, the High Seas Fleet would undertake limited actions in the North Sea in an attempt to lure isolated units of the Royal Navy into a trap.

ACTION OFF SOUTH AMERICA

The German Navy had a number of small squadrons scattered about the oceans of the world that would never be able to run the gauntlet of the Royal Navy and return to Germany. These units attempted to inflict as much damage as possible on Allied interests throughout the world before their inevitable demise. The most powerful German squadron was under the command of Admiral Graf Maximilian von Spee. He moved his squadron, headed by the armoured cruisers *Scarnhorst* and *Gneisenau*, from Tsingtao in China to the coast of Chile to prey upon Allied shipping. The British, aware of Spee's

OVERVIEW

The German High Seas Fleet had been designed to contest the British Grand Fleet for control of the seas. Despite this, on the outbreak of war the Kaiser chose not to risk his beloved fleet in pitched battle. As a result, the naval conflict within World War I consisted, in the main, of small raids until 1916. In that year, a German plan to catch a portion of the Grand Fleet unawares developed into the Battle of Jutland, the largest naval battle ever fought and the last great clash between capital ships. After failing to disable the Grand Fleet at Jutland, the Germans turned to a relatively new weapon of war – the submarine – in their effort to defeat Britain. The resulting First Battle of the Atlantic was very closely run, leaving Britain in danger of losing the conflict.

ADMIRAL JELLICOE, BRITISH COMMANDER AT JUTLAND.

ADMIRAL JOHN JELLICOE

Due to his command and gunnery skill, Admiral John Jellicoe became the protégé of First Sea Lord Admiral John Fisher, and was his first choice on the outbreak of war to command the mighty British Grand Fleet. Jellicoe accepted the position and chose the super-Dreadnought *Iron Duke* as his flagship. However, the popular Jellicoe proved unable to delegate authority and seemed to be rather cautious. While most British people expected glorious naval victory in the best Nelsonian sense, he realised that a showdown with the German High Seas Fleet was fraught with danger. In fact, as Churchill quipped, he was the only man who could 'lose the war in an afternoon'. Many historians contend that when the two fleets squared off in the Battle of Jutland in May 1916, Jellicoe acted with too much caution, allowing the Germans to escape with a draw. Others see him as prudent, unwilling to risk a great defeat for few tangible gains. In 1917 Jellicoe was promoted to the position of First Lord of the Admiralty, specifically to deal with the mounting U-boat threat. Initially he was pessimistic about the Battle of the Atlantic, even forecasting that Britain would lose the war due to submarine actions, but after learning more, he was instrumental in the implementation of the convoy system and the defeat of the U-boat threat. Later, his pessimism and cautious action cost him dearly, and he was replaced as First Lord in December 1917, bringing his career to an end.

actions, ordered their South American squadron, commanded by Admiral Christopher Craddock, to block Spee's access to the Atlantic. The daring Craddock, whose force was much weaker than Spee's, chose instead to seek out battle with the German squadron – before reinforcements had arrived. On 1 November 1914 he got what he wanted, meeting Spee's squadron off the coast of Coronel in Chile. Spee, using superior speed and gunnery,

BELOW: THE BRITISH GRAND FLEET STEAMS BY IN A PRE-WAR REVIEW IN 1914.

ABOVE: SHIPS OF BOTH FLEETS BURNT HUGE AMOUNTS OF COAL TO KEEP THEM AT SEA. 'COALING', AS THE PROCESS OF REFUELLING WAS KNOWN, WAS AN ARDUOUS AND UNPLEASANT TASK SHARED BY MOST OF THE SHIP'S CREW.

forced the British into a disadvantageous position – silhouetted against the setting sun – and pummelled his outmatched opponent. Two British cruisers blew up and sank with all hands; some 1600 men, including Craddock himself. The Germans took no damage and no casualties. Two other British ships managed to escape, but the Battle of Coronel was a disaster for the Royal Navy.

After refuelling, Spee decided to enter the Atlantic Ocean and make for the African coast. The British, however, smarting from their recent defeat, were determined to destroy him and his squadron, and on 11 November, dispatched a much stronger squadron under the command of Admiral Doveton Sturdee to the Falkland Islands in the South Atlantic. Spee rounded Cape Horn in December and decided to launch an attack on undefended Port Stanley in the Falklands before crossing the Atlantic. To their horror, the Germans discovered Sturdee's squadron, which had arrived only the night before, occupying Port Stanley. The outnumbered Germans fled for their lives, but the quicker British ships, sensing imminent revenge, took up the pursuit immediately. After closing to within firing range, Sturdee's ships destroyed Spee's squadron in a one-sided battle, in which the Germans lost 2000 men, while the British suffered no casualties. Only the light cruiser *Dresden* was able to escape, fleeing into the Pacific only to be sunk three months later. The destruction of Spee's squadron served as a morale-boosting victory in an otherwise dismal year for the British. The victory also wiped the oceans clean of German surface warships, leaving the Royal Navy once again undisputed mistress of the seas.

NORTH SEA BATTLES

A secret Admiralty department known as 'Room 40' had succeeded in breaking the German naval codes, and thus Beatty's battle-cruisers were ready when the Germans launched their raid near Dogger Bank off the coast of Northumberland.

Some of the officers of the Royal Navy chafed at the inactivity forced upon them by Jellicoe's decision to follow a defensive strategy. One such officer, Commodore Reginald Tyrwhitt, commander of a cruiser force based at Harwich, developed a plan for an attack. He noted that the German destroyers that patrolled the Heligoland Bight near Wilhelmshaven did so on a regular schedule. He proposed that the Royal Navy take advantage of the German predictability and strike at one of the small patrols. A reluctant Jellicoe gave his approval, and even added Beatty's cruiser squadron to the attack force. On 28 August 1914 the Royal Navy struck. Accurate British fire soon sent two German ships to the bottom, before the High Seas Fleet could send reinforcements. By afternoon, the balance had shifted and Tyrwhitt had to withdraw while Beatty's powerful force entered the melee. As more ships rushed to the scene, the battle became quite confused, and British ships came perilously close to firing at one another. The Battle of Heligoland Bight was a British victory which cost the Germans three cruisers, one destroyer and a total of 1200 men. British forces suffered only 35 fatalities.

Bothered by their own inactivity, several German naval officers, too, pressed for a more daring strategy. Admiral Franz von Hipper, commander of the German cruiser squadron, wanted to take the battle to the Royal Navy and slowly to whittle away at their naval superiority. His plan called for raids upon British coastal towns and he hoped that Jellicoe would respond by sending isolated squadrons to deal with the problem, forces small enough for the Germans to lure them to their doom. The Germans raided the British coast in both November and December, and killed hundreds of British civilians, but failed to lure elements of the British Grand Fleet into a trap.

BELOW: ADMIRAL HIPPER, THE DARING, CHARISMATIC LEADER OF THE GERMAN CRUISER SQUADRON.

The German raid of 24 January 1915 would be different. A secret Admiralty department known as 'Room 40' had succeeded in breaking the German naval codes, and thus Beatty's battle-cruisers were ready when the Germans launched their raid near Dogger Bank off the coast of Northumberland. Stunned to find a superior force awaiting his arrival, Hipper wisely reversed his course and made a dash for home and safety, but Beatty gave chase, and the Battle of the Dogger Bank began. Within minutes, the slowest German ship, the *Blücher*, had been disabled, and the rest were fleeing for their lives. However, the battle turned when Beatty's flagship was disabled. He signalled his second-in-command, Admiral Moore on board the *New Zealand*, to continue the pursuit but Moore misinterpreted Beatty's order and turned the British cruisers to the task of destroying the disabled *Blücher*. No doubt wondering at their good fortune, the remaining German cruisers escaped. A chance for a significant British victory had been missed, and Moore lost his command as a result of this error. Most importantly, however, the Germans had learned something from Dogger Bank. Bursting shells posed a great threat to the ammunition magazines aboard ship. The Germans immediately took measures to counter such problems; the Royal Navy would not take similar measures until after the Battle of Jutland.

JUTLAND

BELOW: THE BLÜCHER CAPSIZING DURING THE BATTLE OF DOGGER BANK, 1915.

It would be 1916 before the Germans once again attempted to alter the British dominance of the North Sea. In that year, Admiral Reinhard Scheer became commander of the High Seas Fleet and once again convinced the reluctant Kaiser that a more offensively

orientated strategy was required in the North Sea. On 31 May the High Seas Fleet left port, led by a scouting force of 41 ships commanded by Hipper. Trailing well behind him were the main elements of the High Seas Fleet commanded by Scheer, consisting of some 59 ships, including 16 Dreadnoughts. The Germans hoped that Hipper would encounter a British cruiser force of similar size to his own. Recreating events of the Dogger Bank, Hipper would turn to flee, enticing the British to pursue. Hipper would then lead the British cruisers into a clash with the might of the entire High Seas Fleet, resulting in a dramatic German naval victory.

Jellicoe had taken the entire Grand Fleet, numbering some 99 ships, including 24 Dreadnoughts, to sea. Neither the Germans nor the British were aware of it, but they were steaming toward the last great clash of capital ships in naval history.

Luck was not with the Germans. Once again 'Room 40' had divined their intentions. Although the British were unaware of the exact location of the German fleet, they knew it was at sea. As a result, Jellicoe had taken the entire Grand Fleet, numbering some 99 ships, including 24 Dreadnoughts, to sea. Sixty miles ahead of the Grand Fleet was Beatty's scouting force numbering 52 ships, including 4 Dreadnoughts. Neither the Germans nor the British were aware of it, but they were steaming toward the last great clash of capital ships in naval history.

Shortly after 1400 hours Beatty caught sight of Hipper's forces and swung southward to pursue. In the confusion, however, Beatty lost touch with his force of Dreadnoughts. Unperturbed, he sped forward to the chase, believing that he had once again caught Hipper at a disadvantage. The Dreadnoughts could catch up later; Beatty had decided that he would not let another chance like Dogger Bank go. Hipper, seeing the German plan coming to fruition, fled southwards, putting Beatty on a collision course with the entire High Seas Fleet. During the run south, the cruiser forces engaged one another at long range and disaster struck for the British. A shell penetrated one of *Indefatigable*'s gun turrets, touching off a huge explosion in the magazine, and the great ship quickly capsized and sank, killing nearly 1000 men. Shortly thereafter, a huge magazine explosion destroyed the *Queen Mary*,

killing 1200. Aghast, Beatty turned to the captain of his flagship and said, 'There seems to be something wrong with our bloody ships today.' He was quite correct, for the British were now suffering from the same problem the Germans had corrected after Dogger Bank.

Undaunted, Beatty continued with his pursuit of Hipper – until he spotted the entire High Seas Fleet emerging from across the horizon. Threatened with total destruction, he quickly turned and fled northward to the protection of the Grand Fleet. Now it was the Germans who took up pursuit, hoping to destroy an outnumbered foe. They chased Beatty for over two hours, unaware that he was leading them into a trap.

As the German ships approached, Jellicoe readied for battle. He decided to arrange his ships in an effort to 'cross the enemy's T', and the Grand Fleet accordingly deployed into a line, stretching out to intercept the onrushing German column of ships. Such a manoeuvre put the British in a position to use every gun on every ship – while the Germans would only have the forward guns of their lead ships – in a satisfactory firing position.

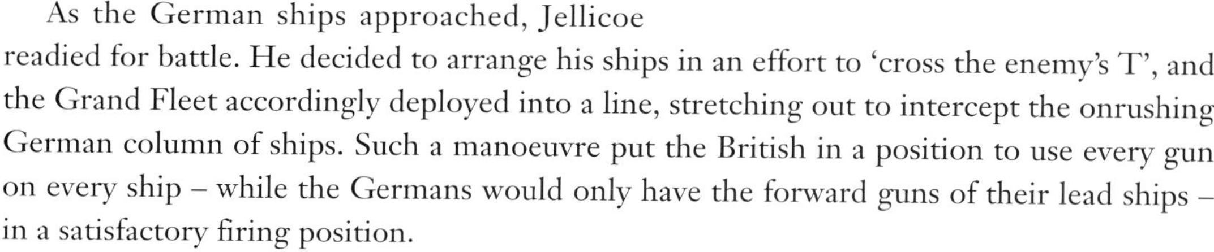

At 1815 hours Scheer was stunned to find the entire Grand Fleet lurking over the horizon, perfectly positioned to assure his destruction. In the ensuing battle, Scheer realised

Above: Admiral Beatty (left) the commander of the British cruiser squadron that faced off with Hipper at Jutland.

Left: The German battlecruiser *Derfflinger* seen at Wilhelmshaven on 3 June 1916 showing the effects of a direct hit from a British shell after the Battle of Jutland.

ABOVE: HMS *NOTTINGHAM* SEEN FROM HMS *BIRMINGHAM* AT JUTLAND.

FAR RIGHT: THE *QUEEN MARY*, STRUCK IN THE POWDER MAGAZINE BY A GERMAN SHELL, BLOWS UP AT THE BATTLE OF JUTLAND.

that all was lost unless he acted quickly. He ordered his fleet to execute a simultaneous 180-degree turn under cover of a smokescreen and a destroyer attack. The daring and difficult manoeuvre succeeded in extricating the German fleet from its predicament, but presented it with another; it was now heading away from its bases in Germany. Jellicoe used the lull to reposition his ships, and when Scheer finally tried to turn towards home, he found his 'T' crossed by the Grand Fleet yet again. Faced with imminent disaster, Scheer ordered another 180-degree turn. To cover the manoeuvre he sent his battle-cruiser force and several torpedo boats on a suicidal 'death ride' directly into the awesome firepower of the Grand Fleet. Although several ships suffered horrific damage, the tactic succeeded, and once again Scheer had avoided destruction.

As day became night, Jellicoe attempted to position the Grand Fleet to cut off any German attempt to escape to home waters. His efforts failed and Scheer was able to pass through the rear echelon of the British fleet in a flurry of confused night fighting and

Q-SHIPS

Initially the Royal Navy had few ways to attack marauding submarines, and thus the Q-ship was born. The Admiralty knew full well that U-boats generally surfaced to strike unprotected merchant ships rather than wasting valuable torpedoes. In an effort to catch U-boats unawares, the Royal Navy converted merchant vessels into disguised ships of war. These Q-ships varied in size and were indistinguishable from ordinary merchant ships, sometimes flying false colours. When an unsuspecting U-boat surfaced to claim its seemingly harmless prize, the Q-ship revealed its deadly nature. Sailors of the Royal Navy would hold their disguise to the last minute - sometimes even having some of their number abandon ship to lure the doomed U-boat into a false sense of security - when suddenly, in a blaze of activity, the Q-ship would fire its concealed guns or torpedoes at the U-boat, either sinking it or driving it underwater. Although Q-ships were first launched in 1914, the converted collier ***Prince Charles*** scored the first Q-ship success by sinking ***U-40*** in July 1915 off the Scottish coast. The Q-ships were few in number; even so, they had a significant impact on the war. Due to the threat posed by the 'mystery ships', German U-boats often resorted to attacking underwater where they were very slow and much less effective. In all, the Q-ships sunk 11 German U-boats before they were withdrawn from service in late 1917.

A Q-SHIP UNDER CONVERSION.

return to port. The Battle of Jutland was at an end. Tactically the battle was a draw, with the Grand Fleet suffering somewhat heavier losses. In total, the British suffered 6800 casualties and lost three battle-cruisers, three cruisers and eight destroyers sunk. The Germans lost one old battleship, one battlecruiser, four light cruisers and five destroyers and suffered 3100 casualties. Using numbers to their advantage, the Germans trumpeted Jutland as a great victory. However, this was not the case. The Royal Navy retained its dominance over the North Sea and the German fleet returned to port, never again to challenge British dominance. For the

NORTH SEA NAVAL OPERATIONS

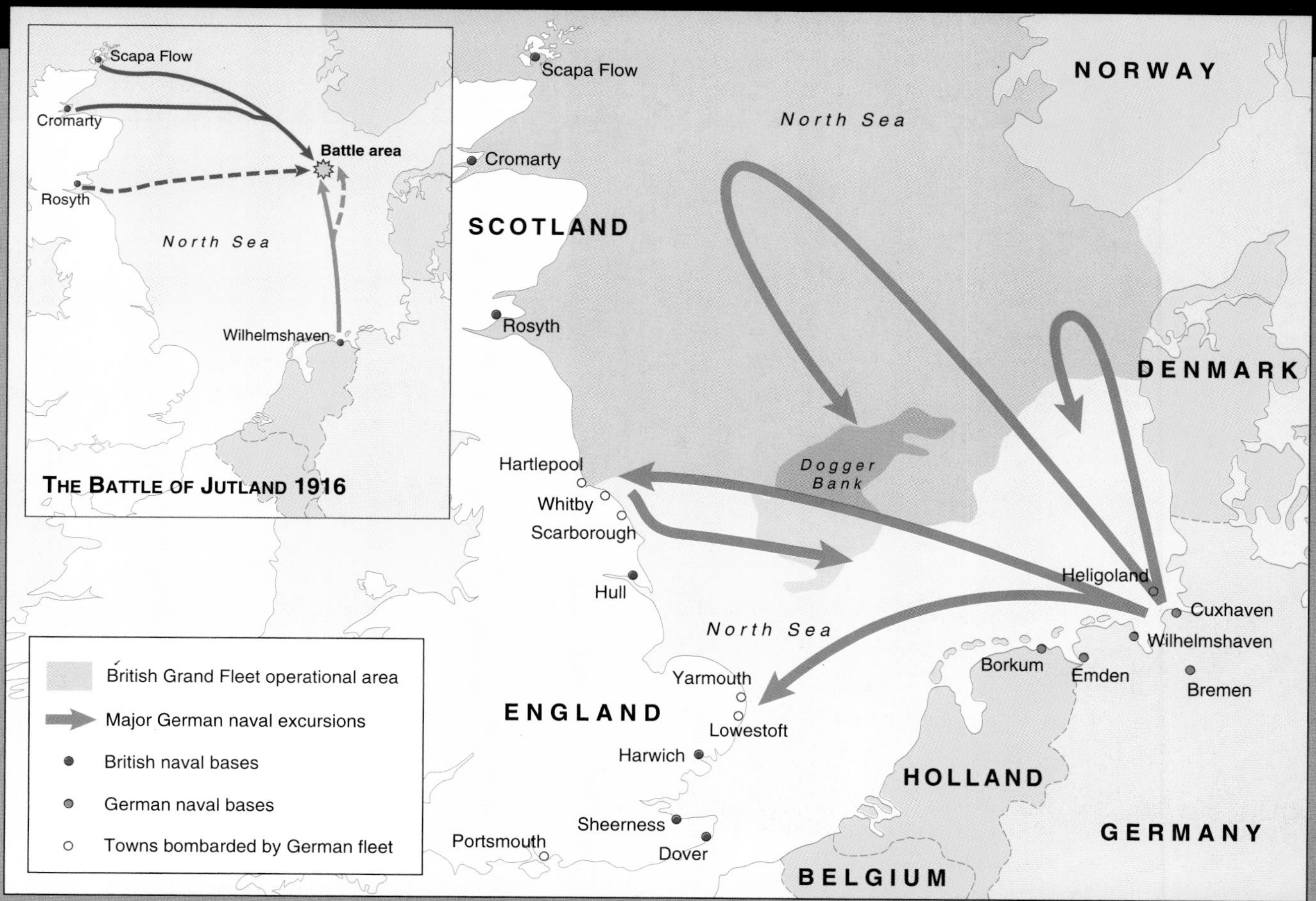

RIGHT:
A U-BOAT'S VICTIM SINKS BENEATH THE WAVES. THE SMALL U-BOATS COULD MAKE NO PROVISION FOR THE RESCUE OF THE CREW OF SUCH SHIPS, LEAVING THEM TO THEIR FATE.

LUSITANIA

The *Lusitania*, reputed to be the most luxurious ship afloat, was a trans-Atlantic liner that sailed between New York and Liverpool for the Cunard Line. Before she sailed in May 1915 the Germans took out advertisements in New York newspapers, warning prospective customers not to sail upon the vessel. Germany had declared a war zone around Britain, and all ships (especially British ones) entering that zone were possible targets for German U-boat attacks. However, the *Lusitania* took no special precautions and sailed to Britain as usual. On 7 May 1915, off the southern coast of Ireland, two torpedoes fired from *U-20* slammed into the *Lusitania* without warning. The stricken ship sank quickly, going down in 92m (300ft) of water in 18 minutes. Most of the passengers aboard were unable to make it to lifeboats and drowned in the chilly water. In all, 1198 passengers and crew, including 124 Americans, died that day. Although the Germans correctly contended that the *Lusitania* carried illegal wartime contraband – including ten-and-a-half tons of rifle cartridges and 51 tons of shrapnel shells – Americans viewed the sinking of the *Lusitania* as murder. All over the nation, newspapers decried the attack, and President Woodrow Wilson had to struggle hard to keep the United States neutral in war. The sinking of the *Lusitania* brought the United States ever closer to the wartime Allies.

THE LUSITANIA.

British, their tactical victory was pyrrhic at best. All had hoped for a victory of epic proportions, in the best Nelsonian fashion. However, even after the Battle of Jutland, the German fleet remained a threat – although an unused threat – and making matters much worse, the Germans were about to mount a very different attempt to seize control of the seas.

ABOVE: A TORPEDO FIRED FROM *U-35* STRIKES ITS VICTIM.

BELOW: A U-BOAT SURFACES TO STOP AND SEARCH A NEUTRAL AMERICAN MERCHANT STEAMER IN MID-OCEAN.

U-BOAT WAR

At the beginning of the war, few strategists paid much attention to a new weapons system: the submarine. Germany, for instance, only possessed 18 submarines of inferior quality when the war began. The strategists who gave the submarine any credit thought that its chief value would be in attacking enemy warships and indeed, a German submarine scored an initial success on 22 September 1914 by sinking three British armoured cruisers. As the German surface fleet was cleared from the seas, more naval strategists, most importantly Tirpitz, turned to the U-boat as a way of striking against valuable Allied merchant shipping and doing great damage to British trade. However, the laws of war were against the Germans. Submarines were weak vessels that succeeded through the use of stealth. International law required a warship to stop a merchant

RIGHT: A U-BOAT OF THE UB-II CLASS FINDS IT DIFFICULT GOING IN ROUGH SEAS OFF HELGOLAND ISLAND.

BELOW: VARIOUS METHODS WERE TRIED TO EVADE THE U-BOAT THREAT BY MERCHANT SHIPS. THE ONE BELOW IS USING A DAZZLE PAINT SCHEME IN AN EFFORT AT CAMOUFLAGE.

ship and make arrangements for its crew before sinking it. German submarines initially followed this pattern, but found themselves quite vulnerable to Allied attack, especially from Q-ships. Thus Tirpitz came to support unrestricted submarine warfare, meaning that merchant ships would be sunk without warning.

Tirpitz campaigned for the institution of unrestricted submarine warfare, but was opposed by several in the government who argued that such indiscriminate sinking of merchant vessels would antagonise neutral nations, most importantly the United States. Eventually Tirpitz carried the day and, on 4 February 1915, Germany declared the waters around Britain to be a war zone. Any ship entering those waters was liable to submarine attack without notice. The German declaration drew the ire of American President Woodrow Wilson. Once American lives were lost in the submarine war, matters became much worse. On 7

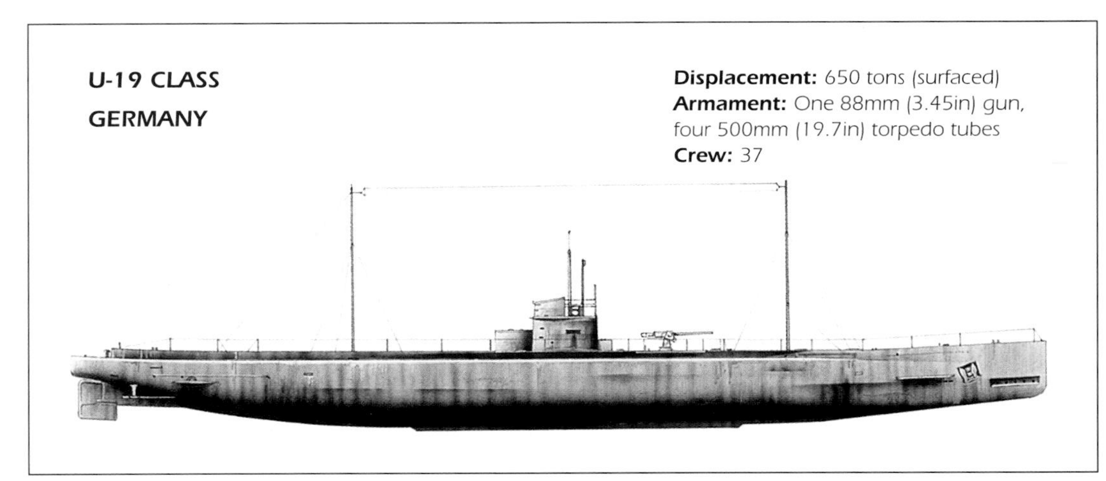

U-19 CLASS
GERMANY

Displacement: 650 tons (surfaced)
Armament: One 88mm (3.45in) gun, four 500mm (19.7in) torpedo tubes
Crew: 37

Above: A convoy escort vessel displays its depth charges (explosives set to detonate at a certain depth) for attacking U-boats. It was the introduction of a convoy system for merchant vessels that decided the Battle of the Atlantic in World War I.

May submarine *U-20* sank the *Lusitania* off the Irish coast with the loss of 1198 lives, including 124 Americans. In August the situation repeated itself with the submarine sinking of the liner *Arabic.* Wilson vehemently protested against the German actions, to the point that the German foreign office worried about a total rupture of relations with the United States. As a result, the Germans called off their unrestricted submarine war in September 1915.

The events of 1916 placed great pressure on every belligerent nation, including Germany. Many in the Empire questioned whether Germany could stand another year of attritional fighting; for this reason, many were willing to accept extraordinary risks to attain victory in 1917. The new command team of Hindenburg and Ludendorff believed that they should make full use of any weapon to win the war; to do otherwise was treasonous. By 1917 Germany had 154 U-boats of superior quality. Naval theorists contended that if these submarines could sink 600,000 tons of merchant shipping per month, Britain would be forced to capitulate due to lack of supplies. The prospect of defeating Britain through the use of the U-boat fleet held great appeal for Hindenburg and Ludendorff, but there was one problem. Any concerted effort to attack shipping bound for Britain would certainly cause American intervention in the conflict. The risk seemed worth the gamble. The United States had but a tiny army and would have no immediate impact on the war.

Above: The positioning of the blockships in the aftermath of the raid on the harbour at Zeebrugge. However, the tiny U-boats could make their way around these blockships.

Also British surrender would mean the end of the war and make American intervention a moot point. The Germans chose to gamble, and on 1 February 1917 resumed unrestricted submarine warfare.

During 1916 Britain was very concerned about the potential threat posed by the submarine. In November submarines had destroyed 175,000 tons of shipping, and to deal with the problem, the Government appointed Jellicoe as First Sea Lord. When he took over his new position he discovered that there were few weapons available for anti-submarine duty. While he began to search for a solution to the submarine problem, the German unrestricted submarine campaign began. Submarines gathered off the approaches to British ports and stealthily took their victims from among the throng of ships travelling singly across the area. Patrols of British warships attempted to provide protection, but were ineffective. Merchant shipping losses to submarine attack skyrocketed and, by April, had reached an astounding 870,000 tons, well above the German forecasts of what was required for victory over Britain. By the end of April Britain's supply of wheat was down to only enough for six weeks. If the submarines could continue to press their advantage, it seemed that Britain would be defeated.

CONVOY

Jellicoe despaired as losses to German submarines began to mount, and he even informed the Government that Britain might be forced to sue for peace by December if no solution to the submarine menace was found. Unbeknownst to the First Sea Lord, however, the solution was at hand, unnoticed and ignored by Admiralty planners: the convoy system. Although the use of warships to guard convoys of merchant ships had proven successful in past wars, the Admiralty had opted against institution of a convoy system in World War I for several reasons. Convoys were slow and cumbersome and many within the Admiralty thought that a group of merchant ships would only provide a bigger target for submarines. In addition, the Grand Fleet could not spare warships to guard convoys, for it always had to be on guard against a battle with the German High Seas Fleet. Now the high losses suffered in the first months of unrestricted submarine warfare were forcing Jellicoe and the Admiralty to reconsider their options.

After conducting a feasibility study and receiving some judicious pressure from the Prime Minister, the Admiralty chose to begin implementation of the convoy system in May 1917. Although it took time to organise the system properly, it had an immediate impact on the war and losses to submarines fell to more manageable levels. While losses remained significant, sometimes topping over 200,000 tons of merchant shipping lost per month, never again did the German U-boats come near forcing Britain out of the conflict.

BELOW: RAMPS LIKE THOSE SHOWN BELOW WERE SPECIALLY FITTED TO HMS *VINDICTIVE* TO ALLOW MARINES TO BE LANDED ON THE MOLE IN ZEEBRUGGE HARBOUR DURING THE RAID.

The convoy system succeeded for two reasons. Firstly, contrary to British expectations, convoys were very hard for the Germans to locate. One convoy sailing across the vast Atlantic presented a much smaller target for the U-boats than a vast number of ships sailing singly. Secondly, the warships protecting the convoys were able to use early versions of sonar and depth charges to attack marauding submarines. Although such weapons were in their infancy, and thus the Allied warships never drove the German submarines from the oceans, the crisis of the naval war had passed. Merchant shipping losses continued throughout the rest of the war, but in the end, the convoy was a war-winning weapon for the Allies. Of the 88,000 ships escorted across the Atlantic during the last two years of the conflict, only 436 were torpedoed. By comparison, the Germans lost 178 submarines. Thus, the German gamble to end the war through an unrestricted submarine campaign against Britain failed. Making matters worse, the submarine effort brought about the expected diplomatic result: the United States entered the Great War in April 1917. It would be nearly one year before American troops could enter Europe in any substantial numbers, and the Germans held a firm belief that they would win the entire conflict before America became a factor.

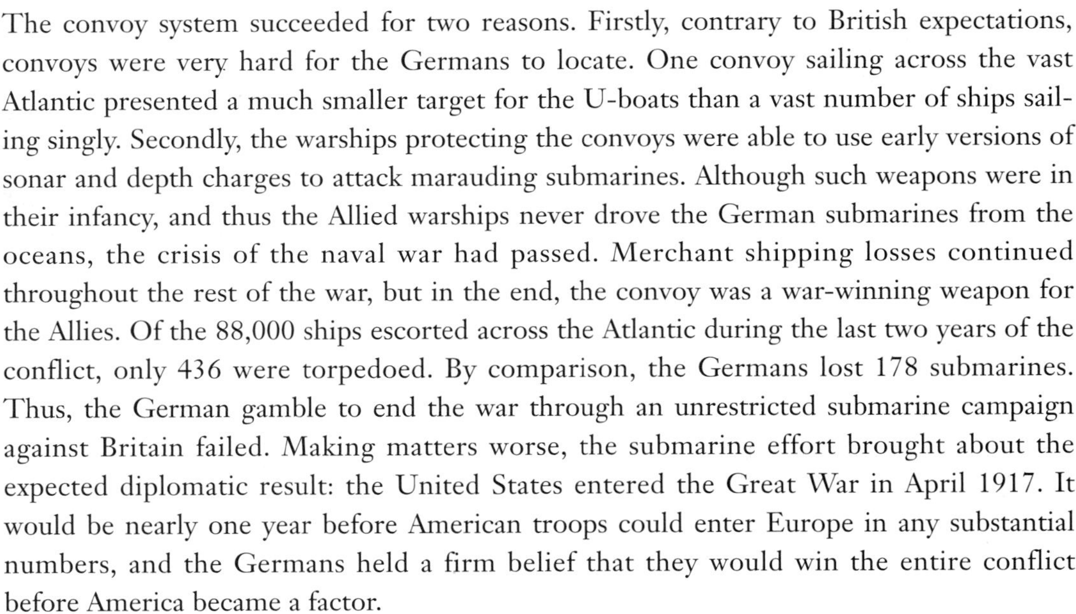

BELOW: A JAUNTY-LOOKING ROYAL NAVY OFFICER FROM THE TIME OF THE BATTLE OF JUTLAND IN 1916.

THE RAID ON ZEEBRUGGE AND THE END OF THE WAR

Though the submarine menace was well in hand and the High Seas Fleet was bottled in its home ports, there remained one final naval act to the war. German possession of the Belgian ports of Ostend and Zeebrugge had long bothered British naval planners, because U-boats based there posed a threat to shipping in the English Channel. However, no direct naval action was taken until 23 April 1918. On that day a flotilla of 75 ships, under the command of Admiral Roger Keyes, launched a raid on the ports designed to deny their use to the Germans. The attack began when some 200 marines landed on the Zeebrugge mole as a diversion. In the resulting confusion, three old cruisers, loaded with concrete, manoeuvred their way into the central harbour towards the important canal entrance protecting the German U-boats. Under heavy fire, two of the ships steamed into the canal and scuttled themselves, hoping to form a barrier blocking German access to the canal. The operation, however, did not succeed. One of the ships never made it to the canal entrance, and the two ships that did failed to block the canal effectively, leaving it still useable for German U-boats and destroyers. Further down the coast, the effort to block the harbour at Ostende was a complete failure, for none of the blockships there were able to reach the harbour entrance.

Although less than successful, the Zeebrugge Raid provided the British with a morale boost amid a time of defeats on the Western Front. It finally seemed to indicate that the Royal Navy was not afraid to flex its offensive muscles. In addition, the exploits of the marines and sailors that day made for wonderful news stories; eight Victoria Crosses were awarded.

After the Battle of Jutland, the German High Seas Fleet was, in the main, confined to its home ports and languished through a period of inactivity. The morale of the fleet that had once meant to challenge British naval dominance began a swift decline, and as the war on the Western Front turned against Germany in 1918, this morale plummeted.

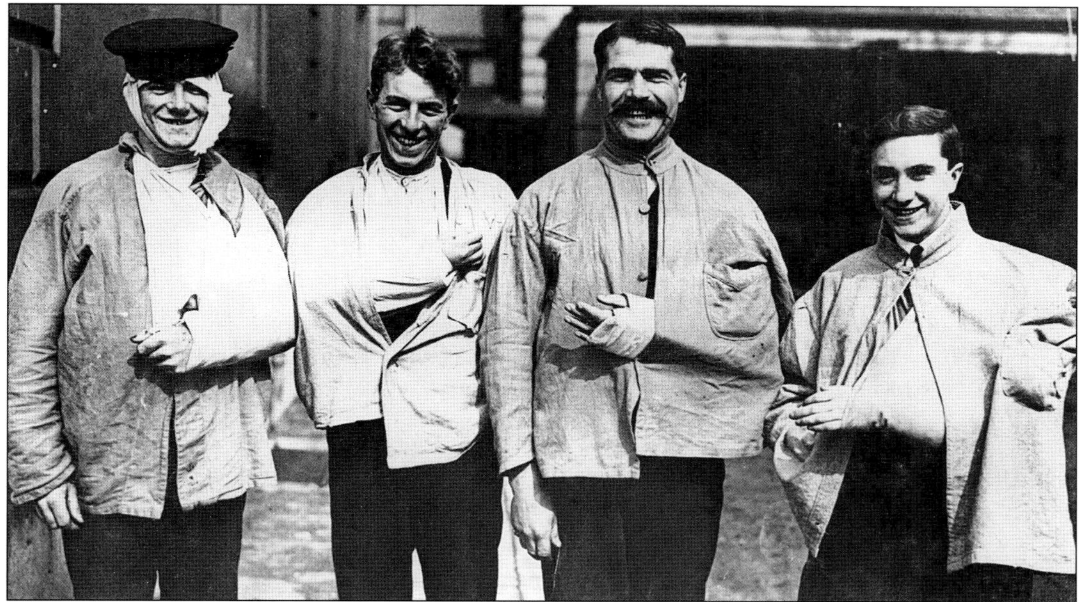

LEFT: MEMBERS OF THE RETURNED RAIDING PARTY ON ZEEBRUGGE SHOW THEIR BANDAGES PROUDLY TO THE CAMERA.

BELOW: HAVING SURRENDERED AFTER THE ARMISTICE, THE GERMAN HIGH SEAS FLEET LIES AT ANCHOR IN SCAPA FLOW. IN A FINAL ACT OF DEFIANCE THE GERMAN OFFICERS WOULD LATER SCUTTLE THEIR VESSELS.

German naval leaders, painfully aware of their fleet's minor role in the war, planned to regain their honour by sending the High Seas Fleet to sea for a suicidal battle with the Grand Fleet. However, the crews of the German ships were not keen to sacrifice their lives for the honour of their officers, and the fleet descended into mutiny. Sailors joined with workers in the nearby cities and formed revolutionary councils, like those seen in Russia. The revolution spread to the rest of Germany and contributed to the decision to end the conflict in November 1918.

The High Seas Fleet was destined to play one last role in the conflict. As part of the peace settlement, the German fleet finally left its harbours to meet the British fleet once again, for the first time since Jutland. On 21 November the High Seas Fleet surrendered to the British and went into internment in the British base of Scapa Flow. There the mighty fleet languished until 21 June 1919 when, in a final act of defiance, its officers scuttled it entirely.

CHAPTER 8

Defeat, Despair and Mutiny

AUSTRIAN MACHINE GUNNERS RUSH OUT OF A DUGOUT TO FACE AN ATTACK BY THE ITALIANS IN 1917. THE FEARSOME CASUALTIES CAUSED BY SUCH MODERN WEAPONS OF WAR CAUSED MANY COMBATANTS AND CIVILIANS ALIKE TO QUESTION THE ULTIMATE WORTH OF THE WAR.

Summoning their last bit of trust and innocence, the French took Nivelle at his word. It was 1914 all over again. Nivelle had raised French hopes to new highs – only to bring them crashing down to disastrous lows.

ALLIED PLANNING AND GERMAN WITHDRAWAL

The confident and articulate new French commander-in-chief, General Robert Nivelle, proposed a plan for certain victory in 1917. The scheme called for a British attack near Arras to draw German attention away from the coming French offensive. In mounting the main attack, Nivelle would use the tactics which had won him such stirring victories at Verdun, but on a greater scale. A punishing barrage, followed by a precise creeping barrage would, he claimed, launch an attack of 'violence, brutality and rapidity', which would rupture the German front lines in, at most, 48 hours, leading to a pursuit of a defeated enemy into Germany. Most importantly, however, he pledged to end his attack if it had not achieved such success within two days. Haig and some within the French Army, including Petain, questioned the wisdom of Nivelle's plan; even so, the French commander proved to be a master of self-promotion. Firstly, he convinced French politicians to back his proposal. He then went on to convince his troops and his nation that victory was at hand. There would be no more Verduns, he said, and no more wasting men's lives for minimal gain; his attack would be different, and French elan and firepower would win the day at last. Summoning their last bit of trust and innocence, the French took Nivelle at his word. In many ways, it was 1914 all over again. Nivelle had raised French hopes to new highs – only to bring them crashing down to disastrous lows.

As the French prepared for their great offensive, the Germans made a move that unhinged many of Nivelle's plans. Worried that another Somme might be too much for Germany to bear, Hindenburg and Ludendorff had decided to straighten their line on the Western Front in an effort to conserve resources. As a result, in February 1917 the Germans withdrew to the highly fortified Hindenburg Line on the Western Front. This was the very area that Nivelle hoped to attack, but such details did not bother the French commander, for he still planned to rupture the German line, no matter where it was or how strong it was. The German withdrawal had posed additional problems for the planned French attack. During their retreat, the Germans had ruthlessly destroyed almost everything of value in the French countryside. Roads were destroyed, wells were poisoned, houses were booby-trapped and the population was removed. The retreating

OVERVIEW

The years of strain in World War I became apparent in the events of 1917. The French, whipped into a fever pitch by Nivelle, expected a great victory along the Aisne River, but instead experienced the same futile slaughter as before. The French Army mutinied as a result, avoiding disaster by a narrow margin. The offensive role of the Allies then fell to the British. After successful offensives at Arras and Messines, the BEF expected great results from its major offensive operation at the Third Battle of Ypres. Instead the battle was a mixed bag that ended in the muddy horror of Passchendaele. Shortly after the close of that campaign, however, the BEF launched an experimental tank attack at Cambrai that signalled a change in the nature of warfare. In the east, 1917 was a year of disaster for the Allies, mitigated only by the British capture of Jerusalem. The Italians were routed at Caporetto, narrowly avoiding a total defeat, while Russia collapsed into revolution and quit the war. Thus at the end of the year it seemed that the Central Powers were poised for victory. There was one bright spot for the Allies: German unrestricted submarine war had brought the United States into the conflict. But could the Americans reach Europe in sufficient numbers in time to have an effect on the war's outcome?

A British casualty.

'SHELL SHOCK'

The horror and brutality of war often inflicts mental trauma and anguish upon the men who fight it. The sheer scale of World War I and its static trench nature ensured that mental casualties would be at an all-time high. The term 'shell shock' was used to describe psychiatric battle casualties, whose symptoms ranged from paralysis, to aimless wandering, to loss of bladder and bowel control. During the war, losses due to mental illness were staggering. The United States sent nearly two million men to Europe in World War I. Of this number 116,516 were killed, and another 159,000 soldiers put out of action due to psychiatric problems. Psychiatrists on both sides of the conflict struggled to determine the cause of the mounting problems. Their answer was that the concussion of exploding shells somehow compressed the brain, resulting in a seemingly mental reaction. Some soldiers received care for their 'shell shock'; the Austrian Army even employed electric shock treatment as a possible cure. Other soldiers had their symptoms ignored, or were put to death for dereliction of duty. In truth, these men had just seen more death and slaughter than their minds could take. Wilfred Owen, a sensitive observer of war, understood this fact and expressed it in his poem 'Mental Cases':

> These are men whose minds the
> Dead have ravished.
> Memory fingers in their hair of murders,
> Multitudinous murders they once witnessed.

Germans left in their wake a wasteland, one that would make French forward movement and logistical operations very difficult.

The ever-confident Nivelle went on with his preparations for and promotion of his offensive. In a move of almost criminal carelessness, he informed several politicians and many newspapers of the basic outline for his coming offensive. The Germans could not fail to notice such publicity and quickly became aware that the French were planning an attack. Making matters worse, a German trench raid in March succeeded in capturing detailed plans for the attack. Hindenburg and Ludendorff arranged their defences accordingly. The French offensive would receive a rude reception indeed.

ARRAS

On 9 April the British launched their diversionary attack at Arras. The BEF had learned more about infantry tactics and, at Arras, brought men into the front lines in secret by using tunnel networks. The combination

Below: General Robert Nivelle, architect of the French attack plan in 1917 that caused the French army mutiny.

of surprise and artillery effectiveness made it one of the most successful attacks to date in World War I. The British Third Army, under General Edmund Allenby, and the Canadian Corps surged forward on a 23km (14 mile) front in the wake of a bombardment by 2800 guns. On the left of the British line, the Canadians did what the French had often found to be impossible and seized the powerful German defences of Vimy Ridge in gallant, often hand-to-hand, fighting. Further south, Allenby's forces penetrated the last line of German defences just north of the Hindenburg Line. In all, the British Third Army advanced 3 miles, the greatest one-day gain on the Western Front since the beginning of trench warfare in 1914. On 11 April Australian units penetrated parts of the Hindenburg Line itself, and the advance in the north continued. However, within days, the Germans had rushed reinforcements to the scene and stood firm against continued British advance. Once again, the defensive rules of the war had intervened and an attack had run its course. In an attempt to draw German reserves away from the main Allied advance under Nivelle to the south, Haig chose to continue the offensive. It went on into May, although few further gains were made. Arras had been a relatively minor operation but it cost the BEF 84,000 casualties and the Germans 75,000. It had been the best British offensive on the Western Front to date and seemed to portend well for the future.

BELOW: THE MASSIVE BARBED-WIRE ENTANGLEMENTS GUARDING THE HINDENBURG LINE AT BEAUREVOIR. THIS SECTION ALONE WAS DEFENDED BY OVER 50 MACHINE GUNS.

ABOVE: BRITISH SOLDIERS GATHER AND INSPECT SHARPENED METAL DEVICES DESIGNED TO DELAY AND DISCOURAGE CAVALRY PURSUIT LEFT BEHIND BY THE GERMANS IN THEIR RETREAT TO THE HINDENBURG LINE.

THE NIVELLE OFFENSIVE

The highly-touted French offensive further south near the Aisne River got underway on 16 April after suffering numerous delays. The massive preparatory bombardment, which began on 5 April, included 7000 guns firing over 11 million artillery shells, but the heavy fire was dispersed over a front of nearly 64km (40 miles), diluting its impact. In addition, the forewarned Germans had constructed defences of great strength, especially on the Chemin des Dames Ridge, and had chosen to man their front lines only lightly, hoping that the French attack would lose its momentum before it reached their main defensive lines to the rear. The initial French advance, then, met with little resistance and lulled Nivelle into a false sense of security. However, trouble lay ahead, for the much-heralded 'creeping barrage' moved too quickly; the advancing forces lost touch with it and found themselves nearly defenceless against the powerful German rear defences. As a result, German machine gunners took a fearsome toll on the advancing French forces.

Few gains had been made on the first day of the attack, but Nivelle pressed on and continued to hope for a great victory. On 17 April the French surged forward again, only to meet with a similar fate. The breakthrough had not come in the required 48 hours, and it

Right: British troops go 'over the top' in the second wave of the successful Arras attack.

Below: Canadians, who had just taken Vimy Ridge, lead some of their haul of German prisoners to the rear in April 1917.

was time for Nivelle to call off his offensive, but the French commander-in-chief was reluctant to do so, and again ordered his soldiers forward. Contrary to the promises he had made before the battle, nothing had changed.

The Nivelle offensive raged on until 9 May and did achieve some success. The French had seized the Aisne River valley and parts of the Hindenburg Line on the heavily defended Cemin des Dames Ridge. Furthermore, the offensive had gained more ground than any ever launched by Joffre. It was not enough; Nivelle had promised his soldiers and his nation victory. If he was unable to produce victory, he had promised his men not to squander their lives needlessly in another futile battle. He had lied.

FRENCH ARMY MUTINY

French casualties in the Nivelle Offensive had been high, nearing 150,000 men. To the French soldier (*poilu*), the slaughter was too grim to bear. The men had fought bravely for three years, and had suffered the hell of Verdun. They would defend their nation, but would not tolerate their lives being sacrificed for the vanity of one man. Mutinies began to break out among the troops in the Aisne area as early as 3 May, when the 21st Division, which had seen heavy action at Verdun, refused to go forward into battle. Other units up and down the French line followed this example. In the end, the French Army Mutiny affected over 50 divisions. Large numbers of soldiers deserted, as many as 30,000, usually attempting to return home to a farm and family they had not seen in far too long. Other units chose to remain in line to defend their territory, but refused to advance to their doom. Finally, other units chose to move forward but bleated like sheep being herded to the slaughter.

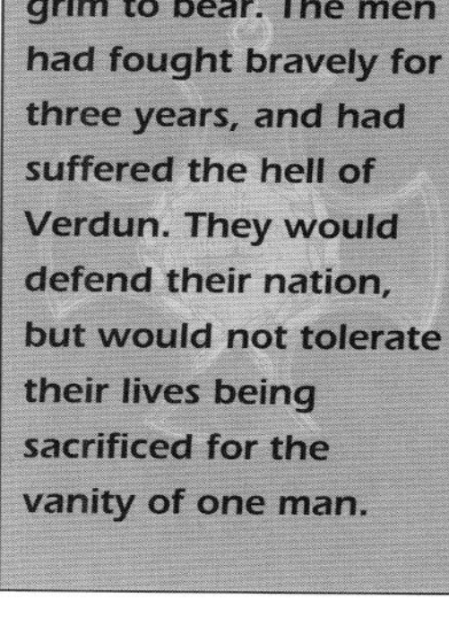

To the French soldier, the slaughter was too grim to bear. The men had fought bravely for three years, and had suffered the hell of Verdun. They would defend their nation, but would not tolerate their lives being sacrificed for the vanity of one man.

The French High Command was shocked by what it referred to as the acts of 'collective indiscipline'. Many feared that the French *poilu*, like his Russian counterpart, had become politicised; revolution might be the end result. In reality, the French Army Mutiny was spontaneous, not led. Soldiers simply baulked at needless human sacrifice. In addition, French soldiers had been harbouring other grievances for years. Their pay was the lowest of any Allied army. Their food was poor but, more importantly to the average *poilu*, their wine was poor. Home leave was almost unheard of; even British soldiers who had to cross the Channel to return home had more. The French soldier felt unappreciated, ill used and, after the Nivelle Offensive, felt a sense of doom.

Due to his failure and its disastrous results, Nivelle lost his position on 15 May, to be replaced by another hero of Verdun, General Petain. Realising that his first task was to end the mutinies, Petain instituted several changes. He remedied the worst of the soldier's grievances and granted many an all-important home leave. Petain was a soldier's general and treated his men with respect and dignity, looking after their personal needs. The results of this simple formula were magical. The new commander leavened his kindness with discipline. An army cannot stand for a mutiny, and over 50 of the worst offenders were executed. Considering the extent of the mutinies, the retribution was slight. Petain knew that he had to keep death sentences to a minimum or the mutinies might continue. Finally, Petain told the *poilu* what he most

BELOW: FRENCH GUNNERS WEARING GAS MASKS FIRE DURING THE NIVELLE OFFENSIVE IN 1917. NO LESS THAN 11 MILLION SHELLS WERE FIRED DURING THE ATTACK.

wanted to hear. No longer would their lives be wasted in futile attacks. Petain, realising the fragility of his army, would only authorise limited attacks. In his words, the Allies had to wait for the Americans and the tanks before once again attempting to seize victory.

Thus the French Army survived its sternest test, and would remain in the field to defend the nation. However, the weight of the Allied war effort now shifted to the British. For the first time in the nation's history, then, Britain's mass army would stand as the main foe against the leading continental land power. The French Army Mutiny also had an effect on Germany. If the Germans had learned of the existence and extent of the mutiny, the war might have ended differently. However, the Germans remained ignorant of the momentous events taking place across no-man's-land. In some cases, French deserters had informed the Germans of mutiny in their area, but the Germans did not believe such reports; they must have been a trick. Such are the fates of war.

ABOVE: THE FIRST WAVE OF THE ATTACK ON THE CHEMIN DES DAMES RIDGE, WHICH HAD STRONG GERMAN DEFENCES TO A DEPTH OF 7000M (7700YDS).

RIGHT: FRENCH SOLDIERS MARCH DOWN A SUNKEN LANE IN NORTHERN FRANCE DURING THE OFFENSIVE.

If the Germans had learned of the existence and extent of the mutiny, the war might have ended differently. French deserters had informed the Germans of mutiny in their area, but the Germans did not believe such reports; they must have been a trick. Such are the fates of war.

MESSINES

The commander of the BEF, Douglas Haig, had long wanted to launch an offensive in Flanders. He hoped that a successful attack there might seize the important ports of Ostend and Zeebrugge and turn the German flank off the coast, thus restoring a war of movement. The French pleaded with Haig to attack, fearing that if the Germans attacked their still fragile army, it might not be able to hold. However, before Haig could launch an offensive in Flanders, he had to make the British position at Ypres more secure. To the right of the salient, the Germans held the heights of Messines Ridge. Although the ridge is only some 46m (150ft) in height, it dominates the flat, marshy land around Ypres. Haig instructed General Herbert Plumer and his British Second Army to take the Messines Ridge in a limited offensive of the bite-and-hold type. Plumer proved to be the right choice. His men dug more than 20 tunnels beneath the ridge and placed more than one million pounds of high explosives under the German lines.

BELOW: FRENCH COLONIAL SOLDIERS AWAIT INSTRUCTIONS NEAR THE FRONT IN FRANCE.

At 0310 hours on 7 June, after a lengthy preliminary bombardment, the Second Army detonated its mines. Huge gouts of earth and flame soared skyward as the top of the ridge was, in many places, shorn away. The titanic explosion could even be heard in London 209km (130 miles) away. Nearly 10,000 German soldiers were atomised or buried by the blast. As British and ANZAC forces surged up the ridge, they found several dazed German survivors wandering aimlessly, unable to offer any resistance. In total, the BEF rounded up an astounding 7500 German prisoners. British and ANZAC soldiers quickly reached the top of Messines Ridge and prepared to face the inevitable German counter-attacks. Fighting lingered on for nearly a week, but the BEF held firm and retained the ridge line.

The Battle of Messines Ridge was the perfect example of a limited, bite-and-hold offensive. Using meticulous preparation, the BEF had seized its goal with low casualties. On one of the few occasions in the war, the attacker took fewer casualties than the defender; the Germans lost nearly 26,000 men compared to only 17,000 for the BEF. After Arras and Messines it seemed that British command had learned its lessons well and that the next offensive could only build on those successes. This was not to be the case.

RIGHT:
BRITISH MINERS TOIL AWAY TO CONSTRUCT ONE OF THE 20 TUNNELS THAT WOULD BE LOADED WITH EXPLOSIVES TO DESTROY THE GERMAN DEFENSIVE POSITIONS AT MESSINES.

THE THIRD BATTLE OF YPRES

Haig warned Gough that the Germans would be utilising a defence-in-depth system, designed to tempt attackers to attempt to seize great gains – as Nivelle had just done. Gough chose to ignore Haig's advice.

Haig was now ready to launch his main offensive from Ypres aimed at seizure of the Belgian coast, and chose the British Fifth Army, under General Hubert Gough, to carry out the majority of the offensive. The choice of commanders, however, was a mistake. Gough was unfamiliar with the Flanders terrain, and tended toward the desire to rush through to deep objectives. While Haig too desired a breakthrough victory, he warned Gough that the Germans would be utilising a defence-in-depth system, designed to tempt attackers to attempt to seize great gains – as Nivelle had just done. Gough chose to ignore Haig's advice. Making matters much worse was the fact that the Germans were expecting a British attack near Ypres and had strengthened their already formidable defences in the area. One final problem was posed by the land itself. Flanders is low-lying and, without an intricate drainage system, would be a marsh. Years of shelling had already done considerable damage to the area, meaning that when the

LEFT:
A BRITISH MINE EXPLODES BENEATH GERMAN LINES THROWING DEBRIS SKYWARD. IT WAS REPORTED THAT PEOPLE AS FAR AWAY AS LONDON COULD HEAR THE EXPLOSIONS AT MESSINES.

rains came, it would become an almost impassable wilderness of mud.

Gough launched his preliminary bombardment, the heaviest to date in the war, on 18 July, further ravaging the ground in the area. On 31 July the BEF went over the top into no-man's-land. Although they had suffered heavy losses due to concrete German pillboxes that dotted the area, Gough's forces made great initial gains. However, that was the intent of the new German defensive system: allow the enemy forward until he loses momentum, then counter-attack. Gough had tried to take too much, not learning the lessons of Arras and Messines, and had played into the Germans hands. Suddenly the unfazed German defenders of the German Fourth Army, under the command of General Friedrich Sixt von Arnim, poured forth and struck the BEF while it was at its weakest. As a result, Gough lost the vast majority of his gains, and the attack was a failure. Making matters worse, that night the rains struck, transforming the battlefield into a sea of mud and water-filled shell holes. Gough allowed his troops to recuperate as he waited for the weather to break. On 16 August, he launched his next major attack and achieved the same dismal results. Haig had seen enough.

At this point, Haig shifted the direction of the battle into the hands of Plumer. The victor of Messines proposed to follow the same pattern of attack that he had used to such success earlier. He scheduled a series of bite-and-hold offensives aimed at the eventual seizure

ABOVE:
SUPPLIES MOVE FORWARD THROUGH THE RUINED CITY OF YPRES, WHICH THE BELGIANS REBUILT AFTER THE WAR AS A REPLICA OF THE MEDIEVAL TOWN.

of Passchendaele Ridge. Haig agreed with the strategy, but held out the hope that a series of effective Messines-like hammer blows would eventually cause the Germans to break. The weather also aided the new command team and the next month was nearly bone dry. Plumer proceeded to launch three wonderfully successful set-piece offensives. He attacked on a narrow front, seizing only limited objectives under the cover of lavish fire support. Simply put, he took what was available and did not play into the Germans' hands. During September and October in the battles of Menin Road Ridge, Polygon Wood and Broodseinde, the British Second Army took all of its objectives and held them against determined German counter-attacks. The battles were so effective that they caused Ludendorff great concern; he wondered whether or not the German line in the area could hold at all.

The set-piece victories had once again emboldened Haig who, against Plumer's advice, decided to press for more, even though the rains had returned. The resulting deluge, referred to by some as a monsoon, transformed the battlefield once again into a nearly impassable wilderness of mud. Slogging through mud that often reached their waists, first ANZAC troops then Canadian troops strove to reach the top of the last ridge and the village of Passchendaele. Due to the muddy horror of this futile portion of the battle, many refer to the entire offensive as the Battle of Passchendaele rather than its proper name the Third Battle of Ypres. Some men fell into water-filled shell holes and due to their slippery sides were unable to clamber out and drowned. Wounded men struggled in the clinging mud only to be dragged down to their horrible deaths. The Germans added to the plight

BELOW: British soldiers work feverishly to remove an artillery piece from the clinging mud of Flanders on 9 August 1917 at Zillebeke.

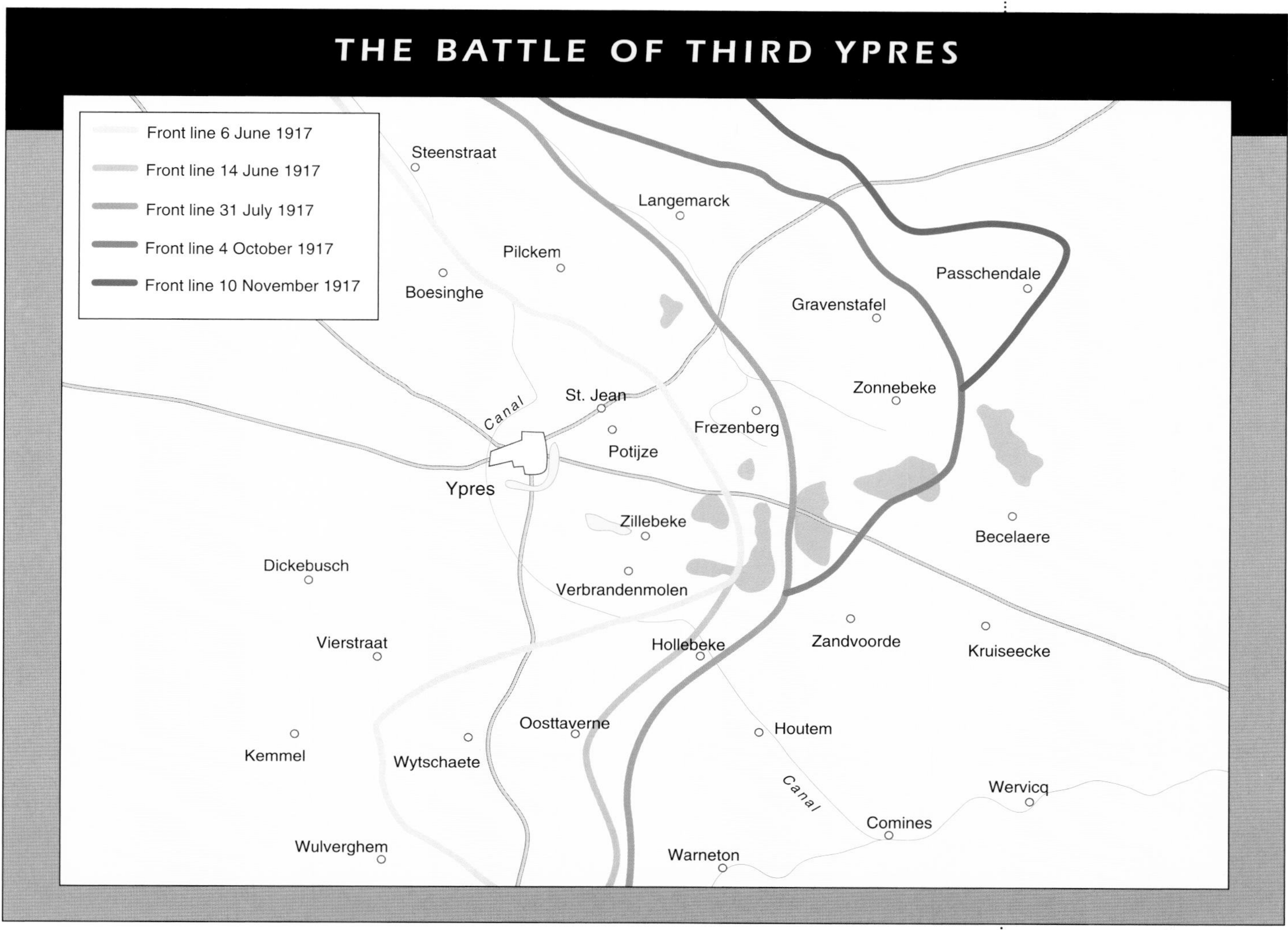

of the forlorn soldiers by using mustard gas for the first time in the war. It had all gone terribly wrong. One soldier remembers his experience at Passchendaele:

> Mud. We slept in it, ate in it. It stretched for miles – a sea of stinking mud. The dead buried themselves in it. The wounded died in it. Men slithered around the lips of huge shell craters filled with mud and water ... [On] each side of the track lie the debris of war ... Here an arm and a leg. It was a nightmare journey ... Finally dawn broke, a hopeless dawn. Shell holes and mud. Round about rifles with fixed bayonets stuck in the mud marking the places where men had died and been sucked down.

In the end the brave Canadian units seized the ruined village of Passchendaele and the Third Battle of Ypres dragged to a halt. Estimates vary widely, but both sides suffered over 300,000 total casualties during the struggle. To many of the British, Third Ypres ranks with the Somme as one of the twin disasters of World War I. The first and last phases of the battle were misguided and horrific. However, often lost in the shuffle are the successful battles fought under Plumer's direction. From these battles, the BEF learned much, lessons that it would put to use in 1918.

CAMBRAI

On 20 November, using no preliminary bombardment, the tanks rolled forward out of the mist. Terror spread quickly through the German lines, and many men fled their positions rather than face the terrible tanks.

There remained one great offensive act on the Western Front in 1917. Proponents of the tank, including Lt Colonel J.F.C. Fuller, had developed a plan for a massed tank raid on the Hindenburg Line near the town of Cambrai. After the end of Third Ypres, Haig gave his approval to the plan and assigned it to the command of General Julian Byng and the British Third Army. Byng hoped for a greater success and transformed the raid into a major offensive.

It was to be the first mass use of tanks in the history of warfare. Byng, under great secrecy, gathered 324 tanks and eight infantry divisions to attack on a narrow front. The surprised Germans only had two defending divisions in the area. On 20 November, using no preliminary bombardment, the tanks rolled forward out of the mist. Behind them the infantry advanced in columns in order to pass through lanes cut in the barbed wire by the advancing tanks. Terror spread quickly through the German lines, and many men fled their positions rather than face the terrible tanks. One soldier remembers the stunning effects of the tank attack:

RIGHT: A BRITISH SOLDIER SLOWLY NAVIGATES THROUGH A SODDEN COMMUNICATION TRENCH IN FLANDERS KNEE-DEEP IN MUD. THE CONSTANT SHELLING HAD DESTROYED THE LAND'S NATURAL DRAINAGE SYSTEM, CREATING A QUAGMIRE OF NIGHTMARE PROPORTIONS.

> The German outposts ... were overrun in an instant. The triple belts of wire were crossed as if they had been beds of nettles ... The defenders of the front trench ... saw the leading tanks almost upon them ... [and] were running panic stricken, casting away arms and equipment.

Within a few hours the tanks had rolled over the formidable defences of the Hindenburg Line. By the afternoon the BEF had advanced over 6.4km (4 miles) and the Germans were reeling. However, in the north, near Bourlon Wood, things were not going so well. Lack of co-ordination between the British infantry and the tanks led to few advances in this area. In addition, the momentum of the attack quickly stalled along the entire front. Tanks were being lost, through mechanical problems or due to enemy action, at a phenomenal rate. On the first day alone, 179 tanks were knocked out or unserviceable. Although impressive in action, the tank was not yet a war-winning weapon.

For the next three days, against stiffening German resistance, the BEF managed to take Bourlon Wood, but that signalled the end of the British advance. Ludendorff was convinced that he had to retake the lost ground and assembled some 25 divisions to do so. Now outnumbered, the British Third Army faced a difficult situation. It occupied only sketchy defences and its artillery support was poor. In many ways it had advanced too far too fast. The German counter-attack met with great success and, in certain areas, pushed the British back beyond their start line. Now the BEF rushed reinforcements to the scene, and by 7 December the Battle of Cambrai had reached its inconclusive end. Both sides suffered nearly 50,000 casualties. Although small in comparison to the Somme and Third Ypres, the Battle of Cambrai is their equal in importance. A new style of warfare was being developed: truly modern warfare that combined tanks and infantry. It was a style of warfare that would change the world.

Above: A British soldier wears his gas-mask high on his chest, ready for action.

Left: A Canadian soldier and his German captive share a light amid the endless mud and shellholes of Flanders.

CHAR D'ASSAUT SCHNEIDER
FRANCE
Weight: 14.6 tons
Armament: One 75mm (2.95in) gun, two MGs

CAPORETTO

On the southern front, the Italians renewed their efforts. Although they had suffered heavy losses and the morale of the army was slipping, they launched two more offensives along the Isonzo front in May and August of 1917. The second attack, known as the Eleventh Battle of the Isonzo, actually made substantial gains, forcing a reaction by the Central Powers. Conrad hoped to counter-attack in the area, and the Germans obliged by despatching the German 14th Army, under General Otto von Below, to the Italian front.

THE TANK

The need to break the trench deadlock led to numerous inventions, some ludicrous and some destined to change warfare. In 1915 the Admiralty Landships Committee took over the task of designing a weapon capable of breaking through trenches, but got nowhere until Ernest Swinton joined the design team. By 1916 the lozenge-shaped, caterpillar-tracked prototype was ready for testing. It was called a tank in an effort to maintain secrecy. The tests went well and the War Office ordered 100 of what became known as the Mark I tank. The hull of the vehicle was armoured and its powerplant consisted of a 105hp Daimler engine that produced a maximum speed of 6kph (3.7mph) and a range of 36km (22 miles). Steering the behemoth required the efforts of four men. Half of the Mark Is, dubbed 'males', sported a six-pounder naval gun on each side, mounted in turrets. The other half of the Mark Is, dubbed 'females', carried four side-mounted Vickers machine guns. A handful of tanks saw action in the Battle of the Somme, but their success prompted Douglas Haig to order 1000 more such vehicles. As the war progressed, tank design modernised, culminating in the British Mark V tank. The much more reliable and powerful Mark V was produced in great numbers in 1918. In the Battle of Amiens in August 1918 the BEF attacked with over 300 tanks and succeeded in shattering the German lines. Oddly enough, the Germans, often the victim of tank attacks, produced very few of their own. During World War I tanks remained too slow and too unreliable to become a truly war-winning weapon. However, interwar military thinkers came to believe that tank forces, with modifications, could make trenches and possibly even infantry obsolete. Thus the tank would become the quintessential weapon of World War II.

AMERICAN TROOPS TRAINING WITH A TANK.

The German and Austrian forces planned to attack near the town of Caporetto, but the odds were against them. The attacking force numbered only 35 divisions, compared to some 41 Italian divisions under the command of General Luigi Cadorna. Making matters worse, Cadorna expected the attack and began to prepare his defences accordingly. However, the area around Caporetto was defended by the substandard Italian Second Army commanded by General Luigi Capello, who chose to ignore Cadorna's warning that an attack was imminent. Thus at the critical point of attack, the Italians were outnumbered and poorly prepared.

On 24 October the Austro-German force attacked out of the mist following a short, but intense bombardment. Utilising infiltration tactics much like those employed by Brusilov in Russia, the German forces advanced quickly. Thick fog prevented the Italian defenders from being able to see the Germans all around them, and panic set in. The advance of the German 14th Army soon became a rout. The Italians' collapse at Caporetto was almost total, and soldiers demoralised by years of slaughter surrendered in droves. This allowed von Below's forces to advance 22.5km (14 miles) in a single day, flanking the Italian defenders to the north and south of Caporetto. A stunned Cadorna decided on a general retreat to the Tagliamento River in an attempt to retrieve the situation. However, in places, the advancing Germans reached the river before the Italians. As a result, Cadorna ordered his troops to fall back all the way to the Piave River, where he hoped to construct new defensive positions and regroup.

LEFT: A BRITISH MARK IV TANK STUCK IN A TRENCH AT RIBECOURT LA TOUR ON 20 NOVEMBER 1917 DURING THE BATTLE OF CAMBRAI.

The Austro-Germans had scored an unexpected enormous victory at Caporetto. The Italians retreated nearly 113km (70 miles) to reach the Piave. No army had moved as far or as quickly since 1914 and it seemed that Italy was on the verge of defeat. Reacting quickly to the disaster, the Italian Government sacked Cadorna and Capello, passing command of the army to General Armando Diaz. Active and effective, Diaz was able to rally his troops so that they held their new defensive positions against fierce German attacks. Italian

The Austro-Germans had scored an unexpected enormous victory at Caporetto. The Italians retreated nearly 113km (70 miles) to reach the Piave. No army had moved as far or as quickly since 1914 and it seemed that Italy was on the verge of defeat.

Above: British troops ready their weapons for advance during the Battle of Cambrai in 1917 – a battle that was a foretaste of modern warfare.

morale went up after the great defeat; for most, the war had changed from one of needless offensives to one in which Italian liberty itself was now at stake. Now a grim determination to see the war through to victory developed. Although Italy lived on, and in some ways the Italian Army improved, Caporetto had been a disastrous defeat. The Italian Army suffered some 40,000 killed and wounded during the battle, but nearly 275,000 men were taken prisoner.

THE COLLAPSE OF RUSSIA

In Russia – in many ways the weakest of the great powers – military disasters and wartime privation strained the body politic to breaking point. In March 1917, 300,000 people took to the streets in the capital, St Petersburg, due to shortages of food and coal. The government of Tsar Nicholas II ordered the army to disperse the crowd, but it would not, and many military units instead chose to mutiny and join the revolution. In a few short days, the Tsar had lost power, and he would eventually formally abdicate and be

ABOVE:
GERMAN TROOPS FIRE THEIR WEAPONS AT RETREATING ITALIAN SOLDIERS IN THE OPEN WARFARE THAT FOLLOWED THE VICTORY AT CAPORETTO.

LEFT:
ITALIAN DEAD LITTER A TRENCH AFTER THE AUSTRO-GERMAN ADVANCE AT CAPORETTO.

placed under arrest. Power then shifted into the hands of the Russian parliament, or Duma, led by the charismatic moderate socialist Alexander Kerensky. He and the Duma did not rule alone, however, for representatives of the workers and the soldiers had gathered together to form the St Petersburg Soviet, or revolutionary council. Other such bodies sprung up across the nation and demanded a role in governance.

The new Kerensky government made a titanic mistake. Underestimating the intense Russian desire for peace, the Duma chose to remain in World War I. Kerensky even hoped that after a series of moderate reforms the people would unite behind his leadership and Russia could yet achieve victory, and his blunder was destined to play into the hands of the more radical revolutionaries in Russia, the Bolsheviks, led by Vladimir Lenin. Exiled in Switzerland, Lenin advocated an extreme Marxist revolution in Russia, one that involved land reform and an end to the war. Although his political party was tiny, Lenin preached what the Russian people wanted to hear, for he offered 'bread and peace'. The Germans, recognising that Lenin could help destabilise Russia even further, provided a sealed train to carry Lenin and other revolutionaries across Germany. On 16 April 1917 Lenin reached the Finland Station in St Petersburg, and one of the most critical series of events in the twentieth century had begun.

THE EASTERN FRONT 1914–18

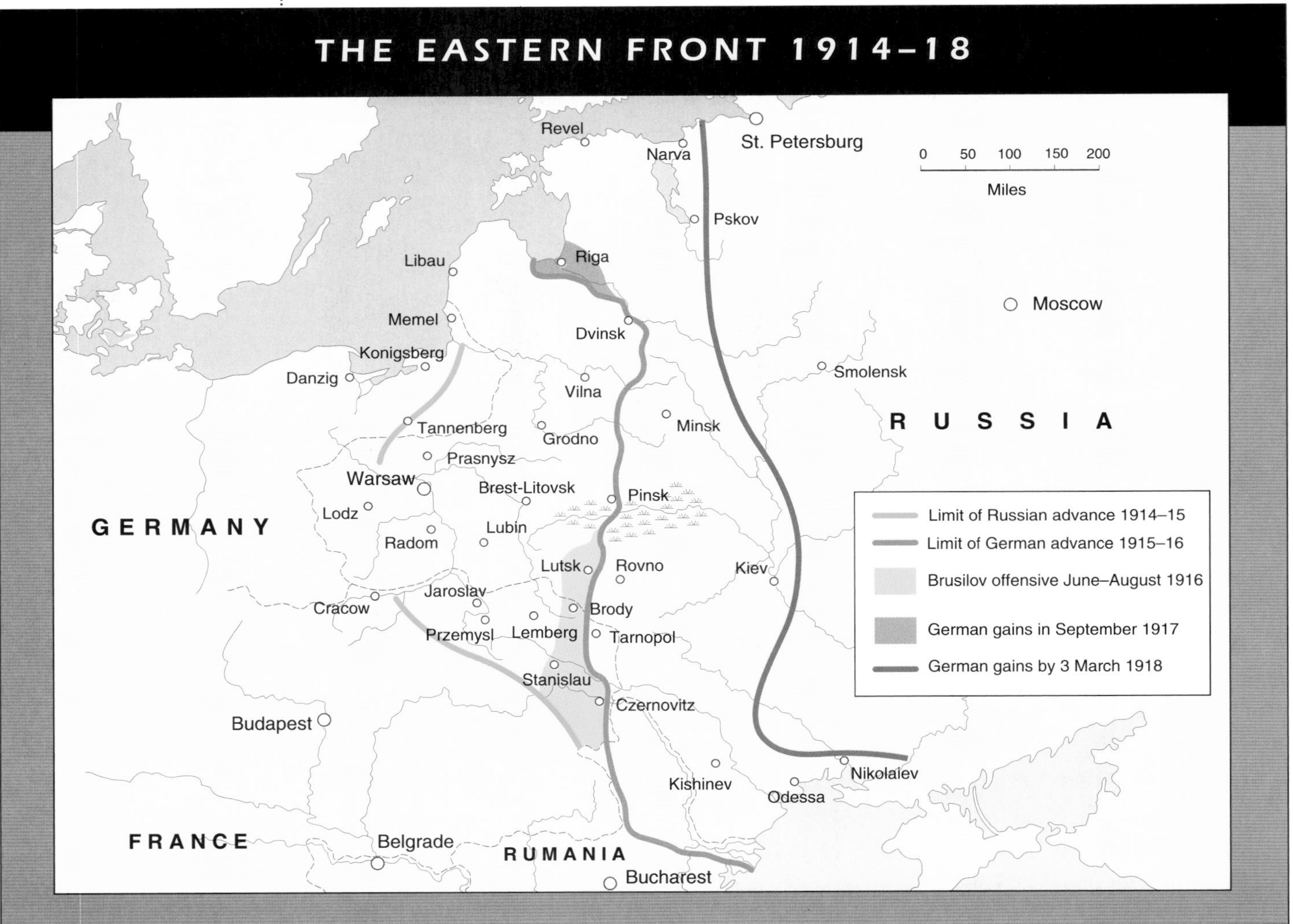

LEFT: ALEXANDER KERENSKY (LEFT WITH MONOCLE) REVIEWS RUSSIAN TROOPS IN 1917.

Kerensky opted to attack the Austrians, placing General Brusilov in charge of the offensive. Brusilov gathered together all the supplies and loyal units he could and launched an attack in Galicia. For the first few days, Russian troops made good progress against equally demoralised Austrians. However, the Germans quickly came to the rescue of their allies and counter-attacked on 19 July, routing the dispirited Russians. The destruction of the Russian Army was now complete. All along the line Russian soldiers mutinied, surrendered or simply returned home. In St Petersburg Kerensky's government was discredited and sporadic violence broke out across the city. As Kerensky launched futile efforts to save the political situation, the Germans continued their general advance in the wake of the crumbling and fleeing Russian Army. The Germans inched ever closer to victory, and more and more people began to listen to Lenin's

The destruction of the Russian Army was now complete. All along the line Russian soldiers mutinied, surrendered or simply returned home. As Kerensky launched futile efforts to save the political situation, the Germans continued their general advance in the wake of the crumbling and fleeing Russian Army.

radical calls for peace. Lenin's star was on the rise, and he realised that the time had come to seize power.

The Bolsheviks in St Petersburg had already taken control of the local soviet and the local military garrison. Under the leadership of Leon Trotsky, on 7 October 1917 these forces launched a new Bolshevik Revolution that was quickly successful. After the victory, Lenin returned to St Petersburg to take control of the new government. As the Bolsheviks sought to consolidate their control over Russia, Lenin also began to make moves toward peace. Russia's collapse into revolution offered Germany a wonderful chance to aim for total victory in the war. Sensing that the Russian threat was gone, the Germans began to remove troops from the east even before a peace treaty was signed. For the first time since the beginning of the conflict, the Germans faced war on only one front. They would use their opportunity to launch a massive offensive in the west.

In March 1918 the Russians signed the humiliating Treaty of Brest-Litovsk with Germany. Under the terms of the agreement, Russia lost the Baltic States, Finland, Poland, the Ukraine and the Caucasus; in all, it parted with 50 million of its people and much of its economic base. The Bolsheviks could do little about the treaty, for they were already being sidetracked by the fighting in their own country which led to the Russian Civil War (which would later give rise to the USSR). The state that rose in Russia's place would come to dominate much of the twentieth century. For their part, the Germans had imposed a harsh treaty on the defeated Russians – setting a precedent for the treaty that would follow their own defeat.

BELOW: RUSSIAN TRENCHES AT THE MOMENT OF A GERMAN GAS ATTACK NEAR BARANOVICHI IN 1917.

LEFT:
RUSSIAN PEOPLE RACE FOR COVER IN FRONT OF THE PETROGRAD WINTER PALACE AS BOLSHEVIKS FIRE UPON THEM WITH MACHINE GUNS DURING THE RUSSIAN OCTOBER REVOLUTION.

BELOW:
GENERAL ALLENBY LISTENING TO THE READING OF THE PROCLAMATION OF OCCUPATION FROM THE STEPS OF THE TOWER OF DAVID, JERUSALEM, 11 DECEMBER 1917.

THE MIDDLE EAST

In a year of Allied defeats, the British sorely needed a morale-boosting victory. In June 1917 David Lloyd George had appointed General Edmund Allenby as commander of British forces in the Middle East. He instructed Allenby to capture Jerusalem by the end of the year as a 'Christmas present' for the British people. Firstly Allenby had to carry the Turkish defensive line at Gaza, the prize that had eluded his predecessor twice before. After thorough preparation, he launched his assault on 31 October 1917. British forces outnumbered the Turks by more than two to one, and used this advantage to break through the Turkish defences near Beersheba. This move threatened to cut off the Turks at Gaza, who were forced to retreat after four days of bitter fighting. The masterful offensive had succeeded in dividing the Turkish forces, leaving relatively few to defend Jerusalem itself.

The Turks hoped that the rugged Judean hills would help their defence of the Holy City, but the British pressed on against the new German commander von

Falkenhayn. Alhough the weather turned bad, and the Turks resisted with fanaticism, the battle had already been decided at Gaza. The Turkish force in Jerusalem was threatened with envelopment and destruction and eventually abandoned the city on 9 December. A victorious Allenby entered the city on foot the very same day, promising to respect the religious practices of Christian, Jew and Muslim alike.

Britain had its Christmas present. Although the battle was small, in terms of World War I overall, it did wonders for British morale. On the other hand, the loss of Jerusalem signalled the end for Turkey. The Turks had already lost the great cities of Baghdad, Mecca and Medina – and now had to give up Jerusalem after 400 years of Turkish rule. It was a blow from which they would not recover.

AMERICA ENTERS THE WAR

The United States had long been isolationist in its international policy, and its President, Woodrow Wilson, had won the last election on a platform of peace. However, as the war dragged on, America found its neutrality under ever-growing pressure. In 1915 German U-boats had attempted an unrestricted submarine war, resulting in the loss of several American lives, most notably in the sinking of the *Lusitania.* Wilson had protested, and the submarine actions were curtailed. The United States also found itself increasingly tied to the economic success of the wartime Allies. Thus, for several reasons Wilson supported the Allies, but even if he did desire entry into the conflict, he would have to overcome the objections of isolationists and a significant German minority in the population.

When the Germans renewed unrestricted submarine warfare, they did so realising that sinking American ships and the loss of American life would result in the United States entering the conflict. However, the German planners thought it worth risking, partly because of their disdain for the pitifully small American Army. Wilson was dismayed with the new development and, after consultation with his cabinet, severed diplomatic relations with Germany. On 24 February the diplomatic situation worsened with the interception of the 'Zimmerman Telegram', which suggested an alliance between Germany and Mexico aimed at the United States. After the telegram was

ABOVE: AN OFFICER FROM THE US 1ST CAVALRY DIVISION IN FRANCE, 1917.

RIGHT: GENERALS PETAIN AND PERSHING IN CONFERENCE IN FRANCE. PERSHING REFUSED TO ALLOW AMERICANS TO BE USED MERELY AS REPLACEMENTS.

PRESIDENT WOODROW WILSON.

ZIMMERMAN TELEGRAM

When Germany declared unrestricted submarine warfare in 1917, few doubted that such a measure would bring the United States into the conflict. The German Foreign Secretary, Arthur Zimmerman, was determined to be ready for such an eventuality. On 19 January 1917 Zimmerman sent a telegram to Count von Bernstorff, the German Ambassador in Washington D.C., notifying the ambassador of the unrestricted submarine campaign, but also suggesting a possible diplomatic solution to American entry into the war. Zimmerman included proposals outlining a possible German–Mexican alliance, suggesting that if Mexico entered the war on Germany's side, she might be able to reconquer Texas, New Mexico and Arizona. He also suggested that Germany might seek a Pacific alliance with the Japanese aimed at the United States. Zimmerman's message was intercepted by British intelligence and turned over to President Woodrow Wilson. Unsure of what to do, Wilson sought confirmation of its authenticity and alliance offers. Unbelievably, Zimmerman himself confirmed that the telegram and its anti-American rhetoric were genuine. On 1 March, Wilson chose to publish the telegram in several newspapers. The American public, already shocked by the submarine campaign, saw it as a virtual declaration of war, and demanded an American response. In a country with a large German minority and a history of isolationism, entering the war on the Allies' side was a difficult prospect, but one made into a near certainty by the Zimmerman Telegram.

made public, Americans began to demand a declaration of war on Germany, and Wilson was forced to act. On 2 April he called Congress to meet in special session and asked for a declaration of war against Germany. Congress debated the proposal for three days and neutralists spoke against American entry; even so, there remained no hope for peace. On 6 April 1917 Congress approved Wilson's request and the United States was at war.

Although the United States boasted a strong economy, it was militarily weak, with a poorly trained army of only 128,000 men. Even these men needed much in the way of training before they could see action on the Western Front. Wilson appointed General John 'Black Jack' Pershing to command the American Expeditionary Force. Pershing toured the trenches in France and returned to announce to a stunned government that the United States would have to raise an army of 3 million men. As a result, Wilson introduced the Selective Service Act to provide men for the armed forces. New training facilities sprung up across the nation as the United States went about raising its first mass army. From all over the nation 'doughboys' entered the service and began their training. The task, however, was daunting. In some ways, the war would be decided by a race. Would the Germans transfer their forces from Russia to the west and achieve victory – or would the Americans arrive in time to tip the balance in favour of the Allies once and for all?

BELOW: UPON ENTRY INTO WORLD WAR I, THE UNITED STATES TOOK ON THE TASK OF TRAINING A MASS ARMY FOR USE IN EUROPE.

CHAPTER 9

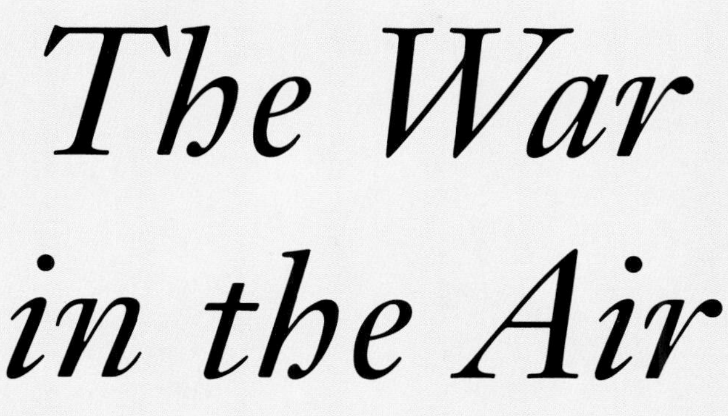

The War in the Air

WORLD WAR I SAW THE FIRST AIR WAR IN HISTORY. AT THE OUTSET OF THE WAR BOTH MACHINES AND MEN WERE RAW AND UNTRIED, BUT ADVANCEMENTS IN AIRCRAFT AND TACTICS HERALDED THE BIRTH OF A NEW KIND OF WARFARE. HERE AN AUSTRIAN ALBATROS TAKES TO THE SKIES OVER THE SOUTHERN FRONT.

DEVELOPMENT OF THE AIRCRAFT

The late-nineteenth and early-twentieth centuries witnessed the height of the Industrial Revolution and the development of new technologies, including everything from chemicals to automobiles. Possibly the most lauded and revolutionary development of the time was powered flight, which began with the invention of the dirigible in France in 1884. The Wright brothers in the United States followed later with the first successful test of an aeroplane in 1903. Interest in aviation grew quickly and flyers the world over were revered as dashing adventurers. It was an era of races, records and larger-than-life heroes. In 1908 a German pilot remained aloft in a dirigible, which the Germans referred to as a Zeppelin after its inventor, for over 12 hours. Even more important was a record achieved in 1909 by Louis Blériot. In that year, the daring French pilot flew an aeroplane across the English Channel.

Such impressive feats caught the imagination of writers and the military alike. Several books spoke of the coming of war from the air. Indeed, in Britain the development of powered flight caused Lord Northcliffe to remark that, 'England was no longer an island'. He envisioned a future war in which aircraft descended upon England like 'aerial chariots'. The novelist H.G. Wells in 1908 published *The War in the Air*, forecasting a lengthy world

BELOW: CAPTAIN PIAZZA OF THE ITALIAN AIR FLOTILLA POSES WITH HIS BLÉRIOT XI, THE FIRST PLANE EVER TO FLY A MILITARY MISSION – AGAINST THE TURKS IN LIBYA IN OCTOBER 1911.

ZEPPELIN RAIDS

THE MARK MADE BY A ZEPPELIN CREWMAN.

The German lighter-than-air craft, known as the Zeppelin, brought a new wartime threat to Great Britain: aerial bombing. The British had always been able to rely upon the English Channel and the Royal Navy to spare them from most immediate effects of war. However, on 31 May 1915, a new era of warfare began when the German military airship LZ38 flew over London and dropped its cargo of bombs without interference from any British defences. The Germans attempted to build upon their success by launching some 53 Zeppelin raids upon Great Britain during World War I. The raiders dropped over 5700 bombs, killing 556 civilians. The peak year of Zeppelin bombing was 1916 when 22 raids were mounted, including the largest single Zeppelin attack on 3 September that involved 16 airships. During that raid, a British aircraft brought down a Zeppelin for the first time. The raids were not serious in a true military sense, but they had a tremendous impact upon the British national psyche. The nearly soundless Zeppelins appeared seemingly out of nowhere, and often left panic in their wake. Absenteeism rose in critical British defence industries and a terrified population took to sleeping in London Underground stations for safety. Forced to scramble to ensure public safety, the British Government developed a host of defensive measures to counter the German threat, including searchlights and anti-aircraft guns. In addition, fighters were taken from the Western Front to defend the cities and towns of the British Isles. In the end, the Zeppelins proved to be too slow, and their highly inflammable gas made them too vulnerable, so the raids were curtailed. The effects of the raids seemed to indicate disaster for Britain in future wars.

war fought by airships that would eventually cause the collapse of civilisation. Military men, often at the behest of pressure groups and aeronautics clubs, came to recognise the military potential of flight somewhat more slowly. France and Germany formed military air services in 1909 and were followed by Great Britain in 1912. Aircraft designers across Europe, from the Dutch engineer Anthony Fokker to T.O.M. Sopwith in Great Britain, began to compete for lucrative government aeroplane contracts, setting the stage for a wartime competition in technological developments. Although military pilots took the place of their civilian counterparts as heroes leading the conquest of the heavens, few tangible gains were made in aircraft design before the war began in 1914. Most military men believed that the war would be won quickly and through the use of unfettered military

OVERVIEW

World War I witnessed the birth of aerial combat. At the beginning of the conflict aircraft were quite flimsy and unarmed, and military commanders did not realise their value. As the war progressed, the uses of air power became apparent. Aided by technological developments, aircraft saw their greatest value in a reconnaissance role. However, both sides realised the need to defend themselves from enemy reconnaissance – and the fighter plane was born. Initially, fighters were lone knights of the air seeking to destroy enemy aircraft, or defend their own. In time, both the Allies and the Central Powers came to recognise the benefit of grouping fighters together for protection and added offensive power. By the end of the conflict, great formations of fighters roamed the skies, setting the stage for later conflicts. The Germans especially had also noted the value of fighter support of ground units. In a separate development, during the early phases of the war, the Germans had sent their Zeppelin airships on bombing raids over Great Britain. The success of these raids led to the development of aircraft specifically designed to bomb behind enemy lines. Although the strategic bombers of World War I had little effect on the outcome of the war, their limited use seemed to suggest that in the future, bombing alone might force a nation to succumb to defeat.

RIGHT: A PICTURE TAKEN FROM *L31*, A ZEPPELIN, DURING A RAID ON ENGLAND. SUCH RAIDS CAUSED A PUBLIC PANIC AT FIRST.

BELOW: JOACHIM BREITHAUPT, COMMANDER OF *L15*, WEARING WARM CLOTHES TO PROTECT AGAINST COLD.

might on land. Thus most production and research resources had gone to the armies of Europe, leaving the air services languishing behind.

At the start of World War I, the European powers had, at best, rudimentary air services. The Germans, who had placed their emphasis on lighter-than-air craft, possessed 11 Zeppelins. These great ships consisted of aluminum frames encased in a fabric covering and contained 17 hydrogen cells that provided the necessary lift. The Zeppelins were powered by two engines and controlled from a gondola that dangled beneath the main frame of the ship. The Germans hoped to use such craft for observation purposes. In addition, each of the main combatant nations possessed a few aeroplanes, none of which were armed. These primitive aircraft, which only reached top speeds of around 80kph (50mph), were usually fragile biplanes constructed of wood with a fabric covering. Many of the first aircraft were so-called 'pushers' with the engine and propeller located behind the pilot. As the war progressed, most air services came to prefer the more efficient 'puller' type, with the engine and propeller in front of the pilot.

The main initial task of military aircraft was reconnaissance. Well suited to the task due to their speed, range and near invulnerability, reconnaissance aircraft provided valuable information to combatant nations during the war of movement in 1914. Pilots of the fledgling French air service made a critical contribution to the outcome of the war in September 1914 by discovering that von Kluck's forces had moved east of Paris, thus offering their flank to the Allies in the pivotal Battle of the Marne.

As the war settled down into a trench stalemate, the main task of air services on both sides of the Western Front remained reconnaissance. It was now their duty to locate and photograph enemy defences and adjust the fall of artillery fire. Such tasks were crucial to the planning of a successful offensive. Initially, reconnaissance flights provided valuable general information on the strength of enemy defences, but were very inaccurate in providing details. Aerial photography was undertaken using regular cameras and the resulting photographs were often off by several hundred feet – enough to ruin an attack. Later, cameras solved the problem by taking the curvature of the Earth into account. Developments in radio technology also kept aircraft in constant contact with the ground. By late 1917 reconnaissance aircraft had provided the Allies with very detailed maps of the entire front, and were increasingly effective in their role as mobile artillery observers. Although the development of fighter aircraft soon seized the public imagination, reconnaissance remained the main role of the military air services throughout the war. It was in that role that the aircraft had its greatest effect – and helped to make possible the great Allied victories of 1918.

At first, air combat was crude and improvised, involving pilots and observers firing at each other using pistols and even shotguns. Some intrepid airmen attempted to drop grenades from above their adversaries into their cockpits.

DEVELOPMENT OF THE FIGHTER

As the reconnaissance value of aircraft became apparent, belligerent nations began to try to develop ways to destroy their enemies' reconnaissance aircraft. At first, air combat was crude and improvised, involving pilots and observers firing at each other using pistols and even shotguns. Some intrepid airmen attempted to drop grenades from above their adversaries into their cockpits. Such efforts understandably met with little success. Both the Central Powers and the Allies began experiments with aircraft armed with machine guns. However, the majority of the aircraft in use were now 'puller' type meaning that forward-firing machine guns simply shot off the aeroplane's propeller. The first great leap forward in fighter design was developed by Roland Garros in France, who used a fixed, forward-firing machine gun but guarded the vulnerable propeller with deflectors.

THE RED BARON

Manfred von Richthofen, a member of the Prussian nobility, joined an elite cavalry regiment in 1912. The astute young man quickly realised that the war would not afford much opportunity for cavalry and transferred to the German Air Service in May 1915. He served as an observer on the Eastern Front, and then with the pioneering bombing unit known as the Ostend Carrier Pigeon Unit, on the Western Front. At the end of 1915 Richthofen qualified to become a pilot, and by August 1916 he was chosen to join the fighters of *Jagdstaffel 2* under the command of the famous German ace Oswald Boelcke. The new unit made its first offensive foray on 17 September 1916, and on the following day, Richthofen scored his first confirmed kill. After this, he averaged one kill per day for the remainder of the year, and often attempted to bring back a trophy from each aircraft he had downed. By January 1917 Boelcke was dead and Richthofen had replaced him as Germany's leading fighter ace. Cool and calculating, he quickly became a hero in his own country, and something of a sensation across the world. To emphasise his status, he had his airplane painted bright red, thus earning him the name 'The Red Baron'. He had now taken command of *Jasta 11* and he and his men went on a rampage through the skies, especially in 'Bloody April' 1917, when his personal kill count rose to 52. In June 1917 he rose to the command of the new *Jagdgeschwader I*, a new fighter grouping consisting of four *Jastas*. It was the top fighter unit in Germany and was moved all over the Western Front to wherever it was needed most. This penchant for moving, coupled with the bright colours of the aircraft, earned the unit the nickname 'The Flying Circus'. By April 1918 the Red Baron's kill count had risen to 80, the highest of the war for any nation, but he had long outlived the average lifespan of a fighter pilot. His luck ran out on 21 April 1918 when he was struck by a single bullet during a dogfight over the Somme. After crashing behind enemy lines, Richthofen received a hero's funeral, complete with British pallbearers and an Australian honour guard. It was a gesture of respect for a gallant enemy that hearkened back to a bygone era of warfare.

MANFRED VON RICHTHOFEN, THE RED BARON.

Allied aircraft now had an advantage over their German counterparts, but it was still quite unnerving to have deflected bullets flying all around as one engaged the enemy. In October 1915 the Germans leapt forward in aircraft design with the introduction of the Fokker Eindecker. Developed by the Dutch engineer Anthony Fokker, working outside Berlin, the new aircraft was a nimble monoplane. Its main advance was the 'interrupter gear' that synchronised the machine gun to fire between the propeller blades. This gave the Germans the upper hand in the air war for the next eight months, introducing a period known as the 'Fokker scourge'. Although German pilots reigned supreme during this time, they were not used to their best advantage. They operated in ones and twos, thus minimising their effect. Had the German air service concentrated their resources, they might have driven the Allied air services from the skies. The Allies responded with the introduction of the French Nieuport and Spad fighters in mid 1916, thus challenging German technical superiority. The pendulum of innovation, however, swung back to the Germans in the autumn of 1916 when they unveiled the improved D.III Albatros. Thus the balance swung back and forth during 1915 and 1916, the heyday of the fighter on the Western Front.

During much of 1915 and 1916 the Allies, who enjoyed greater industrial resources, produced far more aircraft than the Germans. This numerical inferiority often forced the Germans into a defensive mode, only attacking those Allied aircraft that violated German airspace. However, technical dominance, especially the introduction of the Fokker Eindecker, sometimes allowed the Germans to attempt fighter offensives, and helped

RIGHT: CAPTAIN ALBERT BALL OF NO.56 SQUADRON, ROYAL FLYING CORPS, WITH THE PROPELLOR AND SPINNER OF HIS NIEUPORT 17 SCOUT.

AIR COMBAT

A British pilot recalls his first successful kill:

A BRITISH FIGHTER PILOT SCORES A KILL IN 1918.

I got my first Hun today! At last! I dropped into a wide sweeping curve that brought me dead behind the Hun ... I came down closer and closer, holding my fire. My heart was pounding and I was trembling, uncontrollably, but my mind was calm and collected. I closed to ten yards ... He had a dark brown flying helmet, with white goggles-strap round the back of his head. I aimed carefully ... between his shoulders just below where they showed above the fairing. It was impossible to miss. I gently pressed the trigger, and at the first shots his head jerked back, and immediately the plane reared up vertically. He must have clutched the joy-stick right back as he was hit. I followed upwards, still firing until in two or three seconds he stalled and fell over to the left ... I went after him, throttle wide open, firing in long bursts ... then I stopped, there was no point in pumping any more lead into him. But I stayed in the dive and saw that he didn't pull out.

Above: A crippled Zeppelin crash-landed on the North Sea in 1917, dwarfing in size the nearby ships.

to produce the greatest fighter aces of the war. This was the infancy of air combat, a time when lone pilots flew the skies searching for opponents like aerial knights-errant, and imagery of brave warriors engaging in single combat among the clouds gripped the populations of the belligerent nations. Fighter pilots of the war were transformed into national heroes of unbelievable stature. Two men rose to greater prominence than any others during this period: Max Immelmann and Oswald Boelcke.

The German contemporaries, and rivals, were instrumental in the development of modern fighter tactics. Immelmann scored his first kill on 1 August 1915, giving him the distinction of scoring the first victory by an aircraft designed specifically as a fighter. He also became famous for developing the 'Immelmann turn', a half-loop with a roll manoeuvre which allowed a pilot to turn the tables on an aircraft that was attacking him from behind. After having revolutionised fighter tactics, Immelmann lost his life in June 1916 in a dogfight with seven Allied aircraft. The first great German fighter ace had amassed 15 kills. It was Immelmann's rival Boelcke, however, who had the greatest effect on the air war. The young and brash Boelcke chafed at the defensive posture of the German air service in 1915. After the introduction of the Fokker Eindecker, sensing the superiority of the

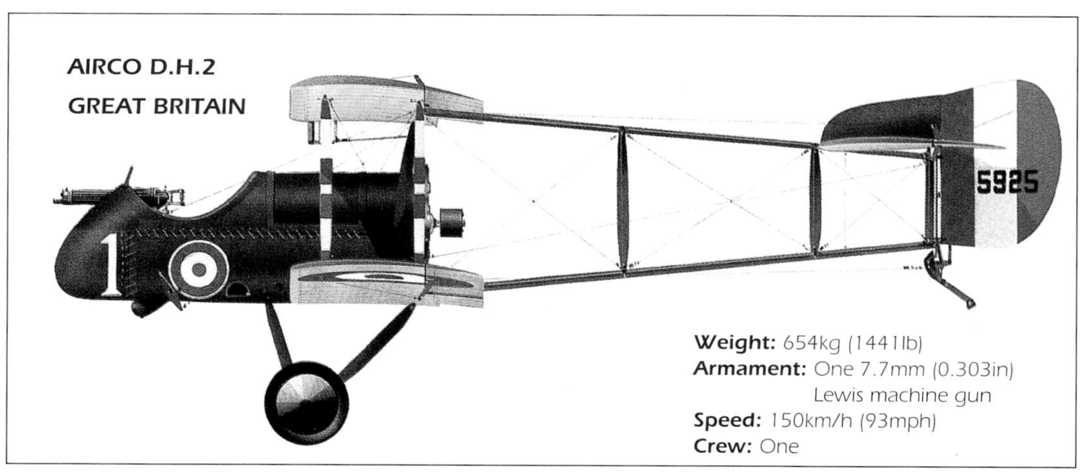

aircraft, he began to ignore his instructions and search out victims across the Allied lines. By the beginning of 1916 he had become a fighter ace and had won the Pour Le Mérite, the highest German military honour. His true impact upon the fighter war would not become apparent until July 1916, when he was asked to command a new fighter unit.

Until this point in the conflict, the air war had been one of individual combat. Boelcke, among others, had long advocated the formation of fighter units. The Germans heeded the advice and formed fighter units, called *Jagdstaffeln* or '*Jastas*', each consisting of 14 aircraft. Boelcke was given command of *Jasta 2*, and the renowned ace gathered together an elite, hand-picked group of pilots, including Manfred von Richthofen. He tutored his new colleagues in fighter tactics, then took to the skies. Under his leadership, *Jasta 2* developed a new style of team flying and fighting rather than emphasising individual heroics. The experiment was a total success; *Jasta 2* became a feared weapon of war, consistently dominating its battle area. Boelcke had struck upon the way of the future: fighter units would come to dominate the skies by the end of the conflict. However, Boelcke would not live to see the fruition of his labours. In October 1916, on his sixth mission of the day, he died after a mid-air collision with one of his own comrades during a confused battle. At the time of his death, he had scored 40 confirmed kills.

ABOVE: AN EARLY BRITISH 'PUSHER' AIRCRAFT, THE F.E.2D, DEMONSTRATING THE FLIMSY NATURE AND AWKWARD FIGHTING CHARACTERISTICS OF SUCH MACHINES.

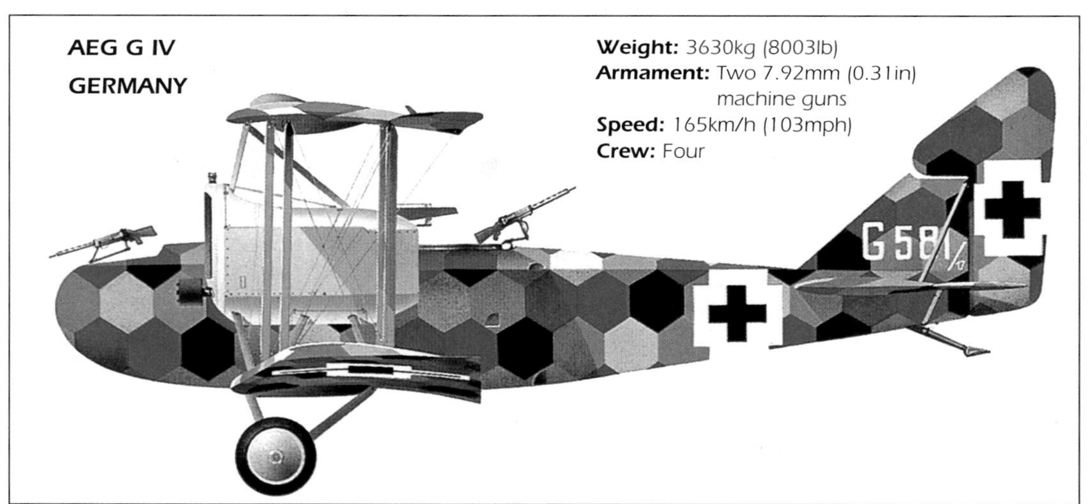

CHANGING FIGHTER WAR

By 1917 the air war on the Western Front was becoming more organised and efficient. General Ernst Wilhelm von Hoeppner, the commander of the German air service, dictated that his new *Jasta* fighter units conserve their strength by remaining on the defensive. On the Allied side, the air services chose to mount operations to support the British at Arras and the French on the Aisne. The result was one of the greatest air clashes of the conflict. In April, near Arras, the Royal Flying Corps (RFC), under the command of General Hugh Trenchard, launched armed aerial raids and reconnaissance missions behind the German lines. The Germans, who enjoyed a momentary technical advantage with the D.III Albatros, put their new group fighter tactics to the test. *Jastas* would climb high into the skies into the sun over their own lines, wait, and then pounce upon the Allied fighter and reconnaissance sorties. The RFC, flying inferior aircraft, persisted in its offensive action but was decimated in 'Bloody April'. Trenchard received great criticism over the high losses; even so, he chose to continue his efforts to support the Arras offensive. During the month of April, the RFC lost nearly one-third of its strength, including its

ABOVE: GERMAN PILOTS AND CREW POSE WITH A FOKKER EINDECKER, WHICH REPRESENTED A QUANTUM LEAP FORWARD IN FIGHTER DESIGN AND BECAME THE SCOURGE OF THE SKIES OVER THE WESTERN FRONT.

LEFT: A GERMAN REAR GUNNER INSTRUCTOR POSES WITH A MACHINE GUN AT DÖBERITZ AIRFIELD NEAR BERLIN IN AUGUST 1918.

Above: A flight of British fighters performing ground support duties fly over a devastated battlefield on the Western Front.

experienced pilots, and most of the losses were permanent. British pilots did not wear parachutes, meaning that nearly all crashes were fatal. In addition, those pilots who did survive a crash usually landed behind German lines and were taken prisoner. As a result, relative newcomers to the RFC were left to face the fearsome *Jastas*, and consequently, the life expectancy of a new front-line RFC pilot varied from only 11 days to three weeks. It would take the RFC nearly an entire year to recover from its losses of Bloody April.

After the close of the Arras offensive, the air war in the west changed yet again. The Allies surged ahead of the Germans with the introduction of the Sopwith Camel and Spad XIII. These new, powerful aircraft gave the Allies the technological edge for the remainder of the war. In addition, the Allies began to modernise their own tactics with the introduction of British fighter squadrons and French *Escadrilles de Chasse*. Thus all up and down the length of the Western Front, fighters now took to the skies in formation. The era of the lone hunter was at an end. These developments placed the Germans once again at a disadvantage, for now that the Allies had caught up in tactics and technology, their superior numbers began to tell. Always at a numerical disadvantage, the Germans again made an organisational leap forward to compensate for it. They combined four *Jastas* to form a new unit called a *Jadgdeschwader* (fighter wing). The first of these units was formed under the command of Boelcke's protégé, Manfred von Richthofen. The new unit was mobile and the Germans shifted it up and down the line as needed to provide local air superiority. Thus, the Germans, who could not hope to achieve complete air superiority, could make use of a large, elite unit to provide air superiority at critical places and times. The Allies came to refer to the new German fighter units as 'Flying Circuses'.

The Germans, who could not hope to achieve complete air superiority, could make use of a large, elite unit to provide air superiority at critical places and times. The Allies came to refer to the new German fighter units as 'Flying Circuses'.

FOUR DAYLIGHT GOTHA RAIDS ON ENGLAND

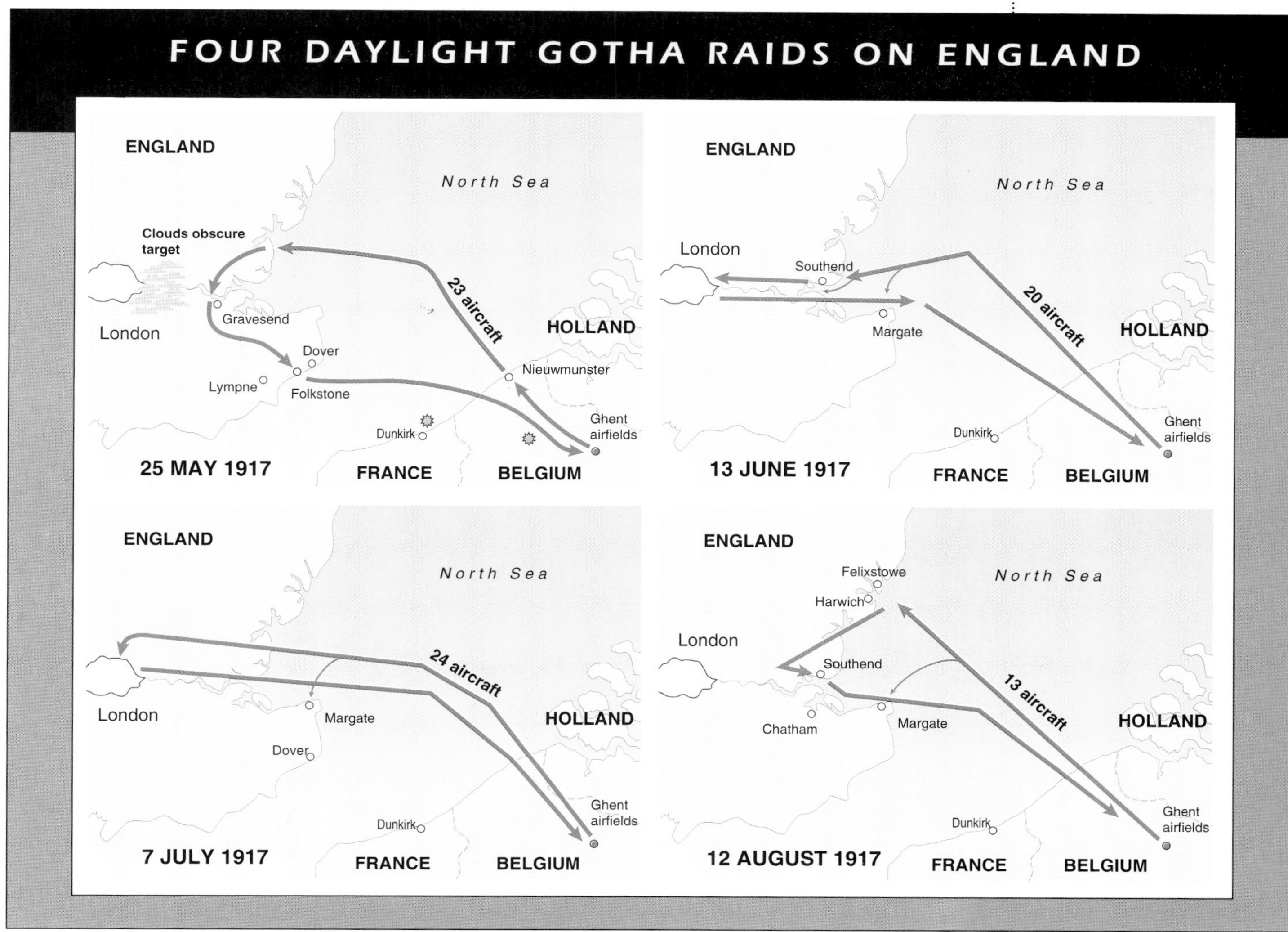

FIGHTER CLASHES OF 1918

The final year of the war saw the renewal of a war of movement and an alteration in fighter tactics. The year opened with Allied superiority in the air in both superior machines and overwhelming numbers. The Allies were able to destroy German efforts at reconnaissance as well as launch aerial offensives over German territory. However, the Germans could wrest momentary air superiority from the Allies by moving a 'Circus' into a given area, although in reality, they were husbanding their strength for their great offensives of 1918. German military planners hoped to use air power in a new way in the coming attacks: in a ground support role. New units, called *Schlastas*, were to fly low over the battlefield using their machine guns and light bombs to aid the advancing infantry. In addition, they were to keep the German High Command constantly informed about the progress of the troops, as well as aiding in directing artillery fire. Thus the *Schlastas* were to provide the Germans with mobile artillery and nearly instantaneous communications.

The new German tactics worked wonderfully well during the initial German offensive on the Western Front in 1918. The Allies, especially the British, responded with overwhelming fighter numbers and new fighter wings of their own. The spring and early summer

Above: A German fighter aerodrome in France in April 1918. The Albatros fighters are lined up in a vulnerable formation, suggesting that this airfield is some miles back from the frontline trenches.

of 1918 was a time of vast aerial clashes between large groups of fighters. However, as with the ground offensives, the German air offensive began to lose momentum due to heavy losses. The Germans had begun their offensives with 4050 aircraft, but wastage was severe during their forays into Allied lines. In April alone, they lost some 659 aircraft, the reverse of the Bloody April of the previous year. Of equal importance, the Germans lost most of their experienced fighter pilots, including the legendary von Richthofen, and had to rely on replacements who were fresh from flying school. As a result, in June 1918 the depleted German air service only had 2551 pilots on its rosters.

When the Allies shifted to the attack in the summer of 1918 they did so with overwhelming air superiority. The British had 1799 aircraft, the Americans 740 and the French 3000; against such numbers, the depleted German air service could put up but a token resistance. The Allied air services rolled forward using ground support methods learned, in part, from their adversaries. In the end, the war in the air finished with no climactic battle, but with the slow deterioration of the German air service, partly due to Allied superiority, and partly to the privations forced upon Germany by the British blockade.

Above: A German Albatros scout performs a loop over the Western Front in 1918.

BOMBING

Both the Allies and the Central Powers realised that aircraft would be valuable in the role of strategic bombing behind enemy lines. The French were the first to create a squadron of aircraft dedicated to bombing, but such efforts quickly shifted to the Germans and the British. At first, bombing efforts were rather rudimentary, often consisting of lone pilots dropping grenades from their cockpits as they overflew enemy territory. Soon bomb racks began to appear beneath aeroplanes and bombing began in earnest.

The Germans were the first to attempt strategic bombing in a systematic way, using Zeppelins to bomb cities and towns in Great Britain. The lighter-than-air craft launched 53 raids on London, Tyneside and the Midlands between 1915 and 1918. The raids only caused minor damage, and resulted in the deaths of 556 civilians. As British air defences and fighter capabilities increased, the weaknesses of the highly inflammable Zeppelins became apparent and the frequency of their raids abated. The raids had, however, caused a public reaction that sometimes bordered on panic. Such results encouraged German military leaders to search for more effective ways to bomb Britain.

By May 1917 the Germans had developed the Gotha GIV heavy bomber and formed an 'England Squadron' dedicated to strategic bombing. From May until August 1917 the Germans mounted eight daylight 'Gotha raids' on England, dropping some 33,112kg (73,000lb) of bombs and causing 1364 casualties. Once again, panic spread across Britain, resulting in demands for better defence and revenge.

At first, bombing efforts were rather rudimentary, often consisting of lone pilots dropping grenades from their cockpits as they overflew enemy territory. Soon bomb racks began to appear beneath aeroplanes and bombing began in earnest.

RIGHT: A BRITISH PLANE DISINTEGRATES DURING A DOGFIGHT. BRITISH PILOTS DID NOT WEAR PARACHUTES, MEANING THAT THE VICTIMS OF SUCH INCIDENTS INVARIABLY DIED.

BELOW: FLYERS ON ALL SIDES TOOK TO DECORATING THEIR AIRCRAFT, LIKE THESE GERMAN EXAMPLES SEEN IN JULY 1918.

THE FORMATION OF THE ROYAL AIR FORCE

The British Government set up a committee under the leadership of General Jan Christian Smuts, the South African statesman and soldier, in an attempt to deal with the situation. He quickly set about modernising the air defences of Great Britain and transferred two of Britain's best fighter squadrons to home defence. Such measures

succeeded in causing the Germans great losses during their raids, forcing them to switch to night bombing attacks, which continued until May 1918.

Smuts also advocated amalgamation of the Royal Flying Corps and the Royal Naval Air Service. Such a force would maximise British air power, and could concentrate much of its resources on a strategic bombing campaign aimed at Germany. As a result, Britain formed the Royal Air Force (RAF) in April 1918, the first independent air service in the world.

ABOVE: A FOKKER D.VII OVERFLIES A GERMAN MACHINE GUN POSITION IN 1918.

Right:
Eddie Rickenbacker, America's leading wartime ace with 22 confirmed kills, posing with his SPAD XIII.

Below:
Bomb damage caused by German raids on London. The level of damage was far less than that caused during the Blitz in 1940, but it nonetheless caused civilian casualties.

ABOVE: MEMBERS OF NO. 1 SQUADRON OF THE ROYAL AIR FORCE – THE FIRST INDEPENDENT AIR FORCE IN THE WORLD – SEEN WITH THEIR SE 5A AIRCRAFT IN JULY 1918.

The RAF worked quickly to begin the revenge bombing of Germany. Using Handley Page bombers, it began to strike at targets on the German homefront by mid-1918. The abrupt end to the conflict meant that the RAF was never to see its bombing campaign reach full fruition. In total, British bombers only dropped some 543 tons of bombs on German targets by the end of the campaign. Indeed, more advanced RAF bombers stood poised to strike Berlin itself as the war drew to a close.

CONCLUSION

Although great strides had been made in aerial warfare since the days of pilots shooting pistols at one another in 1914, World War I ended before the air war had truly come of age. Reconnaissance and counter-reconnaissance remained the chief duty of air services throughout the conflict. Fighter aircraft had contested control of the skies, but it was only in 1918 that new roles for aircraft became apparent. Vast aerial armadas working in conjunction with ground forces seemed to be the way of the future, and caught the imagination of German military planners during the interwar years. Blitzkrieg in World War II would involve a seamless co-operation between air and ground forces that would shock their stunned adversaries. However, it was strategic bombing that seized the attention of most in the west. It seemed, given the reaction of British civilians to a few German raids during the Great War, that a sustained bombing offensive against enemy civilian targets would undermine the people's will to resist. Thus was born the idea that the enemy could be bombed into submission, which led to the thousand-bomber raids of World War II, and even the nuclear strikes upon Japan.

Strategic bombing seized the attention of most in the west. It seemed, given the reaction of British civilians to a few German raids during the Great War, that a sustained bombing offensive against enemy civilian targets would undermine the people's will to resist.

Chapter 10

Last Battles

The Germans had one last chance to secure victory on the Western Front in the great offensives of spring 1918 before American troops began arriving in significant numbers. Here German infantry in Picardy wait to go 'over the top' and into the fateful assault.

PLANNING FOR BATTLE

The German command team of Hindenburg and Ludendorff understood that 1918 would be decided by a race for time. Rejecting the idea of attempting a negotiated peace in the west, while retaining gains in the east, the Germans chose instead to aim for total victory.

The German command team of Hindenburg and Ludendorff understood that 1918 would be decided by a race for time. Rejecting the idea of attempting a negotiated peace in the west, while retaining gains in the east, the Germans chose instead to aim for total victory.

The German command team of Hindenburg and Ludendorff understood that 1918 would be decided by a race for time. Rejecting the idea of attempting a negotiated peace in the west, while retaining gains in the east, the Germans chose instead to aim for total victory. However, Ludendorff realised that his troops would have to achieve victory before the American Army could become a true factor in the war. He thought that he could achieve his goal for, due to the Russian collapse, Germany enjoyed a numerical superiority on the Western Front for the first time since 1914. The question was, how would the Germans choose to use that superiority to achieve victory?

On 11 November 1917 Ludendorff called a staff conference to discuss offensive plans for the coming year. At the conference, he decided to attack the BEF, believing that they were more determined to fight than the French. If he could defeat the British – better yet drive them into the sea – France would prove to have little stomach for the war and capitulate. Ludendorff chose to strike near the old Somme battlefield, at the vulnerable juncture between the British and French armies. The attack would be made on a grand scale involving three armies and 78 divisions. There was one weakness to the plan: there were no goals of strategic significance in the area.

The Allies realised that the Germans would attack, and did their best to prepare. Haig believed that the attack would take place in Flanders, and positioned his best units there. As a result, he mistakenly placed the weakened British Fifth Army of General Gough in what he hoped would be a quiet area of the front: at the juncture of the British and French armies. Thus Gough stood astride the axis of the coming German advance with a mere 14 divisions defending a front of over 67.5km (42 miles). To make matters worse, Gough was instructed to employ a sophisticated defence-in-depth scheme like the Germans had used at the Third Battle of Ypres. However, he did not fully understand the system, nor did he

BELOW: SOME OF THE MASSIVE NUMBERS OF GERMAN INFANTRY THAT HAD BEEN MOVED TO THE WEST FROM THE RUSSIAN FRONT PAUSE DURING THEIR MARCH TO THE FRONT LINES IN FRANCE.

OVERVIEW

In 1918, by moving troops west from Russia, the Germans had gained the numerical superiority over the Allies on the Western Front for the first time since 1914. Eschewing prospects for a negotiated peace, Ludendorff chose to gamble all on total victory. He realised that the Germans were racing against time, for they had to defeat Britain and France before American manpower could decide the conflict. Using stunning new tactical innovations, the German spring offensives gained much territory, but never succeeded in destroying the Allied lines. By summer, the German offensives had ground to a halt, and the initiative passed to the Allies, aided by increasing numbers of Americans. While these events played out in the west, Allied attacks from Mesopotamia to Italy forced the lesser nations of the Central Powers to sue for peace, one by one. Finally, Germany stood alone as the Allies, led by the British at Amiens, unleashed a firestorm of continuous offensives. Even the vaunted Hindenburg Line could not hold the Allied tide back, and Germany sunk into an oblivion of despair and revolution. Seeing no way out, the Kaiser fled his throne and Germany requested an end to the war.

have time to implement it fully before the Germans struck. Thus a small, tired British force that manned sketchy defences and had expected only a quiet sector of the front stood between the Germans and possible victory.

NEW TACTICS

The attacks made by both the Germans and the Allies on the Western Front in 1918 were quite different to the attritional affairs of 1916, for technological developments had once again intervened to alter the modern battlefield. At the Somme and Verdun, a scant two years past, infantry had been seen as almost powerless against an entrenched enemy. However, by 1918 the infantry soldier was once again a force to be reckoned with. There were now truly portable machine guns that gave advancing infantry more firepower. In addition, infantry could now carry their own artillery in the form of hand grenades and mortars. Such weaponry enabled infantry to deal with an enemy strongpoint or machine-gun nest, rather than have their forward momentum stop while awaiting artillery assistance. Finally, the infantry of 1918 carried more exotic weaponry such as flame-throwers and bangalore torpedoes.

The Germans are often credited with being the first to experiment with updated infantry tactics that used the strength of new technological developments. It was General Oskar von Hutier who codified the new methods and, as a result, they bear his name: Hutier tactics. To be fair, however, all sides were busy developing more modern methods of attack throughout the war. Historians call the process 'the learning curve'. One can see ample evidence of the advance in tactics throughout the war, with the Brusilov offensive and Cambrai standing out as examples. It was, however, in the Ludendorff offensive of 1918 that the new tactics gained fame. Hutier tactics called for the German infantry to attack in bursts, rushing from cover to cover, rather than in waves. In the van of the attack were elite German storm troops. Their job was to use their firepower and speed to probe the enemy defences for weakness. Once located, the storm troops would infiltrate the weak spots and advance through to depth. Such tactics, it was hoped, would shock and dislocate the enemy defensive system. It was a far cry from the waves advancing at the Somme. The Germans were, in effect, planning to use Blitzkrieg without tanks.

THE GERMANS STRIKE WEST

Ludendorff's Operation Michael began at 0500 hours on 21 March 1918 with a withering artillery barrage. The artillery fire was directed by Colonel Georg Bruchmuller and took the form of what he referred to as a 'fire waltz'. The goal of the bombardment was not to obliterate the enemy; so many previous barrages had attempted that and failed. The German barrage was designed to keep the British heads down and to disrupt their command and reinforcements, allowing the shock troops to advance quickly. At 0940 hours, the German infantry poured forth to attack the surprised British Fifth Army. Hutier tactics, aided by British mistakes, immediately proved their worth. Attacking out of a dense fog that helped confuse the dazed British defenders, the shock troops achieved rapid progress. By nightfall, German forces had advanced nearly 11km (7 miles). At this point Ludendorff had hoped to turn his advance to the north, aiming at the seizure of the pivotal transportation hub of Amiens. However, British forces in the north, under the command of Byng, had not given way so quickly. As a result, Ludendorff altered his plan, choosing to reinforce the gains made by Hutier in the south.

BELOW: UNDERGOING AN ECONOMIC CRISIS AT HOME, GERMANY SENT MUCH OF ITS DWINDLING FOOD SUPPLY TO ITS MEN ON THE WESTERN FRONT IN THE EFFORT TO SECURE VICTORY. THESE SOLDIERS ARE MAKING USE OF A CAPTURED ALLIED SUPPLY WAGON.

The Germans continued to make rapid gains against the depleted British Fifth Army and by 6 April had advanced an amazing 64km (40 miles). It was a great tactical victory by World War I standards, but it suffered the same fate as the German advance of 1914. After a few initial defensive mistakes, the BEF rushed reinforcements to the scene and eventually stemmed the German tide. Also, the German advance encountered the typical problems of supply and organisation that bedevilled commanders in that war. Ludendorff's choice to reinforce Hutier proved to be a failure. The German forward movement had netted no gain of true strategic value; it had only formed a vulnerable salient jutting out into the Allied lines. The great advance cost the Germans over 200,000 men, a price they could ill afford after nearly five years of war.

For the Allies, the near-defeat in Operation Michael led to a momentous decision. The fact that the Germans had struck at the hinge joining the French and British armies called for a level of Allied defensive co-operation that simply did not exist. Until this point in the war, British and French forces had often argued over what military path to take; it had not been a true coalition war effort. During Operation Michael, the lack of co-operation had almost caused a fatal defeat. Knowing that the Germans would attack again, the Allies realised that they had to remedy the situation. At a meeting at Doullens on 26 March, a unified command was formed. Haig took the remarkable step of placing the BEF under the overall command of the French General Ferdinand Foch who became the Supreme Allied Commander. German pressure had caused the age-old enemies Britain and France to unite in the cause of victory.

THE MASSIVE PARIS GUN.

PARIS GUN

The Germans had been working since 1916 to develop a 'super artillery piece' capable of shelling Paris. In the end, they modified a 38cm (15in) naval gun for the task. With additions, the gun barrel was 39m (43yds) long and the whole weapon weighed some 142 tons and had to be carried on special rail cars. The gun fired a projectile with a muzzle velocity of 1645mps (5400ftps) enabling shells to fly nearly 128km (80 miles). The shell reached into the upper stratosphere, 38km (24 miles) high, during flight and fell silently to the ground. On 23 March 1918 the massive gun, six of which eventually entered service, began the bombardment of Paris. The terror weapon, designed to undermine French morale, fired a total of 367 shells at Paris, the last falling on 9 August. As a result of the shelling, 256 Parisians were killed and nearly 630 were wounded. However, the shelling was so sporadic and its effects so limited that it did not have the intended effect. The Paris Gun, a miracle of modern engineering, thus did not aid materially in the German war effort, although its purpose would be copied by Hitler late in World War II, when he too decided to place emphasis on revenge weapons aimed at crushing British morale.

The German Fourth Army under the command of General Ferdinand von Quast had the good fortune to strike part of the front guarded by two tired, substandard Portuguese divisions who quickly broke and ran under the strain of the attack.

CONTINUED GERMAN OFFENSIVES

After the eventual failure of Operation Michael, Ludendorff chose to strike the British further north near the town of Lys. On 9 April two German armies struck, hoping to reach the critical British rail centre at Hazebrouck. The German forces once again utilised Hutier tactics, but on this occasion the offensive met with more mixed results. The German Fourth Army under the command of General Ferdinand von Quast had the good fortune to strike part of the front guarded by two tired, substandard Portuguese divisions who quickly broke and ran under the strain of the attack. Further north, the BEF fought stubbornly but was forced to give up much of the ground they had gained at such a high cost during their Flander's offensives of 1917. By 12 April the German

LEFT: GENERAL OSKAR VON HUTIER, WHO DEVELOPED AND CODIFIED THE NEW STORMTROOP TACTICS.

offensive reached to within 8km (5 miles) of Hazebrouck, causing Haig great misgivings. Realising the danger of the situation, he issued an emotional appeal to his troops to stand firm:

> Every position must be held to the last man: there must be no retirement. With our backs to the wall, and believing in the justice of our cause, each one of us must fight on to the end. The safety of our homes and the freedom of mankind alike depend on the conduct of each one of us at this critical moment.

ABOVE: A GERMAN FIELD GUN PREPARES FOR ACTION DURING THE GERMAN ADVANCE IN FRANCE.

RIGHT: GERMAN INFANTRY MASS IN A NEWLY DUG TRENCH FOR AN ATTACK AGAINST BRITISH LINES DURING 1918.

The Allied command change helped to save the day. After some delay, Foch decided to send French reinforcements to the scene of the crisis. The BEF, aided by its allies, now stood firm, and by 29 April, Ludendorff was forced to abandon his offensive. Like Operation Michael, the Lys offensive had failed to achieve any strategic gain, and had only formed a vulnerable salient into Allied lines, at the cost of over 100,000 German casualties.

Ludendorff now planned two co-ordinated offensives. He decided to strike French lines near the Chemin des Dames Ridge, locking the French into place. Then the Germans would once again strike in Flanders against the British. On 27 May some 41 German divisions struck lightly held French defensive lines on the ridge, and the attack came as a total surprise to the Allies. In addition, the French commander in the area, General Duchene, like Gough before him had failed to ready his defences accordingly. By the end of the first day of the offensive, German forces had retaken the ridge and had advanced nearly 21km (13 miles), creating a gap nearly 40km (25 miles) wide in the French line. The great success convinced Ludendorff to eschew an attack in Flanders to concentrate his resources on a continued drive toward Paris. For the next three days, the Germans made astonishing gains, even reaching the Marne River for the first time since 1914, only 88km (55 miles) from the French capital.

RIGHT: GERMAN MACHINE GUNNERS, WHO HAVE BROKEN THEIR WEAPON DOWN, RACE THROUGH A CAPTURED TRENCH TRYING TO KEEP THE SPEED OF THE GERMAN ADVANCE ALIVE.

BELOW: A SMALL GROUP OF GERMAN STORMTROOPS DASH ACROSS NO-MAN'S-LAND DURING THE OPERATION MICHAEL OFFENSIVE.

The attack would go no further. Once again, logistic difficulties set in and the unified Allied command rushed reinforcements to the scene. The Germans had created yet another vulnerable salient – 56km (35 miles) deep but only 32km (20 miles) wide – into the Allied lines without achieving any strategic goals. Allied forces quickly struck at the vulnerable German flanks. One such Allied counter-attack took place on 6 June at Belleau Wood. Here, American marines launched six successive assaults against superior German forces but captured the tactically important objective. This battle, along with actions at Cantigny and Chateau-Thierry, signalled impending doom for the German war effort. The great gamble was failing; the Americans were arriving in France before the Germans had achieved victory on the Western Front.

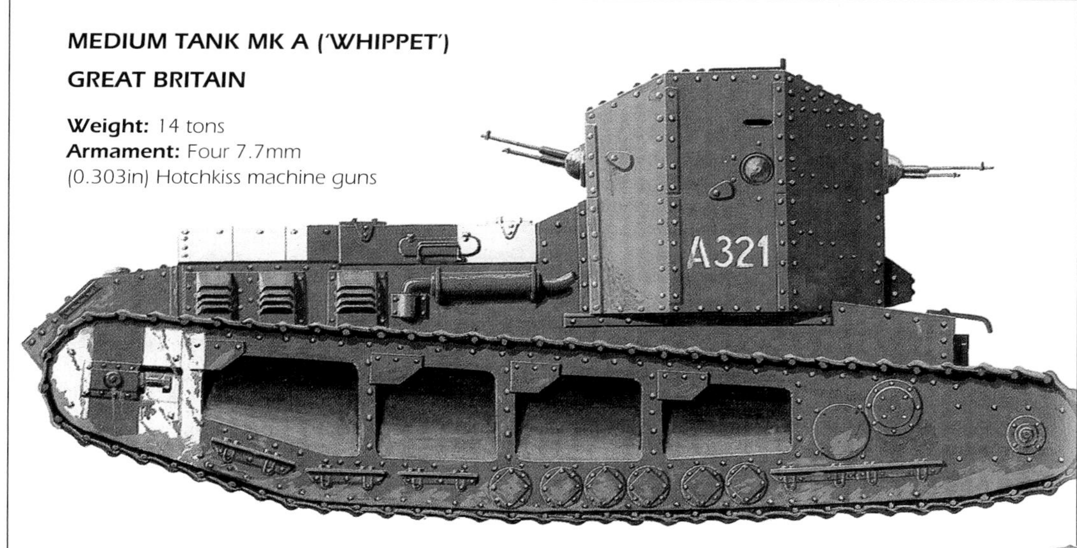

MEDIUM TANK MK A ('WHIPPET')
GREAT BRITAIN

Weight: 14 tons
Armament: Four 7.7mm (0.303in) Hotchkiss machine guns

Below: A British private from the Tank Corps in 1918. The chain mail face mask was to protect the wearer against splinters from enemy machine gun fire.

THE INITIATIVE PASSES TO THE ALLIES

After launching a fourth, ineffective offensive near Montdidier, Ludendorff ceased offensive operations for nearly one month to lay plans for one last, great effort to win the war. It was, however, too late. German losses in the previous offensives had been devastating, totalling nearly 700,000 casualties. Also, Germany's ability to supply its forces was on the wane due to the continuing effectiveness of the British blockade. Finally – and of greatest importance – the Americans were arriving in France in increasing numbers. In May and June alone, over 500,000 American 'doughboys' had arrived on the shores of France, commanded by General John 'Black Jack' Pershing. America and its almost unlimited resources had tipped the manpower balance irrevocably against embattled Germany. It was now the Allies who would attempt to use their superiority to gain victory.

On 15 July the Germans launched their last great offensive of the war in the Second Battle of the Marne. Some 52 German divisions moved forward under a protective barrage. The Allies had learned their lessons; active air reconnaissance had discovered the German's intentions. Effective and determined defenders blunted the German advance, causing considerable loss. Few gains were made and Ludendorff had, in fact, played into the hands of Foch. The Supreme Allied Commander had been planning an offensive of his own aimed at the vulnerable flanks of the Marne salient and the German advance, therefore this only took them further into a trap. While the Germans moved forward, on 18 July Allied units, spearheaded by Americans, struck the German's flanks. Supported by 350 tanks, the Allies advanced over 8km (5 miles) on the first day, threatening to envelop the Germans within the salient. Ludendorff quickly realised the danger of the situation and ordered his forces to withdraw. By 4 August, the entire Marne salient had ceased to exist, as had German hopes for victory in the war.

It was obvious in the Amiens offensive that Rawlinson, who had commanded British forces at the Somme, had learned from his mistakes. In previous battles, the British had been too reliant upon artillery to win the day; this was not the case in 1918.

THE ALLIES STRIKE EAST

The British planned to keep the pressure on the Germans by launching an offensive near Amiens. The attack fell to Rawlinson and his 27 divisions. It was obvious in the Amiens offensive that Rawlinson, who had commanded British forces at the Somme, had learned from his mistakes. In previous battles, the British had been too reliant upon artillery to win the day; this was not the case in 1918. Haig and his commanders planned the coming battles using unprecedented levels of all-arms co-ordination. The new plan called on infantry to use infiltration tactics. Where the Germans had been elitist and trained only a small proportion of their army in infiltration, all British infantry received such training. The role of the artillery too had changed. At the Somme, the artillery had to do it all. In 1918 artillery was much more effective, and was called upon to do less. It no longer had to defeat the enemy, only force him to keep his head down until the newly powerful infantry arrived at his trenches. The British also made use of massed tank formations to aid in breaching the enemy trench systems and the destruction of bunkers and machine-gun nests. Finally, air supremacy allowed the British to use aerial communications and interdiction raids to augment the offensive.

In preparation for the attack, the British had employed false radio traffic to deceive the Germans. In addition, British artillery did not fire ranging rounds prior to the battle; unlike the Somme, there was no preliminary bombardment to warn the Germans of the coming cataclysm. Finally, while the British amassed their tank forces, aeroplanes swooped over the German lines to cover the tanks' engine noise.

The secrecy had worked and the Germans were caught unaware when, on 8 August, the British infantry rushed forward under cover of a massive barrage accompanied by 400

GENERAL JOHN 'BLACK JACK' PERSHING

GENERAL PERSHING

John 'Black Jack' Pershing saw service in the campaign in Cuba in 1898. As America lurched toward war in 1917, he was one of the few officers in the US Army to lead forces in combat, having led the chase for the Mexican bandit Pancho Villa during the previous year. Chosen by Wilson to command the American Expeditionary Force, the dour, strict Pershing made his way to France to view the front lines. He came home with the realisation that the United States had to train and equip an army of millions to have an effect on the European war. After overseeing the massive build-up, Pershing then went with his forces to France. He caused friction among the Allies by not allowing the American forces to be amalgamated with those of the British and French, standing firm in his desire to see an independent American force operating on its own section of the Western Front. When the Germans launched their final offensives and threatened the Allied lines in France, however, he relented. Understanding the dire situation, he offered his forces to the Allied Supreme Commander, Ferdinand Foch, by saying, 'Everything that we have is at your disposal to use as you like - we are here to be killed.' This infusion of manpower was instrumental in stemming the German tide. Eventually Pershing got his sector of the front and launched his most notable attack at the Meuse-Argonne. Here he failed his men, for he believed that he had little to learn from the experience of the British and French in their four years of fighting. As a result, the American offensive used outdated tactics and was very costly, even though, in the end, Pershing led the force that tipped the balance in Europe, and contributed greatly to the Allied victory in World War I.

LEFT:
THE GERMANS, NOT REALISING THE VALUE OF TANK WARFARE, PRODUCED VERY FEW OF THEIR OWN TANKS. HERE THE GERMANS HAVE REPAINTED CAPTURED BRITISH TANKS TO USE THEM IN BATTLE.

BELOW:
A SCENE OF NEW ALLIED CO-OPERATION – BRITISH AND FRENCH SOLDIERS AT REST IN FRANCE PLAY CARDS AFTER THE CRISIS ON THE WESTERN FRONT HAD PASSED IN SPRING 1918.

tanks. The swift blow pinned the Germans in place as the infantry found and exploited weakpoints to advance to depth. The slow-moving tanks created havoc, while artillery and air strikes silenced German artillery and took a heavy toll on German reinforcements moving forward to the front lines. The British had launched a well-coordinated whirlwind of battle and the Germans broke. By 12 August the British had advanced over 24km (15 miles) and had inflicted terrible casualties upon the German defenders. In a development of the greatest importance, the Germans suffered significantly higher numbers of casualties than the British. Such a result is astounding in a war in which the defenders possessed all the advantages. Ludendorff himself referred to 8 August as 'the black day of the German Army'.

Despite this, within three days the attack had bogged down, succumbing to the realities of combat in World War I. Unlike Ludendorff, who had chosen to continue attacking in the same area once hope for

ABOVE: BRITISH PRISONERS, SOME LOOKING HAPPY TO HAVE LEFT THE FIGHTING.

Blaming impending German defeat on 'agitators' and a breakdown of civilian morale rather than on his own misguided military efforts, Ludendorff warned the Kaiser that Germany could no longer win the war and offered his resignation.

strategic victory had passed, Haig chose to halt his offensive over the strenuous objections of Foch. The battle had reached its logical conclusion, and there would be no clear breakthrough. But Haig had a new plan in mind. On the German side of the front, Ludendorff saw the end at hand. Blaming impending German defeat on 'agitators' and a breakdown of civilian morale rather than on his own misguided military efforts, Ludendorff warned the Kaiser that Germany could no longer win the war and offered his resignation. The Kaiser refused.

Not quite one week later, on 18 August, the British renewed their offensive to the north of Amiens, repeating their earlier performance. German reinforcements from Amiens were rushed north to face it. When they arrived in force, Haig ended the assault, and the French under Petain attacked further south, forcing the Germans to react yet again. The Allies had struck upon a war-winning strategy to go with their new tactics. A breakthrough was not possible due to German speed in reinforcement. However, new methods made it possible to rip away great chunks of the German lines before they could react. Attacks up and down the line kept the Germans guessing. The Allies were not fighting battles for their own sake any longer. One battle logically led to, and helped prepare the way for, another. The beginning of an unbroken string of Allied victories, usually referred to as the 100 days, forced the Germans to retire to the Hindenburg Line for protection. Here they hoped to ride out the winter – but only a miracle could save them.

ALLIED VICTORY IN THE MIDDLE EAST

General Allenby, commander of British forces in the Middle East, had planned to launch an offensive designed to capture Damascus shortly after the fall of Jerusalem. However, the German offensives on the Western Front had intervened, robbing him of troops. It was September 1918 before Allenby and his 69,000 troops and the Arabs under Faisal and T.E. Lawrence were ready to launch a co-ordinated action. The Turks in the area were rather dispirited and numbered only 44,000, under the command of the German General Liman von Sanders. Allenby planned to assault the Turkish defensive lines near Jaffa while the Arabs were to capture the important rail centre of Derra, disrupting Turkish efforts either to resupply or retreat.

The offensive, known as the Battle of Megiddo, was launched on 19 September, heralded by an intense artillery barrage. British forces attacked along a weak section of the Turkish front and caught their foes by surprise. Within a few hours the demoralised Turkish Eighth Army saw its front broken, and British cavalry poured through the resulting gap. In

BELOW: KAISER WILHELM II, WHO HAD LONG SINCE LOST CONTROL OVER GERMANY'S WAR EFFORT, AWARDS IRON CROSSES DURING A VISIT TO THE FRONT.

the greatest cavalry action of the war, the Desert Mounted Corps wheeled through and behind the Turkish lines, covering 112km (70 miles) in 36 hours. This bold manoeuvre succeeded in cutting off any Turkish avenue of retreat to the north, allowing escape only to the east where British and Arab forces slowly cut the Turks to ribbons. The Battle of Megiddo was one of the greatest single victories of the war. The Turkish Army in the Middle East was destroyed as a fighting force, losing some 75,000 prisoners to the British, who suffered only 5500 casualties of their own. There was now nothing to stop Allenby from advancing on Damascus. The victorious British forces, however, did not stop there and

BELOW: GERMAN MACHINE GUNNERS BREAK DOWN THEIR WEAPON AND MAKE A HURRIED RETREAT AS FRENCH ARTILLERY SHELLS EXPLODE NEARBY.

made their way to Allepo 320km (200 miles) further north by 26 October. The defeat had left Turkey almost defenceless in the Middle East and therefore hastened its downfall. However, mistrust had already developed between the British and their Arab allies; how would the spoils of Turkish defeat be divided?

In Mesopotamia, British forces also pressed forward to victory. Having already captured Baghdad in 1917, the British commander, Sir William Marshall, now chose to advance on the oilfields of Mosul. It was hoped to eliminate all Turkish influence over the sensitive area before the expected peace settlement. An Anglo-Indian force left Baghdad

LEFT:
BRITISH SOLDIERS OF THE 62ND DIVISION TAKE THE OFFENSIVE IN GROUND UNMARRED BY SHELLFIRE IN THE BOIS DE RHEIMS.

BELOW:
A GERMAN STORMTROOPER FROM OPERATION MICHAEL IN SPRING 1918.

on 23 October and covered 124km (77 miles) in only 39 hours, against only token Turkish resistance. Only at Sharqat, nearly 97km (60 miles) further north, did the Turkish force under General Ismael Hakki stand and fight. Even then, the Turks realised that the war was over and that resistance at the eleventh hour was futile. After one day of fighting, Hakki and his force surrendered, bringing the war in Mesopotamia to an end. The important oilfields were now securely in British hands.

LAST FIGHTING IN THE BALKANS

In the Balkans, disaster loomed for the Central Powers. Although they had done little throughout the war, the Allies had nearly 500,000 men based in Salonika. After the failure of the German advances on the Western Front, the men in the 'greatest Allied internment camp' suddenly swung into action. On 14 September 1918 French, British and Serbian forces forged into a mountainous area of Macedonia, attacking a force of dispirited Bulgarians. The tiny nation of Bulgaria had already suffered 250,000 casualties in the conflict and was ready for peace. Once again, defenders saw little cause to resist for a doomed cause, and the Allies quickly broke through. By 19 September the Bulgarian force had been cut in two and routed. On 26 September Bulgaria sued for peace, becoming the first of the Central Powers to quit the war. In the terms of the peace, Bulgaria agreed to offer the Allied force a free hand to pass through its territory to attack Turkey.

After having suffered bitter defeats in the Middle East and Mesopotamia, the Turks now faced an Allied force driving on Constantinople. A rising tide of discontent in Turkey swept the existing 'Young Turk' government from power, and the new government sued for peace. On 30 October, British officials – since Britain had carried the main burden in the war with Turkey – signed a peace agreement with the Turks on board the battleship *Agamemnon*.

The victory over Bulgaria also led to an Allied invasion of Serbia. Few Austrian and German troops remained in the area to oppose an Allied advance up the Vardar River, thus weakened Austria now faced yet another threat. The political situation in Austria had been worsening since the death of Emperor Franz Joseph in the winter of 1916. His successor, Emperor Charles, firmly believed that his embattled nation had to seek a negotiated peace to survive the conflict intact. He had sent out peace feelers to the Allies as early as spring 1917, but this had been discovered by the Germans. Embarrassed and under great pressure from his erstwhile ally, Charles agreed to attempt a final offensive against the Italians in June 1918. Dispirited and low on supplies of every kind, the Austrian offensive gained but little ground at the cost of 140,000 casualties.

The most recent setback proved to be too much for Austria. Rationing across the nation was strict and wartime dissent was on the rise. Matters were so bad that Austria made a final appeal for a separate peace with the Allies on 14 September 1918. It was, however, too late. The many nationalities within the Austrian Empire made bids for independence, ripping Austria apart from within. Czechs, Slovaks, Magyars, and Slavs all demanded their freedom. In addition the Allies, in response to the Austrian appeal for peace, supported the claims of the various nationalities to self-rule. Austria, it seems, would have to die to survive.

Making matters worse for Austria, Italian forces chose this very time to launch a punishing attack along the Piave River. General Diaz, the Italian commander, had 57 divisions

BELOW:
THE TABLES HAVE TURNED – SOME OF THE GERMAN PRISONERS TAKEN IN THE BATTLE OF AMIENS ARE MARCHED TO THE REAR BY THEIR BRITISH CAPTORS.

The Italians had succeeded in blowing a gap into the Austrian lines. At this point the Austrian Army ceased to function as a coherent fighting force, and fell into a rout. Austrian soldiers deserted and surrendered in droves.

LEFT: British gunners wearing protective gas masks in action in Macedonia.

BELOW: The face of defeat – realising that further resistance was futile these Turkish soldiers surrender to British forces in Mesopotamia.

at his disposal and a wealth of artillery support. The Austrians, already reeling, countered with 52 understrength, poorly supplied and dispirited divisions. The first Italian attack fell on the Trentino front on 23 October and served as a diversion. The main blow fell on 25 October against initially strong Austrian resistance. However, by 29 October the Italians had succeeded in blowing a gap into the Austrian lines near the village of Vittorio Veneto. At this point the Austrian Army ceased to function as a coherent fighting force, and fell into a rout. Austrian soldiers deserted and surrendered in droves. Italian forces advanced as far as the Tagliamento where, on 2 November, they received an Austrian truce. The victory at the Battle of Vittorio Veneto had been complete – the Italian forces had lost 38,000 casualties – but had captured an unbelievable 300,000 Austrian prisoners.

The collapse of the Italian front, along with the Allied advance through Serbia, spelled the end for the Hapsburg Empire. On 28 October both Czechoslovakia and Yugoslavia proclaimed their independence. Poland and Hungary also quit the tottering empire. In Vienna itself, a provisional assembly led by Karl Renner proclaimed an Austrian Republic. Similar events ended the rule of the Hapsburgs in Budapest. On 3 November the Austrian High

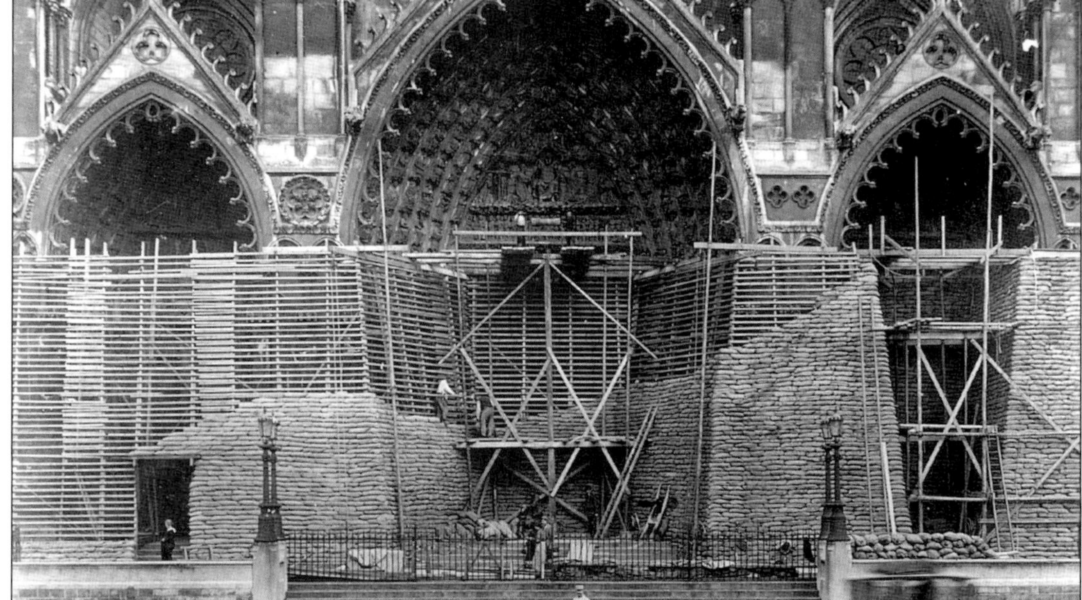

RIGHT:
NOTRE DAME IN PARIS WAS PROTECTED BY A LAYER OF SANDBAGS AFTER THE PARIS GUN BEGAN TO SHELL THE CITY IN 1918.

BELOW:
EMPEROR CHARLES OF AUSTRIA, THE LAST OF THE HAPSBURG EMPERORS, OBSERVES THE PROGRESS OF AUSTRIAN FORCES ON THE ISONZO FRONT DURING THE WAR.

Command agreed to the terms of an overall armistice, but the empire that they purported to represent had been wiped away. Emperor Charles was finally forced into exile in Switzerland, and the multi-national empire of Austria was no more, having shattered into its component parts. The war that Austria had started in an effort to seize Serbia had destroyed both the Austrian Empire and the long-lived Hapsburg dynasty.

AMERICAN OFFENSIVES

By September Pershing had received what he had always wanted: an American sector of the front. The American First Army began planning for its first attack. Pershing proposed to reduce the German salient around Saint Mihiel. On the other side of the lines, Ludendorff realised that the Saint Mihiel salient was very vulnerable and divined that the fresh American Expeditionary Force would launch an offensive there. As a result, on 8 September he ordered his troops to withdraw. The complicated operation was not yet complete when, on 12 September, 16 American divisions struck on both flanks of the salient. Although some German formations resisted the advance, many others attempted to quit the salient with all due speed. By 16 September it had ceased to exist, and the American had scored a remarkable victory. In the biggest American operation since the Civil War, the Saint Mihiel offensive had netted some 15,000 German prisoners at the cost of only 7000 US casualties. To Pershing it seemed that attacks in World War I were not so difficult. In the next American offensive, however, the Germans chose to stand and fight, altering Pershing's opinion.

With the Germans now occupying very strong defensive positions up and down the line, Foch chose to launch a series of four co-ordinated offensives designed to overthrow them. The Americans, along with the French, were to attack the Germans in the area of the Meuse River near the Argonne Forest. It was hoped that an American advance to Sedan, nearly 48km (30 miles) away, would unhinge the German defensive line further north. Pershing agreed to the plan and through a monumental effort, shifted American forces north from Saint Mihiel. This quick move meant that US forces had little time to prepare for the new offensive.

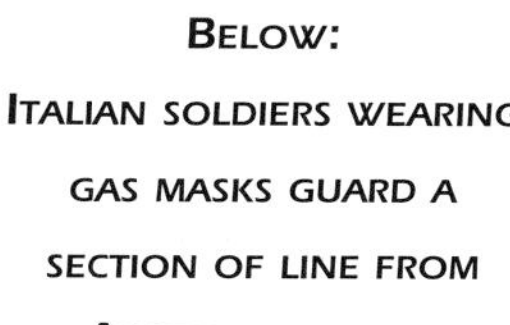

BELOW: ITALIAN SOLDIERS WEARING GAS MASKS GUARD A SECTION OF LINE FROM AUSTRIAN ATTACK.

US and French forces moved forward on 26 September, supported by 189 tanks. In the attack, the Americans exhibited a lack of subtlety. Not having the wartime experience of their Alliance partners, their forces still advanced in waves into the still-effective German 'storm of steel'. Despite considerable gains on the first two days of the Meuse-Argonne offensive, the cost to the Americans was very high. In addition, unlike Saint Mihiel, the Germans chose to stand and fight, recognising the importance of the area, and brought up reinforcements to face them. As a result, using their superiority in numbers, US forces ground slowly forward against determined German resistance in a battle rather reminiscent of the Somme.

In early October, after clearing the Argonne Forest, the Americans attempted to make good several logistic problems. The battle had died down somewhat, so after taking over more line and creating an American Second Army, they renewed their attack on 14 October. It was met with stiff resistance and made few gains. Some within the Allied ranks questioned Pershing's command abilities when they noted the slow pace of the American advance. However, the US forces renewed their assault once again on 1 November,

RACE AND THE US ARMY

Many of America's black citizens rushed to join the armed forces at the outbreak of war in 1917, eager to serve their country. Many hoped that military service would make the white population see them more as equals, but this was not to be the case. Although the United States Army chose to place black soldiers in segregated units with white officers, the sight of armed black men was too much for some supporters of separation of the races. In August 1917, an all-black unit stationed near Houston, Texas, roundly ignored the city's strict race laws. Local whites were horrified to see black soldiers riding on the streetcars with them and sitting down with them in theatres. On 23 August the Houston police chose to make an example of one of the black soldiers, imprisoning and beating him. Incensed at their comrade's treatment, the black soldiers fought back and a massive gun battle ensued, killing two soldiers and 17 townspeople. The US Army chose to treat the incident as a mutiny, immediately disarming the entire unit and court-martialling more than 100 soldiers. They hanged 13 of the accused before they even had a chance to appeal. During the unrest, several black leaders attempted to intercede with President Woodrow Wilson. One black university professor wrote, 'The Negro, Mr President, in this emergency, will stand by you and the nation. Will you and the nation stand by the Negro?' The President never replied.

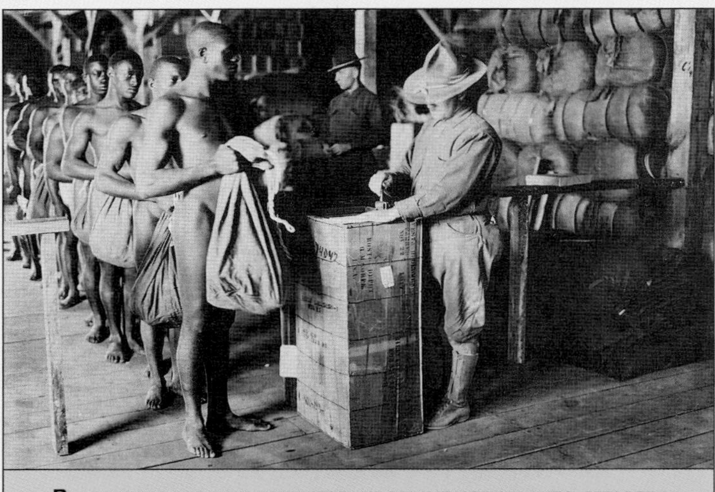

BLACK SOLDIERS ARE INSPECTED UPON INDUCTION INTO SERVICE.

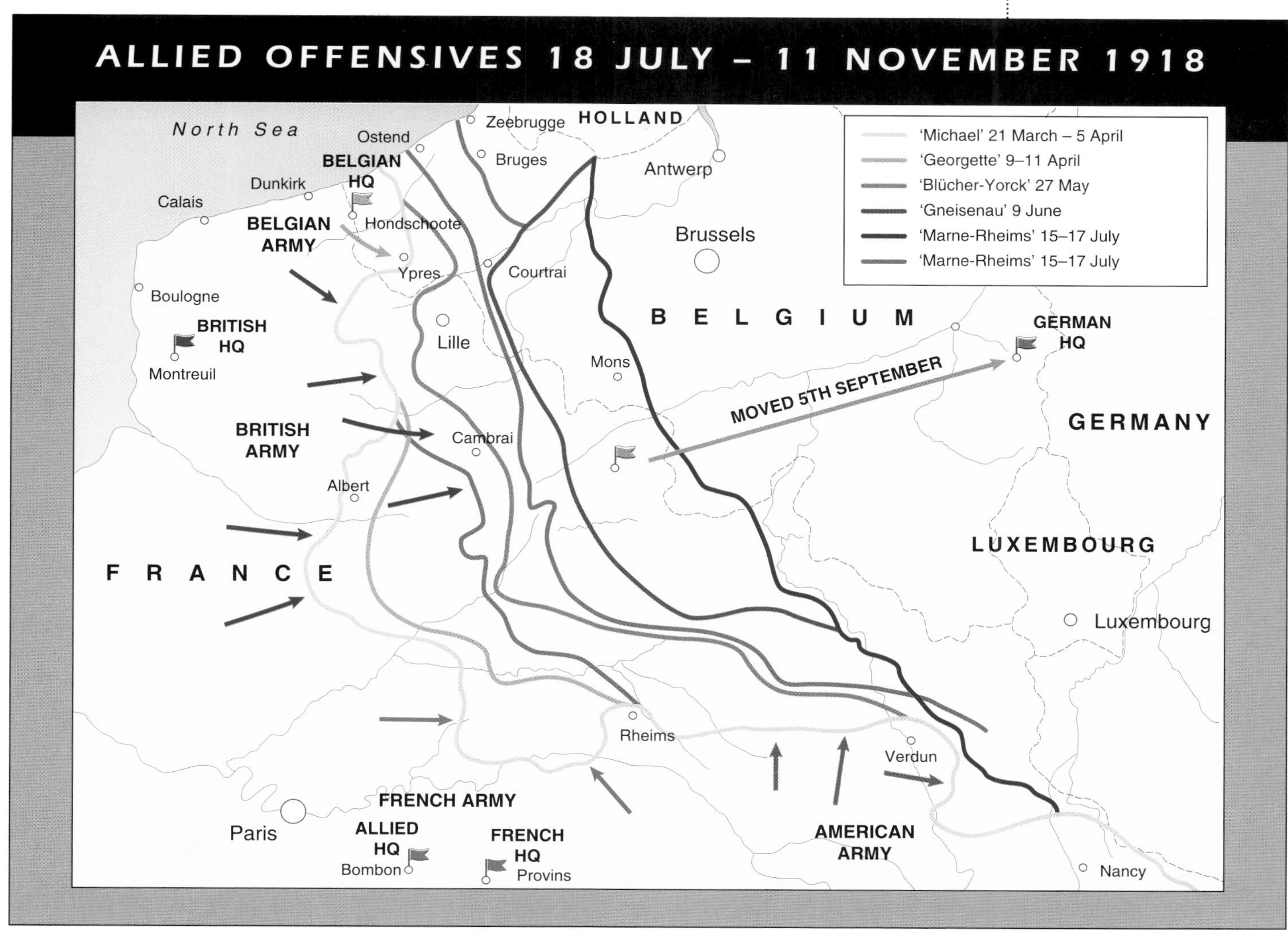

and this time results were quite different. The Germans, sensing that the end was at hand, lessened their resistance, and the Americans made great gains. By 6 November US forces stood outside their goal of Sedan, but American General Hunter Liggett allowed the French to liberate the famous city.

Initially, their advance during the Meuse-Argonne offensive had been disappointing, but the tenacity and difficult on-the-job training of the US forces had resulted in a resounding victory. Even so, the cost of their initially misguided tactics was high, resulting in 117,000 US casualties.

FAR LEFT: AMERICAN TROOPS ADVANCE WITH FRENCH-BUILT RENAULT TANKS IN SEPTEMBER 1918.

FINAL ATTACKS

Further north, British forces, who themselves had lost some 600,000 casualties since March, assaulted the vaunted Hindenburg Line. Making matters worse, on the front of the British attacks lurked two formidable obstacles – the Canal du Nord and the St Quentin Canal – which the Germans had incorporated into their defensive system. On 27 September, using a punishing artillery barrage for cover, the forces of General Henry Horne's British First Army struck the Canal du Nord. With the Canadian Corps leading

On 4 October Rawlinson did the seemingly impossible and broke through the entire Hindenburg Line. In many ways, this great British victory sealed the fate of the Germans. No longer could they hope to hold out along a set defensive line for the winter.

the way, the First Army forced the barrier and made astounding gains, breaking into the Hindenburg Line proper. Further south, the British Fourth Army under Rawlinson met with even greater success. Using rafts and portable bridges, some soldiers even swimming with life vests, British forces succeeded in crossing the St Quentin Canal. Following this surprising victory, the BEF pressed forward and carried the first two lines of the Hindenburg Line.

On 4 October Rawlinson did the seemingly impossible and broke through the entire Hindenburg Line. In many ways, this great British victory sealed the fate of the Germans. No longer could they hope to hold out along a set defensive line for the winter. New tactics and a co-ordinated strategy had been too much for the German Army to bear, and along the entire front, the Germans were obliged to give ground. For the remainder of the war, Allied armies rolled forward remorselessly on all fronts. Sometimes the fighting was heavy and the Allied advance slowed to a crawl, but the demoralised Germans were being soundly and completely defeated in the field. As the defeat grew ever worse, the morale of the German people and even the German High Command broke.

THE COLLAPSE OF GERMANY

Ever since 8 August, the so-called 'black day of the German army', Ludendorff had warned that Germany could no longer win the war and should sue for peace. However, no tangible steps had been taken by Germany toward peace until late September, after all was lost. Several factors added to the German rush towards peace. Firstly, the German population, tired, hungry and dispirited, plainly desired peace and an overhaul of the German governmental system leading to a greater level of democracy. It became clear to many,

BELOW: GERMAN FORCES WATCH WITH SOME TREPIDATION AS THEIR COMRADES COUNTER-ATTACK THE ALLIES IN LATE 1918.

including both Hindenburg and Ludendorff, that the population could follow Russia into revolution unless steps were taken towards political reform and ending the war. The military machine in Germany also hoped that their nation might receive rather lenient treatment at peace talks. In January 1918 President Woodrow Wilson, much to the chagrin of other Allied leaders, publicly declared his unselfish set of war aims: the famous Fourteen Points. Wilson did not demand harsh retribution in his peace plan; on the contrary, he called for ideals such as self-determination and an end to secret treaties. On 3 October the Germans sent a 'Peace Note' to Wilson, offering to end the war based on his Fourteen Points. Ludendorff even dared hope that such a peace might allow Germany to retain Alsace-Lorraine. He was quite mistaken.

ABOVE: GERMAN DEFENDERS ARMED WITH HAND GRENADES AND WEARING STEEL BODY ARMOUR MAN A FORWARD TRENCH ON THE WESTERN FRONT IN LATE 1918.

As the Allied armies won victory after victory, and the other members of the Central Powers all quit the war, Allied political leadership considered the German offer of peace. Understandably both Clemenceau, the Premier of France, and David Lloyd George wanted more out of a peace agreement with Germany. Their nations had been fighting and suffering for nearly five years; a peace agreement that went back to the status quo of 1914 was simply unacceptable. Wilson's reply to Germany's peace note, then, was rather equivocal and called for a German withdrawal from France and constitutional reform of the German Government. Other peace notes flashed back and forth, but Ludendorff considered them all to be demands for unconditional surrender and asked his army to resist to the end. The Kaiser and others thought Ludendorff's bravado went too far; Germany faced utter destruction if she chose to resist much longer.

On 26 October the Kaiser accepted Ludendorff's resignation. On that same day Germany passed a law making the Chancellor responsible to the Reichstag, transforming

Above: Men of the 45th Australian Battalion snipe at retreating Germans near Bellenglise, France, on 18 September 1918.

Germany into a constitutional monarchy along the lines of Great Britain. Even so, the change had come too late. In Kiel, the German High Seas Fleet considered going to sea to face the British in one last suicidal attempt to regain their honour. The sailors of the fleet, whose morale had been plummeting since Jutland in 1916, decided against wasting their lives in a futile display of bravery. Mutiny overtook many of them and spread into the surrounding towns. Sailors and workers began to form revolutionary councils along the lines of the soviets which had brought down Russia, and revolution spread like wildfire among the hungry, disheartened and desperate German populous. Workers in several cities, including Cologne, were joined by disgruntled soldiers. By 7 November the revolution had even spread to distant Munich where an uprising, led by the socialist Kurt Eisner, caused the downfall of the Bavarian monarchy. A mere two days later the unthinkable had happened: revolution had broken out in Berlin.

On 4 November the Allies sent their terms for an armistice to Germany. Considered quite harsh by the Germans, they called for immediate German withdrawal from

LEFT: THE CROSSING OF THE ST QUENTIN CANAL BY MEN OF THE 46TH DIVISION ON 29 SEPTEMBER 1918. BY DUSK THAT DAY THEY HAD CAPTURED ANOTHER 5KM (3 MILES) OF TERRITORY.

Allied territory and an Allied occupation of the Rhineland. In addition, the Allies demanded the surrender of the German fleet and a repudiation of the Treaty of Brest-Litovsk with Russia. Finally, the Allies demanded German compensation for damages to Allied civilian properties. On 8 November a German delegation, led by Matthias Erzberger, arrived at Allied headquarters in Compiègne where they hoped to bargain over the coming peace agreement. Foch informed the Germans that there was no room for negotiations: they could accept the Allied offer, or continue to fight.

In Germany itself events had proceeded at a breakneck pace. The growing revolution threatened to overtake the army and lead Germany down a road to communism. The only way to stave off such an event seemed to be by giving in to most of the revolutionary demands and totally democratising the government. In addition, the war would have to be concluded very quickly so that the front-line army, still mainly loyal, could return home to help destroy the more radical aspects of the revolution. On 9 November the socialists, partly in an effort to head off a further communist bid for power, proclaimed the German republic on the steps of the Reichstag in Berlin to a huge, revolutionary audience. The socialist Friedrich Ebert became the new Chancellor. Later that evening, realising that the Allies would never negotiate with the Kaiser, Hindenburg was able to convince Wilhelm II that he should abdicate for the good of Germany. The Kaiser reluctantly agreed and the next morning left for exile in the Netherlands. Thus the Hohenzollerns, along with the Romanovs and the Hapsburgs, became casualties of the war.

Realising that the Allies would never negotiate with the Kaiser, Hindenburg was able to convince William II that he should abdicate for the good of Germany. Thus the Hohenzollerns, along with the Romanovs and the Hapsburgs, became casualties of the war.

With Germany disintegrating more each day, the new Ebert government gave its consent to the Allied armistice terms. At 0500 hours on 11 November the two delegations met at Compiègne and signed the fateful agreement. It stipulated that a ceasefire would take place at 1100 hours that same day: the eleventh hour of the eleventh day of the eleventh month 1918. At that exact moment, the guns of the Western Front fell silent in a 'stillness heard around the world'.

To many on the Western Front in November 1918 the event was difficult to believe and to understand. After nearly five years of fighting, peace seemed surreal to

It suddenly seemed strangely quiet and still – almost uncomfortable. It took me a moment to realise that the guns whose roar and concussion had kept the operating room shivering like a leaf in the wind almost without interruption for two months had ceased firing forever.

combatants on both sides of 'No-man's-land'. One corpsman remembers the end of the fighting:

> About nine o'clock we got the rumour that Germany had signed, hostilities to cease at eleven o'clock. But meanwhile the barrage was getting fiercer. We hardly believed the news ... I was half-way through [a postoperative report] when it suddenly seemed strangely quiet and still – almost uncomfortable. It took me a moment to realise that the guns whose roar and concussion had kept the operating room shivering like a leaf in the wind almost without interruption for two months had ceased firing forever.

All along the front lines, German, French, British and American troops came out of their trenches to meet each other. There were handshakes all around and the exchange of souvenirs, pictures and addresses. Although some soldiers actively hated their enemy, most

RIGHT: A GATHERING OF GERMAN CITIZENS DEMANDING CHANGE DURING THE NOVEMBER REVOLUTION IN GERMANY IN 1918.

ABOVE: PEACE COMES TO THE TRENCHES – BRITISH TROOPS CELEBRATE ON 11 NOVEMBER 1918 AS AN OFFICER READS THE OFFICIAL ANNOUNCEMENT OF THE ARMISTICE.

respected him as a worthy adversary who had suffered through a common hell. Victors and vanquished alike met as friends on that day.

> Then a quite startling thing occurred. The skyline of the crest ahead of them grew suddenly populous with dancing soldiers and down the slope, all the way to the barbed wire, straight for the Americans, came the German troops. They came with outstretched hands, ear-to-ear grins and souvenirs to swap for cigarettes ... They came to tell how glad they were [that] the fight had stopped, how glad they were [that] the Kaiser had departed for parts unknown, how fine it was to know that they would have a republic at last in Germany.

From Paris to London and Washington, wild, spontaneous celebrations broke out in the streets when news came of the armistice. Soldiers were greeted with great joy as saviours of the world. However, in many capitals from Berlin to St Petersburg, there was no joy, only continuing revolution and hardship. The war had come to an end, and while the victors celebrated with an enthusiasm not seen since 1914, it became apparent to many that there was much left to be accomplished before the world would truly be at peace.

Chapter 11

Reparation

Soldiers and civilians celebrate victory in Birmingham, England, after the announcement of the Armistice. Though the war was now over, much work remained to be done to craft a lasting peace for Europe.

Five foot ten of a beautiful young Englishman under French soil. Never a joke, never a look, never a word more to add to my store of memories. The book is shut up for ever and as the years pass I shall remember less and less.

THE COST OF WAR

People greeted the end of the war with enthusiasm, but it was a joy tempered with sorrow. The first modern, industrial war had ripped Europe asunder and slaughtered nearly an entire generation of the best and brightest. Nearly everyone, it seems, had lost a family member or friend to the fighting, thus Europe grieved in the wake of a calamity of nearly unbelievable proportions. One English woman, mourning the loss of her beloved brother wrote,

> Five foot ten of a beautiful young Englishman under French soil. Never a joke, never a look, never a word more to add to my store of memories. The book is shut up for ever and as the years pass I shall remember less and less, till he becomes a vague personality; a stereotyped photograph.

The aftermath of the killing can still be seen across Europe today. Nearly every English village or French town contains a memorial to the fallen, a memorial that family members still visit and adorn with flowers.

The now peaceful countryside near the sites of major battles also bears stunning witness to the devastation of war. At Verdun, the massive French cemetery surrounds a building known as the Ossuary – or bone yard – a sombre, brooding structure that contains the

BELOW: THE VERDUN MEMORIAL – RECOGNISING THE BRAVERY OF THOSE WHO FOUGHT TO DEFEND THE STRICKEN CITY IN THE WAR.

OVERVIEW

Europe had entered the war almost gleefully in 1914, expecting a quick, cathartic struggle that would end in an easy victory. Instead the continent suffered through the first industrial, total war. Mighty, resilient nations were locked in mortal combat for nearly five years. In the end, millions had perished and the economic, political and social fabric of Europe lay in ruins. In the aftermath of the conflict, the wartime Allies faced the daunting task of formulating a peace plan that restructured the chaos that was Europe. The Allies were torn on how severely to punish Germany, and in the end developed a compromise peace. The Treaty of Versailles was stringent enough to humiliate the German people and leave them hungry for revenge; however, it was lenient enough to leave Germany powerful enough to pursue that revenge. It was hoped that a democratic Germany would pursue a path of peace, but the immediate post-war years were ones of turmoil and economic hardship in Germany, leading many to abandon hope for German democracy and turn to more radical political solutions. Toiling in near-anonymity, the leader of the Nazi Party, Adolf Hitler, eventually convinced many Germans that he was the man who could destroy the hated Treaty of Versailles and lead Germany back to greatness. Thus in the Treaty of Versailles were sown the seeds of World War II.

remains of over 100,000 French unknowns who fell in the battle. Near Verdun are road signs that indicate that one is passing through the remnants of a village destroyed in 1916. One can also visit the 'Trench of Bayonets' where rifle barrels protrude from the ground, marking the spot where a regiment was buried where it stood as a trench collapsed. At Ypres one can find the Menin Gate, a memorial to British soldiers who fell in the fighting there and have no known grave. Over 50,000 names are inscribed upon its walls. Every evening, buglers sound the Last Post in a moving ceremony to honour the fallen. At the Somme one finds the Newfoundland Memorial paying mute tribute to the cost of the battle to that small province. The memorial overlooks preserved trenches where the brave men fought and died.

The cemeteries near the battlefields tell their own stories. The American cemeteries are massive, moving places reflecting the American choice to bury all of the fallen together in one place, aiding in a family's efforts to visit their fallen loved one. The gleaming white crosses seem to march off into the distance in eternal formation. German cemeteries are dark, brooding affairs. The crosses are dark brown and the statuary seems to reflect a torture not seen in cemeteries reserved for victors. British cemeteries are altogether different. The British chose to bury men near to where they fell, meaning that many of the cemeteries are quite small. In addition the British chose to make their cemeteries closely resemble an English garden, with roses blooming everywhere as a touching, final reminder of home. British cemeteries also contain a moving individuality, for the families of loved ones were allowed to add a special inscription on each headstone. The grave of V.J. Strudwick, who was only 15 when he died in 1916, reads 'Not gone from memory, nor from love.'

Finally, some of the reminders of war are more sinister, for the massive shelling left its mark. As in all wars, much of the ordinance fired in World War I failed to explode, leaving behind a landscape littered with hazards of all types. As recently as the early 1980s, the Belgian Government had to dispose of over 500 tons of unexploded munitions per year.

The cost of the war in terms of lives, as illustrated by cemeteries and memorials, was staggering. Nearly 15 million people, soldier and civilian alike, perished in the cataclysm. That simple number does not indicate the true level of wartime loss and grief. Each soldier

ALLIED INTERVENTION IN RUSSIA

When Russia left the war in early 1918, the Western Allies were quite concerned that mountains of supplies they had sent them might fall into German hands. In addition, they hoped that the judicial use of force might cause the Bolshevik Revolution in Russia to fail. In April 1918 the British sent troops to Murmansk to protect supplies there. Within a few months, the intervention came also to include the ports of Archangel and Vladivostok with French, Czech, Japanese and American forces joining the fray. The Allies were able to aid counter-revolutionaries under the pretence of protecting supplies until the collapse of Germany in November, when it became increasingly obvious that the Allied forces were in Russia to combat communism. It was in Siberia, at Vladivostok, that the situation became worst. Here the Japanese hoped to seize land from a vulnerable Russia, while US forces hoped to stop them. At many points the US and Japanese forces were at cross purposes, but both gave aid to the counter-revolutionary leader in the area, Admiral Alexander Kolchak. Allied aid notwithstanding, Kolchak and the other so-called 'White Russian' leaders were no match for Bolshevik forces and the communist forces slowly began to triumph in the bitter Russian Civil War. Noting the inevitable end of the conflict, Allied intervention forces had left Murmansk and Archangel by October 1919. In Siberia, matters too had worsened. Kolchak was captured and shot, prompting an American withdrawal in early 1920, although the Japanese force remained until 1922. The Allied intervention in Russia was tiny by the standards of World War I; for example, United States forces suffered only 174 dead. However, the Bolsheviks would long remember the intervention and would become stalwart enemies of the West.

lost represents parents and grandparents stricken by loss. Wives and children were crushed by the death of a husband and father. The lives that were cut short by the war affected hundreds of millions of people across the world, leaving many with a sense of futility and frustration. In addition, nearly 30 million soldiers returned from World War I having been wounded, some seven million of whom were permanently disabled. Although advances in medicine had kept many wounded soldiers alive, medicine often could not repair faces and limbs that had been ripped apart by shrapnel. Thus many veterans, although not considered disabled, lived the remainder of their lives as ghastly reminders of the horror of war. Finally the war resulted in innumerable cases of psychological wounding. The brutality of the trenches and the terror of battle often overwhelmed the minds of combatants, leaving strong men scarred forever. The world now recognises the perils of post-traumatic stress disorder, but the World War I era did not. Brave men were forced to wander through the remainder of their lives in a mental hell which nobody understood but them.

The war resulted in innumerable cases of psychological wounding. The brutality of the trenches and the terror of battle often overwhelmed the minds of combatants, leaving strong men scarred forever.

The nations of the world also paid a steep price for the war in other ways. The monetary price-tag for the conflict was almost unbelievable, totalling over 350 billion dollars, a truly staggering amount, especially in the light of inflation. A historian put this mammoth price into better terms; the cost of World War I 'represented about six and a half times the sum of all the national debt accumulated in the world from the end of the eighteenth century up to the eve of the First World War'. In addition, the inflationary spiral begun by the war did not relent with the coming of peace. European economies lay shattered, having lost their markets to the new economic powerhouses in the world: the United States and Japan. Fighting men from all over Europe returned home to find limited employment opportunities and poor housing in some places, and societal chaos and revolution in others. This economic turmoil contributed greatly to the chaotic nature of the interwar years, threatening to bring down even the nations that had won the war.

THE INFLUENZA PANDEMIC

In March 1918 American troops at Camp Funston, Kansas noted an outbreak of influenza in their midst. These men were transshipped all over the nation and then to the world as America readied hurriedly for war. As a result, the disease, which would become known as 'Spanish influenza' swept across the nation like wildfire. Soon citizens were falling sick in droves, and taking the elementary precaution of wearing gauze masks almost everywhere. When the disease finally reached the crowded battlefields of Europe and the

BELOW: THE PRINCE OF WALES AND 11,000 PILGRIMS ATTEND A SERVICE OF REMEMBRANCE AT THE MENIN GATE IN YPRES IN AUGUST 1928.

RIGHT:
TO THIS DAY REMNANTS OF THE TREMENDOUS CATACLYSM THAT WAS WORLD WAR I ARE REGULARLY FOUND. THESE UNEXPLODED SHELLS AND BARBED WIRE SUPPORTS NEAR THIEPVAL ON THE SOMME BATTLEFIELD WERE FOUND IN 1938 AFTER A BRUSH FIRE.

backwaters of the Third World, it struck with a vengeance never before seen, becoming the world's worst pandemic. The disease felled even more people in Europe than had the famed 'Black Death' during the Middle Ages. However, coming as it did during the climactic end of a mighty war, the influenza pandemic of between 1918 and 1919 is often lost in history.

Worldwide the pandemic killed over 22 million people, and sickened over a billion more, thus affecting nearly one half of the world's population. In European nations where the food ration was the lowest, and thus people had less resistance, the death toll was the worst. Russia suffered over 400,000 fatalities, while Germany lost nearly 300,000 dead. For civilians who had suffered great privations for the war effort, to be struck down by a silent killer as the conflict wound down was devastating. In London when the disease hit, over 18,000 people died in a matter of weeks. One woman remembers the horror:

> Things here are in a terrible state, this new flu as they term it is quite a plague and taking people off as they walk along the streets, in fact the undertakers can't turn the coffins out or bury the people quick enough. There's families of 6 or 7 in one house lying dead, it's really terrible dear and makes one nervous of going out.

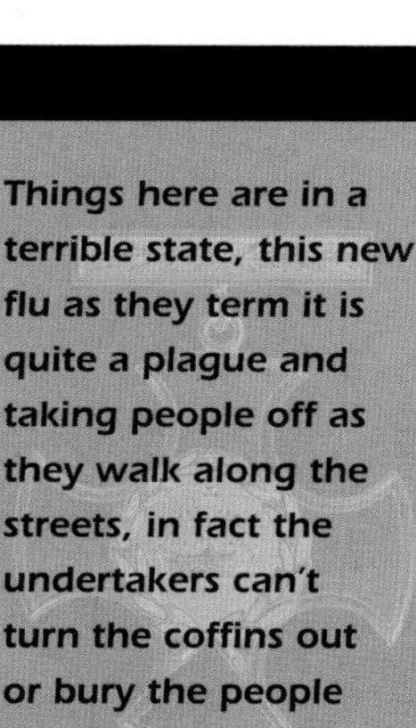

Things here are in a terrible state, this new flu as they term it is quite a plague and taking people off as they walk along the streets, in fact the undertakers can't turn the coffins out or bury the people quick enough.

For soldiers, the disease was even more fearsome. They had always known that their families were safe at home awaiting their return, but now even that solace was taken from them. Also for many, the flu represented the ultimate sad irony; after fighting and surviving war for years, it was disease that was destined to kill them in their hour of victory. A doctor with the BEF was stricken with sorrow and had to watch young, fit soldiers die and remembered, 'enormous ANZACs, the flower of colonial England, were dying like flies, having escaped all the hazards of war'.

THE PARIS PEACE CONFERENCE

In January 1919 representatives of the victorious Allies met in Paris to hammer out a peace treaty for a world shattered by war. Although 27 nations attended the conference, it was notable in part for the nations excluded from the ongoing negotiations. The defeated Central Powers, most notably Germany, were not invited. Thus the Allies made ready to dictate peace to the defeated nations of Europe. In addition, Russia was not represented. None of the Allies recognised the legitimacy of the new Bolshevik regime in Russia; indeed, several nations, including Britain and the United States, sent troops to Russia in aid of counter-revolutionary forces. Thus from its inception, the Paris Peace Conference alienated several of the most important nations on the European continent.

The leaders of the conference faced a daunting task: the rebuilding and reshaping of Europe. Not since the Congress of Vienna after the Napoleonic Wars had such a fundamental redrawing of the European map been undertaken. Almost immediately, the conference fell under the sway of three leaders: Wilson of America, Lloyd George of Britain and Clemenceau of France. Initially, Orlando, the Prime Minister of Italy, joined the trio. He was, however, concerned mainly with the land that Italy had been promised along the Dalmatian Cost for entering the conflict. Orlando was shocked to learn that the Allies, led by Wilson, rejected the majority of Italy's territorial claims; Italy settled for far less than it had been promised in 1915, and mattered little in the overall peace negotiations. Thus the wartime Allies of Italy and Russia would join Germany – as the so-called 'Revisionist Powers' – in the belief that the Treaty of Versailles was an unfair, dictated peace. These powers would often join forces to redress the perceived inequities of the Treaty of Versailles during the interwar years.

BELOW: 'FORTY THOUSAND SONS OF THE CITY LOST THEIR LIVES FOR YOU, 1914–1918' – A NAZI MEMORIAL TO WAR DEAD IN HAMBURG, 1935.

Wilson, the head of a nation that had not suffered much during the war and in fact had made several economic gains, could afford to be quite idealistic. He truly believed that the war had been fought to make the world safe for democracy.

ARGUMENT

The 'Big Three' – Wilson, Lloyd George, and Clemenceau – entered into negotiations in Paris with fundamentally different goals which led to constant bickering and inevitable compromise. Wilson, the head of a nation that had not suffered much during the war and in fact had made several economic gains, could afford to be quite idealistic. He truly believed that the war had been fought to make the world safe for democracy. He wanted a peace based on self-determination for nations and a lack of recrimination. A democratised Germany would be punished for its role in starting the war, but only mildly and would, in the end, be welcomed back into the family of nations. Future war would be avoided through collective security after the formation of the League of Nations. Such a body would represent the world's democracies working together to put an end to war.

The French, led by Clemenceau, rejected the idea of a lenient peace. France had suffered greatly in the war. Invading German forces had brought ruination to a great area of the country. In a more fundamental sense, France had suffered through the devastating loss of nearly an entire generation of its young men, and the war had ended before French forces were able to exact their just retribution upon the German nation and people. In short, Clemenceau sought to continue the war through the imposition of a harsh peace treaty. He wanted to see Germany stripped of much of its land area, wealth, industrial base and military might. Germany should never again be allowed to rise from the ashes to attack France as it had done in 1870 and 1914.

David Lloyd George, the Prime Minister of Great Britain, could have occupied a pivotal middle ground between the extremes represented by Wilson and Clemenceau. Britain had lost much in World War I, but had not suffered an invasion. Indeed, Lloyd George was inclined to moderate the harsh demands of the French. However, politics conspired to intervene. The British held an election in November 1918 which ended up hinging on the nature of the looming peace conference. In an effort to hold his fragile coalition together, Lloyd George pandered to the anti-German feeling of the British electorate. In the peace conference, he promised British voters, he would squeeze Germany 'until the pips

RIGHT: SURGERY FAILED THIS FRENCH SOLDIER WHO FOUND HIMSELF HORRIBLY DISFIGURED BY HIS WOUNDS. IN THE SECOND PHOTOGRAPH HE WEARS A MASK IN AN EFFORT TO PUT FORWARD A MORE NORMAL APPEARANCE.

squeaked'. Although hamstrung by his own political policy, Lloyd George did, as he said, sometimes feel the strain of occupying the middle ground, 'as might be expected, seated as I was between Jesus Christ and Napoleon Bonaparte'.

In the end the Treaty of Versailles resulted in a compromise peace, lodged between the extremes of Wilson and Clemenceau. During months of argument and bickering, both gave in on crucial points. Clemenceau agreed to the formation of the League of Nations, while Wilson agreed to several aspects of the treaty that restricted Germany's size and power. Thus was fashioned what is possibly the worst peace treaty in modern history. It would be harsh enough to inspire great German dissatisfaction; indeed, the fledgling Weimar government in Germany nearly rejected the treaty in favour of continued resistance. However, it would also be too lenient. It left Germany very strong in terms of population and economic might, strong enough eventually to seek its military revenge on the wartime Allies.

LEFT: AN AMERICAN INFANTRYMAN, PART OF THE OCCUPYING FORCE ALONG THE RHINE RIVER IN GERMANY, FLIRTS WITH ONE OF THE LOCAL CIVILIAN WOMEN.

BELOW: BLANKETS AND MEDICINE TO COMBAT THE INFLUENZA EPIDEMIC ARE GATHERED FOR EUROPEAN HOSPITALS BY THE RED CROSS.

THE RAILWAY CARRIAGE USED TO SIGN THE ARMISTICE.

PEACE

A British soldier, learning of the armistice, wrote of what peace meant to him:

> No more slaughter, no more maiming, no more mud and blood, and no more killing and disemboweling of horses and mules – which was what I found most difficult to bear. No more of those hopeless dawns with the rain chilling the spirits, no more crouching in inadequate dugouts scooped out of trench walls, no more dodging of sniper's bullets, no more of that terrible shell-fire. No more shoveling up bits of men's bodies and dumping them into sandbags, no more cries of 'Stretcher-bear-ERS!', and no more of those beastly gas-masks and the odious smell of pear-drops which was deadly to the lungs, and no more writing of those dreadfully difficult letters to the next-of-kin of the dead.
>
> There was silence along the miles and miles of the thundering battle-fronts, from the North Sea to the borders of Switzerland. There would be silence in Ypres, and over the whole haunted area of the dreaded salient this silence must seem positively uncanny ... The whole vast business of the war was finished. It was over.

THE TREATY OF VERSAILLES

Five separate treaties, one with each of the Central Powers, ended the Great War, but no agreement was as important as that with Germany, known as the Treaty of Versailles. The flawed, compromising agreement stripped Germany of all of her overseas colonies. In addition, the treaty altered the map of central Europe in a fundamental way. Alsace and Lorraine were ceded to France, and an important German coal-mining area, the Saar, fell under League of Nations supervision for 15 years. Clemenceau wanted more: a buffer zone between France and Germany, so the treaty stipulated that Allied troops would occupy the Rhineland, the area between the Rhine River and the French border, for 15 years. After that time, although still in German possession, the area would be permanently demilitarised. The most significant territorial changes took place in the east. Poland, like a phoenix, rose from the ashes of history, carved from land taken from both Germany and Russia. Germany lost a great deal of land, including a 'Polish Corridor' to the sea, demanded by Wilson. The cession of this land, ethnically German, to Poland did not fit well with Wilson's desire for self-determination. However, access to the sea was deemed essential for the fledgling Polish state. The only port in the area, the solidly German city of Danzig, was also a thorny issue. The population there had no desire to become part of Poland, so it was transformed into a free city under the League of Nations, and its port facilities were placed at the disposal of Poland. Thus, by this treaty, Germany had lost a great deal of territory, although far less than it had seized from Russia in the Treaty of Brest-Litovsk. The losses, especially in the east, rankled the Germans and would become a source of ongoing controversy. However, they had not stripped Germany of its population or its economic might. She remained the greatest economic power on the continent and was second to only Russia in population. Germany retained its latent power.

The most significant territorial changes took place in the east. Poland, like a phoenix, rose from the ashes of history, carved from land taken from both Germany and Russia. Germany lost a great deal of land, including a 'Polish Corridor' to the sea.

The French hoped to crush all remnants of German strength by the destruction of her military machine. Thus the Treaty of Versailles contained a number of provisions that effectively disarmed Germany. The army was forbidden to conscript young men or form a reserve, was limited to a 100,000-man force, barely enough to keep order in the revolution-stricken nation. In addition, Germany was not allowed to have a General Staff, a military air force, or tanks. Finally, the navy was limited to a force of only six ships, none of which could be submarines. Thus Germany's military power was gone. However, the ability to rearm remained, and the Allies would have to be ever-vigilant if the Germans chose to test the limits of the agreement.

Finally, the Allies decided that Germany had to pay war reparations, just as the Germans themselves had imposed upon France after the Franco-Prussian war and upon Russia at Brest-Litovsk. It

ABOVE:
GERMAN SOLDIERS RETURN TO BERLIN AT THE CLOSE OF WORLD WAR I. MANY OF THESE DISILLUSIONED VETERANS WOULD JOIN ORGANISATIONS SUCH AS THE *FREIKORPS* OR, LATER, HITLER'S STORMTROOPERS.

LEFT:
CLEMENCEAU (LEFT) AND HIS WIFE AFTER THE PROCLAMATION OF THE TREATY OF VERSAILLES.

Above: Ceremonies for the signing of the Treaty of Versailles take place in the Hall of Mirrors in the Palace of Versailles outside Paris.

Far right: A German crowd has to be held in check by the Berlin police in demonstrations following the acceptance of the Treaty of Versailles.

was such a thorny problem that the Big Three left it to a special Reparations Commission to solve in 1920. However, the Allied leaders did impose several immediate obligations upon the Germans in the Treaty of Versailles, including a cash payment of five billion dollars.

By 1921 the Reparations Commission was ready with its verdict, deciding that Germany owed the Allies an unbelievable sum of 33 billion dollars. Germany was ordered to make steady payments on the principle, with accrued interest, until 1987. The severity of the reparations figure shocked many, including the famous economist John Maynard Keynes, who doubted Germany's ability to pay such a stupendous bill. The payments, he argued, could dislocate the entire global economy. As harsh as the reparations seemed, worse was yet to come. The Allies, in an effort to justify the reparations, blamed the entire war upon Germany alone in the famous 'War Guilt Clause', in article 231 of the Treaty. Of course, the Germans realised that the war was not entirely their fault, and that the war guilt clause simply represented their final humiliation at the hands of the victors. Thus humiliated, weakened, angered and wracked by revolution, Germany began its first experiment with democracy.

CHAOS IN GERMANY

To the fighting men of Germany, peace was welcomed, but was also mourned. One soldier noted in his diary, 'The war is over ... How we looked forward to this moment; how we used to picture it as the most splendid event of our lives; and here we are

now, humbled, our souls torn and bleeding, and know that we've surrendered. Germany has surrendered to the Entente!' Such men found the situation to be worse than they had ever imagined upon returning home. The new, democratic Weimar Germany had little to offer its returning soldiers other than hardship and societal insecurity. Disgruntled, jobless, and often violent, former soldiers found common cause with each other and formed *Freikorps* (free corps), bands of fighting men that owed their loyalty to no one, but often sided with the political right.

Below: French forces take up occupation of German territory near Frankfurt in accordance with the Treaty of Versailles.

ADOLF HITLER (RIGHT) AS A SOLDIER IN 1916.

ADOLF HITLER

Adolf Hitler was born in 1889 in Austria, the son of a minor customs official. In 1908 he moved to Vienna to pursue a career as an artist. However, the art institute there rejected his application and the young man became a vagrant, living off the meagre sales of his artwork. During his stay in Vienna, he became swept up into a bizarre political mixture of anti-Semitism and radical German nationalism. In 1913 Hitler moved to Munich, hoping to rekindle his artistic career, but soon became engulfed by world events. When World War I broke out, he rushed to join the German Army. In November 1914 the youthful volunteer took part in the First Battle of Ypres where he won the Iron Cross, Second Class for bravery. He wrote to his landlord, 'It was the happiest day of my life. True most of my comrades who had earned it just as much were dead.' Hitler achieved the rank of corporal and went on to serve the remainder of the conflict, sometimes occupying the dangerous position of runner, and only narrowly escaped the war with his life. As the war neared an end, he again found himself near Ypres and on 14 October 1918 was blinded in a gas attack and evacuated to a military hospital in Pasewalk, Germany. Later, when he learned of the German defeat, he turned his face to the hospital wall and wept bitterly. After his recovery, on his return to Munich he was hired by the authorities to investigate extreme political movements in the city. One of the groups he was sent to investigate, the obscure German Workers Party – a small anti-Semitic, ultranationalist group – appealed to him and he eventually became the party's seventh confirmed member. Hitler believed that the Jews and the communists had betrayed Germany, contending even at this early stage that some 15,000 Jews should be held 'under poison gas'. He would prove to be an impassioned and inspiring orator, and provided Germans of the Weimar period with an alternative to democratic government. His goal for Germany, as illustrated in his book *Mein Kampf*, was a return to greatness and the domination of Europe.

Meanwhile the fledgling Weimar government lurched from crisis to crisis as radical groups sought to seize control of the young nation. During January 1919 in Berlin, the Spartacists, a communist group, launched a revolution. The leaders of the coup, Karl Liebknecht and Rosa Luxemburg, hoped that soldiers would join the revolution as they had the previous year. However, government forces, with considerable aid from the *Freikorps*, crushed the uprising with great brutality and killed both of its leaders. During the remainder of the year, the *Freikorps* put down several such revolutions in Germany, becoming something of an informal and brutal police force. By the end of 1919, the threat of a takeover from the left had abated, leaving the *Freikorps* and the political groupings of the right as the legitimate government's chief rivals for power.

Even in the midst of the chaos, all Germans noted the severity of the Treaty of Versailles. The loss of land, reparations and war guilt were simply unacceptable to many, who blamed the failure upon their new government. Although the German Army had been defeated and revolution stalked the streets, many Germans felt that the new government, led by the crafty socialists, had betrayed the brave German fighting man. Many leaders of the political right, led by Ludendorff himself, contended that the army had not been defeated, and that Germany had been forced to end the war due to a cowardly 'stab in the back' by the socialists. For many, such reasoning was quite comfortable and reassuring; they could believe that Germany had not been beaten, but betrayed.

RIGHT:
SPARTACIST REBELS TAKE TO THE STREETS OF BERLIN IN 1919.

BELOW:
REVOLUTIONARIES TRY TO STORM THE REICHSTAG BUILDING IN THE KAPP PUTSCH OF MARCH 1920.

As trouble brewed on the right, the Weimar government faced its sternest test. Post-war Germany found itself wracked with inflation; the German mark had fallen from 9 to the US dollar, to 191 to the US dollar, and in less than three years. The problem was made worse, for the weak German economy led to a slow rate of payment of the reparations bill. The French, feeling quite ill used, demanded satisfaction and in 1923 occupied the German industrial area of the Ruhr, hoping to force compliance with the agreed payment schedule but workers there chose to fight back with strikes. As a result, the German economy spiralled out of control in one of the worst inflationary periods ever seen in the world's history. By November 1923, the German mark hit a low of 4.3 trillion to the dollar. Money was, in essence, worthless. People even burned the paper bills in their fireplaces, for it was cheaper to burn than firewood. The monetary crisis destroyed the middle class, usually staunch in their resistance to radical change. Savings were gone, salaries were worthless, and millions of people who had worked hard all of their lives were destitute. In the end, the government, with massive aid from the wartime Allies, eventually saved the situation and the middle class made a slow recovery. However, in the process many more blamed the government for their problems, and abandoned it in support of radical organisations.

The German economy spiralled out of control in one of the worst inflationary periods ever seen in the world's history. By November 1923, the German mark hit a low of 4.3 trillion to the dollar. Money was, in essence, worthless.

Almost lost in the political shuffle was a tiny, right-wing party in Bavaria named the National Socialist German Workers Party. Led by the spellbinding orator Adolf Hitler,

LEFT: HYPERINFLATION GRIPS GERMANY – HERE GERMAN WORKERS MUST COME TO WORK WITH LAUNDRY BASKETS TO CARRY HOME MASSIVE PILES OF WORTHLESS PAPER MONEY IN PAY.

Above: Hitler poses for a photograph in the 1920s after his release from prison, before his rise to power.

Far Right: Faces of the old war and the new – aged German President Hindenburg along with his new chancellor Hitler and Hermann Goering in 1933.

the Nazi Party, as it became widely known, gained support only slowly and made several initial mistakes. At first Hitler advocated violent revolution through the use of his own burgeoning party political army, the SA, similar to the *Freikorps*. The Nazis put their beliefs to the test in the hopelessly botched 'Beer Hall Putsch' in 1923, but all of the major leaders of the party were arrested and imprisoned. It was during his nine-month stay there that Hitler developed his master plan for the takeover of Germany. He chose to play down the party's rabid anti-Semitism and hammer home the political issues that he knew would resonate in post-war Germany. He preached that the weak, democratic government and its lackeys had betrayed an undefeated army during the war. He swore that the Nazis would make Germany great again by the destruction of the Treaty of Versailles; the lost land would be recaptured and the economy and army would be rebuilt. His words, his tireless speaking schedule, and the aura of militarism that surrounded his uniformed party colleagues, gained the upstart Nazis national notoriety and support. A nation disgusted with Versailles and radicalised by economic hardship turned to the charismatic Hitler as a viable alternative.

Alhough Hitler had gained great fame and the government seemed weak, most Germans seemed willing to offer the government a second chance. However, in 1929 worldwide economic tragedy struck in the form of the Great Depression. For the second time in six years, the German middle class was destroyed. Support for Hitler rose sharply, making the Nazi party the largest single party among a bewildering array of German political groups. Economic problems, mixed with hatred of the Treaty of Versailles, had raised Hitler to the brink of power. He stood ready to reshape a vengeful Germany left powerful by the Treaty of Versailles into a military powerhouse that could destroy its perceived oppressors and dominate the entire continent of Europe, if not the world.

CHRONOLOGY

1914

June 28 Archduke Franz Ferdinand of Austro-Hungary assassinated at Sarajevo
July 6 Kaiser promises German support for Austro-Hungary against Serbia
23 Austro-Hungary sends Serbian government a ten-point ultimatum
25 Serbia replies to Austro-Hungary
28 Austro-Hungary declares war on Serbia
The First World War Begins
30 Russia begins general mobilisation
31 Germany demands that Russia ceases mobilisation
August 1 Germany declares war on Russia
Germany mobilises
France mobilises
Italy declares her neutrality
German–Turkish treaty signed
2 Germany invades Luxembourg
British fleet mobilises
3 Germany declares war on France
Germany invades Belgium
British ultimatum to Germany
4 Britain declares war on Germany
Germany declares war on Belgium
5 Turkey closes the Dardanelles
6 Austro-Hungary declares war on Russia
Serbia declares war on Germany
7 British troops arrive in France
Montenegro declares war on Austro-Hungary
10 France declares war on Austro-Hungary
Goeben and Breslau enter Dardenelles
11 Montenegro declares war on Germany
12–21 Austrian invasion of Serbia halted at the Battle of the Jadar
12 Britain declares war on Austro-Hungary
14–25 Battle of the Frontiers
14–22 Battle of Lorraine
16 Liège surrenders
17 Russians invade East Prussia
Battle of Stallupönen
20–25 Battle of the Ardennes
20 Battle of Gumbinnen
Germans occupy Brussels
22–23 Battle of the Sambre
23 Germans invade France
Battle of Mons
Namur captured
Austro-Hungary invades Russian Poland
Japan declares war on Germany
23–24 Battle of Krasnik
25–27 Battle of Le Cateau
25 Austro-Hungary and Japan at war
26–31 Russians defeated at the Battle of Tannenberg
27 Austro-Hungary declares war on Belgium
28 Battle of Heligoland Bight
29 Battle of Guise
September 3–11 Austrians defeated at the Battle of Rava Russka
5–10 Battle of the Marne
8–17 Austria's second invasion of Serbia halted
9–14 First Battle of the Masurian Lakes; Russian retreat from East Prussia
14 Falkenhayn replaces Moltke as German chief of staff
15–18 First Battle of the Aisne
15 Australians seize New Guinea
October 9 Germans capture Antwerp
9–19 Battle of Warsaw
October 18–November 30 Battle of the Yser
October 29 Turkey enters war on the German side
Trench warfare begins on the Western Front
30 First Battle of Ypres begins; fighting ends 24 November
November 1 Battle of Coronel
Hindenburg assumes command on the Eastern Front
2 Britain begins blockade of Germany
3 Montenegro declares war on Turkey
November 5–December 15 Serbia repels third Austrian invasion
November 6 France declares war on Turkey
Britain declares war on Turkey
Japanese attack Tsingtao
9 Emden destroyed
11–25 Battle of Lodz
December 3–9 Battle of Kolubra River
8 Battle of the Falkland Islands
16 German fleet shells Scarborough and Hartlepool
20 First Battle of Champagne begins; concluded 10 March 1915
29 Battle of Sarikamish; continued 1–3 January 1915

1915

January 19 First Zeppelin raid on Britain
23 German and Austrian offensive in the Carpathians
24 Battle of the Dogger Bank
February 4 German submarine warfare against merchant vessels begins
7–21 Winter Battle of the Masurian Lakes
19 Britain bombards Turkish forts in the Dardanelles
March 10–14 Battle of Neuve Chapelle
22 Przemysl surrenders to Russians
April 22–May 25 Second Battle of Ypres
April 25 Allies land in Gallipoli
Treaty of London
May 2–June 27 German breakthrough at Gorlice-Tarnow
May 7 Lusitania sunk by German U-boat
May 9–June 30 Second Battle of Artois
May 23 Italy enters war on Allied side
June 22 Lemberg recaptured by the Central Powers
23 Italy begins operations on the Isonzo front
July 9 German forces in South-West Africa surrender
August 5 Germans capture Warsaw from the Russians
6–21 Second Allied landings on Gallipoli fail
21 Italy declares war on Turkey
25 Germans capture Brest-Litovsk
September 1 Germany ends unlimited submarine warfare
September 25–November 6 Allied offensives at Loos and in Champagne
September 28 Allied troops enter Kut
October 6 Serbia invaded by Germany, Austria and Bulgaria
9 Allied troops arrive at Salonika
15 Britain declares war on Bulgaria
22 Battle of Ctesiphon
23 Allied evacuation of Gallipoli approved
November 27 Serbian army collapses and is evacuated to Corfu
December 3 Joffre becomes French commander-in-chief
7 Siege of Kut begins
17 Haig replaces French as British commander-in-chief in France

1916

January 8 Austro-Hungarian offensive against Montenegro; capitulates 16 January
11 Corfu occupied by Allies as a base for the Serbian army
Russian offensive in the Caucasus begins
24 Scheer appointed commander of the High Seas Fleet
27 Military Service Act introduces conscription in Britain
February 21–December 18 Battle of Verdun
February 28 German Cameroons surrenders
March 1 German submarine

INDUSTRIAL WAR

World War I was the first major conflict after the Industrial Revolution. Advances in both agricultural and industrial production made it possible, by 1914, to raise, equip and sustain mass armies at war. Never before had a nation been able to keep an army numbering in the millions in the field for nearly five years. By 1914 seven countries were able to accomplish such a feat. The new industrialised war pitted nation against nation, not army against army.

The twin battles of Verdun and the Somme serve to illustrate the new era of total, industrial war. The two battles lasted a combined 16 months and cost nearly 2 million casualties. When normal wastage along the remainder of the front is added, the number of casualties on the Western Front in 1916 rises to over 2.5 million. The amount of munitions expended during the two battles is staggering. Both sides fired off a total of more than 35 million shells, and 60 million machine gun rounds. Add to this the industrial might that it took to supply these men at war, from the countless bullets they fired to the food they consumed. In the end the battles of 1916 cost well more than the yearly Gross National Products of most countries in the world. Such immense numbers represent another revolution in war. World War I was the first modern total war. The societies and industries in all combatant nations had to work for and sacrifice for the war effort. Europe had reached a new, horrific level of warfare.

warfare extended; abandoned 10 May
9 Germany declares war on Portugal
18 Battle of Lake Naroch
April 23 Easter Rising against British in Ireland
29 British troops at Kut surrender to Turks
May 10 Austrian offensive in the Trentino begins; ends 9 July
May 31–June 1 Battle of Jutland
June 4–September 20 Russian (Brusilov) offensive
June 5 Arab revolt in the Hejaz begins
Hampshire sunk off Orkneys; death of Lord Kitchener
June 24–November 13 Battle of the Somme
July 25 Battle of Erzincan
August 3 Battle of Romani
27 Rumania enters war and invades Transylvania
Italy declares war on Germany
29 Hindenburg becomes Chief of the German General Staff; Ludendorff appointed his deputy
30 Turkey declares war against Rumania
September 1 Bulgaria declares war against Rumania
6 Central Powers create unified command
September 10–November 19 Allies launch offensive on Salonika front
September 15 British use tanks for the first time (at Somme)
October 15 Germany renews U-boat war according to prize rules
24 Fort Douaumont, Verdun, recaptured by the French
November 1 Allied forces capture Monastir
25 Beatty replaces Jellicoe as commander of the Grand Fleet; Jellicoe appointed First Sea Lord
December 3 Nivelle succeeds Joffre as French commander-in-chief
6 Bucharest captured
7 Lloyd George becomes British Prime Minister
13 British begin offensive in Mesopotamia
Nivelle replaces Joffre as French commander-in-chief

1917

January 31 Germans resume unrestricted U-boat campaign
February 23–April 5 Germans withdraw to the Hindenburg Line
February 22–25 British recapture Kut
March 1 Zimmermann telegram
11 British enter Baghdad
12 First Russian Revolution
15 Tsar Nicholas II abdicates
April 6 USA declares war on Germany
Nivelle offensive on Western Front begins
9–16 British offensive at Arras
16–20 Nivelle offensive unsuccessful
April 29–May 20 Mutinies in the French army
May 5–15 Allied offensive on Salonika front
10 Britain introduces convoy system
12 Tenth Battle of the Isonzo begins
15 Pétain becomes French commander-in-chief
June 4 Brusilov replaces Alekseev as Russian commander-in-chief
7–8 British capture Messines Ridge
12 King Constantine of Greece abdicates
25 American troops land in France
July 1 Second Brusilov offensive
20 Pact of Corfu
22 Battle of Marasti
31 Third Battle of Ypres begins; ends 10 November
August 2 Kornilov replaces Brusilov as Russian commander-in-chief
6–20 Battle of Marasesti
19 Eleventh Battle of the Isonzo
September 1 Riga offensive
8 Kornilov coup attempt fails
27–28 Battle of Ramadi
October 24 Italians defeated at Caporetto
November 4 British forces arrive in Italy
5 Allies agree to establish a Supreme War Council at Versailles
7 Bolsheviks seize power in Russia
British seize Gaza
19 Clemenceau becomes French premier
20 British tanks gain victory at Cambrai
December 2 Fighting ends on the Eastern Front
7 USA declares war on Austro-Hungary
9 British capture Jerusalem from the Turks
Rumania signs armistice
15 Armistice signed between Germany and Russia
22 Russia and the Central Powers start peace talks at Brest-Litovsk

1918

January 8 President Wilson outlines his Fourteen Points
February 18 Fighting between Russia and Germany resumes
21 British capture Jericho
March 3 Treaty of Brest-Litovsk signed by Russia and Germany
21 German breakthrough on the Somme
23 Artillery bombardment of Paris begins; ends 7 August 1918
29 Foch becomes supreme Allied commander on the Western Front
April 9 Germans Lys offensive in Flanders
23 Zeebrugge/Ostend raid
May 7 Treaty of Bucharest concluded by Rumania and the Central Powers
May 27–June 6 German Aisne offensive
May 28 Battle of Cantigny
June 9–13 Germans launch Noyon-Montdidier offensive
15–22 Italians repulse Austrian attack across the Piave
July 13 Turkish army launches final offensive in Palestine
15–18 Second Battle of the Marne
German retreat begins
July 18–August 5 Allied Aisne-Marne offensive
August 8 Allied Amiens offensive on Western Front successful: 'black day of the German army'
September 12–16 American offensive at St Mihiel
15–29 Allied offensive against Bulgarians
19–21 Battle of Megiddo
25 Bulgaria seeks armistice
26 Foch begins final offensive on Western Front
29 Bulgaria concludes armistice
October 1 British forces enter Damascus
5 British troops breach the Hindenburg Line
6 Germany requests armistice
9 Allies seize Cambrai
20 Germany abandons submarine warfare
26 Groener replaces Ludendorff
29 German High Seas Fleet mutinies
Battle of Vittorio Veneto; ends 4 November
30 Turkey makes peace
November 3 Austro-Hungary makes peace
4 Armistice concluded on the Italian front
9 Kaiser Wilhelm II abdicates
German Republic proclaimed
10 Emperor Charles of Austria abdicates
11 Germany signs armistice
Fighting ends
12 Austria proclaimed a republic
13 Hungary signs armistice
14 Czechoslovakia proclaimed a republic
Lettow-Vorbeck surrenders in Rhodesia
German U-boats interned
21 German High Seas Fleet surrenders to Britain
27 Germans evacuate Belgium
December 1 Yugoslavia proclaimed an independent state

1919

January 4 Peace conference convenes in Paris
June 21 German fleet scuttled at Scapa Flow
28 Treaty of Versailles
July 9 Germany ratifies Treaty of Versailles
21 Britain ratifies Treaty of Versailles
September 10 Treaty of St Germain signed by Austria and Allies
November 19 US Senate refuses to ratify the Treaty of Versailles
27 Treaty of Neuilly signed by Bulgaria and the Allies

WAR AND CHANGE

The post-war world of 1919 was vastly different to the one that had entered the conflict some five years earlier. The changes wrought by war rendered much of the world, especially Europe, almost unrecognisable. A stable civilisation that had been in place since the end of the Middle Ages came to a quick and violent end. Nations that had withstood nearly a millennium of turmoil simply ceased to exist. Families that had ruled Europe for centuries were no more. Political systems that had stood up to numerous revolutions crumbled to be replaced by new, experimental regimes that would help lead to another European conflagration. The economic superiority that had cemented European global dominance collapsed – ushering in a new age of global superpowers. Societal taboos across the world disintegrated in the face of the demands placed on the world body politic by the war. Even modes of expression, from poetry to painting, had to change to reflect the bestial nature of the war and humanity as a whole. World War I destroyed the very fabric of modern Europe, cutting society adrift from centuries of political and cultural stability. The world would never be the same again.

THE COST OF WORLD WAR I

	Total Numbers Mobilised	Military Deaths in Combat[2]	Military Wounded	Civilian Dead[3]	Economic/ Financial Cost[4] ($ million)
Allied Nations					
France	8,410,000	1,357,800	4,266,000	40,000	49,877
British Empire	8,904,467	908,371	2,090,212	30,633 [5]	51,975
Russia	12,000,000	1,700,000	4,950,000	2,000,000 [6]	25,600
Italy	5,615,000	462,391	953,886	[7]	18,143
United States	4,355,000	50,585	205,690	[7]	32,320
Belgium	267,000	13,715	44,686	30,000	10,195
Serbia	707,343	45,000 [8]	133,148	650,000	2,400
Montenegro	50,000	3,000	10,000	[7]	[7]
Rumania	750,000	335,706	120,000	275,000	2,601
Greece	230,000	5,000	21,000	132,000	556
Portugal	100,000	7,222	13,751	[7]	[7]
Japan	800,000	300	907	[7]	[7]
Total	42,188,810	4,888,891	12,809,280	3,157,633	193,899
Central Powers					
Germany	11,000,000	1,808,546	4,247,143	760,000 [9]	58,072
Austria-Hungary	7,800,000	922,500	3,620,000	300,000 [10]	23,706
Turkey	2,850,000	325,000	400,000	2,150,000 [11]	3,445
Bulgaria	1,200,000	75,844 [12]	152,390	275,000	1,015
Total	22,850,000	3,131,889	8,419,533	3,485,000	86,238
Cost to **Neutral Nations**					1,750
Final Total	**65,038,810**	**8,020,780**	**21,228,813**	**6,642,633**	**281,887**

1 *Many of these figures (compiled from various sources) are approximations or estimates.*
2 *Includes only killed in action or died of wounds.*
3 *Figures vary greatly; deaths from epidemic disease and malnutrition, probably not completely attributable to the war, are included in some instances and not in others. See specific notes below.*
4 *Includes war expenditures, property losses, and merchant-shipping losses.*
5 *About two-thirds of these were lost to U-boats, the remainder to naval and aerial bombardment.*
6 *Includes approximately 500,000 Poles and Lithuanians.*
7 *No reliable figures available; there was relatively small loss.*
8 *Approximately 80,000 additional were non-combat deaths: typhus, influenza, malnutrition, frostbite.*
9 *Asserted by German sources to be due to the Allied blockade through 1919; a handful of deaths were caused by Allied air raids.*
10 *At least two-thirds of these were Polish; many of the remainder have been attributed to Allied blockade.*
11 *More than half of these were Armenian; most of the remainder were Syrian or Iraqi.*
12 *At least 25,500 additional were non-combat deaths.*

ECONOMIC CHANGE

The endless appetite of the war for munitions and manpower forced the combatant nations to devote their economies to war production in a way never before seen. The resultant economic strain had numerous unforeseen consequences. Russia, and to a lesser extent Germany, suffered near economic breakdown, resulting in revolution. Among the Western allies the economic strain led to subtler, yet equally as important, results. Great Britain, the world's economic powerhouse, espoused classical economic liberalism in which the government had little control over a free economy. British leaders hoped that a 'business as usual' supply-and-demand economy would suffice for wartime production needs. However, as the conflict grew, it became obvious that Britain, like all other belligerent nations, would have to turn to state control of the economy. The government took control of factories, controlled transport and even limited the opening hours of public houses. The chief indicator of the collapse of liberalism was the introduction of conscription. The government simply took control of people's lives as never before. By the end of the conflict every nation had turned to a type of wartime socialism to answer their economic needs. What had once been unthinkable had in five years become the norm. After 1918, governments across the world attempted to return to more traditional economic forms, but the power of state involvement had become apparent. The populations of Europe and America began to demand that the state use its economic power for their benefit – the Welfare State was born.

The economic consequences of the war also helped to bring about the end of European global dominance. The small, but advanced, nations of Europe had used their economic and industrial power to subjugate much of the world. As a result the riches of the world flowed into Europe assuring its continued preeminence. However, during World War I Europe squandered the wealth accumulated over centuries in attempting to solve once and for all the question of who was to control the destiny of the continent. Powerful economies were shattered. While Europe bickered, new nations stepped in to claim the lucrative markets abandoned by the combatants. As a result Japan and the United States stepped on to the world stage as true economic superpowers. One simple fact serves to best illustrate the scale of the European economic catastrophe. Before 1914 Great Britain had been the leading creditor nation in the world – at the close of the conflict, Great Britain was just another nation in debt to the United States.

SOCIAL CHANGE

The political and economic strains of World War I gave impetus to several dramatic social changes throughout the world. Women in the western world had long been striving for equality and the franchise, but had made little headway. The onset of war, though, broke down existing barriers and brought a transformation that few had expected. All over Europe the war's insatiable demand for manpower left many nations on the brink of collapse. Into the breach stepped patriotic and determined women. For women of the poorer classes hard work outside of the home was nothing new. However, the typical middle class woman in the pre-war era lived under a sometimes stifling regime of Victorian morality. Women were to bear and nurture children and act as the helpmeet for their husbands. As women flooded into wartime employment, though, the Victorian mould was shattered. Women took on new jobs that had previously been the purview of men, including secretarial work. In addition many women for the first time earned their own salary and enjoyed the measure of independence that came with wages. Unescorted women appeared in movie theatres and pubs, smoked, cut their hair short and even wore trousers – all unheard of behaviour in the very recent past. Many historians argue that at the close of the conflict most middle class women lost their new jobs to returning soldiers. That is certainly true, but attitudes toward women and their attitudes about themselves had changed. The most visible manifestation of this new reality was the enfranchisement of women in most western nations after the war's end.

In the United States, on joining the war in 1917, the American government had a very important decision to make. Should the armed forces make use of its black soldiers? Southern legislators decried such action, worried that black soldiers could experience greater equality in Europe. Over Southern objections, though, the nation chose to send its black soldiers abroad, albeit in mainly a non-combat role. In Britain they were called 'Yanks', not 'niggers'. In France they could attend the same functions as other soldiers and even dance with white women. In short, black soldiers received a kind of dignity and respect that had been so long denied them at home. After the war, uniformed blacks returned to the segregated South where little had changed. White Southerners viewed the returning blacks as dangerous due to the inappropriate ideas they had picked up overseas. Several black soldiers were lynched for simply wearing their uniforms in public. Black troops had seen that there was an alternative to the existing system in the South, and knew that the South was not ready to change. Thus for the first time in American history a black exodus began, and thousands of blacks fled the South for the 'promised land' of Chicago and other, more socially liberal northern urban areas. The first seeds of the Civil Rights Movement had been sown.

BIBLIOGRAPHY

Asprey, Robert, *The German High Command at War.* William Morrow: New York, 1991.

Bidwell, Shelford and Graham, Dominick, *Fire-Power.* Allen and Unwin: Boston, 1982.

Blake, Robert, *The Private Papers of Douglas Haig.* Eyre and Spottiswoode: London, 1952.

Bourne, J.M., *Britain and the Great War.* Edward Arnold: London, 1989.

Bruce, Anthony, *An Illustrated Companion to the First World War.* Michael Joseph: London, 1989.

Churchill, Winston, *The World Crisis.* Scribner's: New York, 1992.

Clark, Alan, *Aces High.* Weidenfeld and Nicholson: London, 1973.

Cruttwell, C.R.M.F., *A History of the Great War.* Clarendon: London, 1936.

Dunn, Captain J.C., *The War the Infantry Knew.* Abacus: London, 1994.

Farwell, Byron, *The Great War in Africa.* Norton: New York, 1986.

Ferguson, Niall, *The Pity of War.* Allen Lane: London, 1998.

Fridenson, Patrick, *The French Home Front.* Berg: Providence, 1992.

Gilbert, Martin, *First World War.* Weidenfeld and Nicolson: London, 1994.

Griffith, Paddy, *Battle Tactics of the Western Front.* Yale: London, 1994.

Griffith, Paddy, *British Fighting Methods in the Great War.* Frank Cass: London, 1996.

Harris, J.P., *Amiens to the Armistice.* Brassey's: London, 1998.

Herrmann, David, *The Arming of Europe and the Making of the First World War.* Princeton: Princeton, 1996.

Herwig, Holger, *The First World War.* Arnold: London, 1997.

Higonnet, Margaret, *Behind the Lines.* Yale: London, 1987.

Horne, Alistair, *The Price of Glory.* St. Martin's: New York, 1963.

Hough, Richard, *The Great War at Sea.* Oxford: New York, 1983.

Jensen, Geoffrey and Wiest, Andrew, *War in the Age of Technology.* New York University Press: New York, 2000.

Johnson, Hubert, *Breakthrough.* Presido: San Marin, 1994.

Junger, Ernst, *The Storm of Steel.* Zimmerman: New York, 1985.

Lewis, C. Day, ed., *The Collected Poems of Wilfred Owen.* Chatto and Windus: London, 1963.

Liddle, Peter, *Passchendaele in Perspective.* Leo Cooper: London, 1997.

Lyons, Michael, *World War I.* Prentice Hall: New York, 1999.

Manning, Frederic, *The Middle Parts of Fortune.* Penguin: London, 1990.

McCarthy, Chris, *Passchendaele, The Day by Day Account.* Arms and Armour: London, 1995.

Middlebrook, Martin, *The First Day on the Somme.* Allen Lane: London, 1971.

Middlebrook, Martin, *The Kaiser's Battle.* Allen Lane: London, 1978.

Moorehead, Alan, *Gallipoli.* Ballantine: New York, 1956.

Morrow, John, *The Great War in the Air.* Smithsonian: Washington, 1993.

Moyer, Laurence, *Victory Must be Ours.* Hippocrene: New York, 1995.

Prior, Robin and Wilson, Trevor, *Command on the Western Front.* Blackwell: Oxford, 1992.

Sassoon, Siegfried, *Memoirs of an Infantry Officer.* Faber and Faber: London, 1965.

Shaffer, Ronald, *America in the Great War.* Oxford: New York, 1991.

Simkins, Peter, *Kitchener's Army.* Manchester: Manchester, 1988.

Simpson, Andy, *The Evolution of Victory.* Tom Donovan: London, 1995.

Stone, Norman, *The Eastern Front.* Scribner's: New York, 1975.

Terraine, John, *The Road to Passchendaele.* Leo Cooper: London, 1977.

Terraine, John, *White Heat.* Guild: London, 1982.

Travers, Tim, *The Killing Ground.* Unwin Hynan: London, 1987.

Tuchman, Barbara, *The Guns of August.* Macmillan: New York, 1962.

Weintraub, Stanley, *A Stillness Heard Round the World.* Oxford: New York, 1985.

Winter, Denis, *Death's Men.* Allen Lane: London, 1978.

Winter, Denis, *Haig's Command.* Viking: London, 1991.

Wiest, Andrew, *Passchendaele and the Royal Navy.* Greenwood: Westport, 1995.

Wilson, Trevor, *The Myriad Faces of War.* Polity: Cambridge, 1988.

INDEX

Note
Page numbers in *italics* refer to picture captions; those in **bold** refer to subjects which are treated in depth in boxes.

PICTURE CREDITS

AEROSPACE PUBLISHING: 16, 17 (t), 37, 43 (b), 66-67, 70, 71, 75, 101 (t), 105, 114-115, 124 (t), 125, 127, 128, 130, 138 (t), 164 (t), 168, 169 (b), 170, 172, 180, 187, 200 (t), 213 (b), 217 (t), 226.

HUGH W. COWIN: 186.

POPPERFOTO: 8, 9, 10 (both), 11, 12-13 (both), 15, 28, 31 (t), 36, 39, 43 (t), 47, 59, 72, 73, 83 (b), 88 (both), 93 (b), 97 (b), 98, 101 (b), 102 (b), 131, 135 (both), 138 (b), 139 (t), 143 (t), 150 (b), 157 (b), 162, 173, 175, 179, 181 (t), 183 (t), 201, 207 (b), 212, 220 (b), 228, 229, 232, 235, 236, 240, 242, 243, 244, 245, 246 (both), 247, 248.

PRIVATE COLLECTION: 26, 32-33 (b), 38 (t), 40, 48 (t), 58, 69 (b), 76, 78, 80 (b), 81, 82, 83 (t), 86 (b), 117, 118, 119, 120 (b), 122 (both), 123, 132, 137 (t), 161 (b), 165, 166 (both), 188 (l), 217 (r), 219 (b), 221, 227, 238 (both).

SÜDDEUTSCHER VERLAG: 6-7, 17 (b), 18, 19, 20, 21, 22, 24-25, 27, 30 (b), 31 (b), 32 (t), 44-45, 49, 50, 51 (both), 52, 53 (t), 54 (both), 55, 56, 57 (both), 61, 62, 63, 64, 65, 69 (t), 84, 85, 86 (t), 90-91, 93 (t), 94, 95, 96 (t), 97 (t), 100 (both), 106, 107, 108, 109, 110, 112, 113, 133, 134, 136, 137 (b), 158-159, 184-185, 189, 190, 191, 193 (b), 194, 196, 197, 198 (both), 199, 202-203, 204, 206, 207 (t), 208 (both), 210 (both), 213 (t), 214, 215, 216, 219 (t), 220 (t), 222 (b), 224, 225, 234, 237, 239 (b).

TRH PICTURES: 14 (both), 23, 30 (t), 34, 38 (b), 41, 42 (both), 48 (b), 60, 74, 77, 79 (both), 80 (t), 87, 96 (b), 99, 102 (t), 103, 111, 116, 120 (t), 124 (b), 129, 139 (b), 140-141, 143 (b), 144, 145, 146, 147 (both), 148 (both), 149, 150 (t), 151 (both), 152 (both), 153, 154, 155, 157 (t), 161 (t), 163, 164 (b), 167, 167, 169 (t), 174, 176, 177 (both), 181 (b), 182, 183 (b), 188 (t), 192, 193 (t), 200 (b), 218, 222 (t), 230-231 (Robert Hunt Library), 239 (t), 241 (both), 249.

ART WORKS:
AEROSPACE PUBLISHING: 29 (b), 78, 109, 130, 152, 174, 191, 192, 211 (t).

DE AGOSTINI UK: 35, 58, 89, 95, 123, 156, 173, 182, 190, 211 (b).

JOHN BACHELOR: 53 (b).

All maps by Peter Harper